I0818997

FOR BETTER AND WORSE

Also by
STEPHANIE COONTZ

The Way We Never Were: American Families and the Nostalgia Trap

A Strange Stirring: The Feminine Mystique and American Women at the Dawn of the 1960s

American Families: A Multicultural Reader

Marriage, a History: How Love Conquered Marriage

The Way We Really Are: Coming to Terms with America's Changing Families

The Social Origins of Private Life: A History of American Families, 1600–1900

For BETTER *and* WORSE

THE COMPLICATED PAST AND CHALLENGING FUTURE OF MARRIAGE

Stephanie Coontz

Afterword by Haley Swenson

VIKING

VIKING
An imprint of Penguin Random House LLC
1745 Broadway, New York, NY 10019
penguinrandomhouse.com

Designed by Amanda Dewey

LIBRARY OF CONGRESS CATALOGING-IN-PUBLICATION DATA

Names: Coontz, Stephanie author
Title: For better and worse: the complicated past and challenging future of marriage / Stephanie Coontz.
Description: New York: Viking, [2026] |
Includes bibliographical references and index.
Identifiers: LCCN 2025047111 (print) | LCCN 2025047112 (ebook) |
ISBN 9780593299098 hardcover | ISBN 9780593299104 ebook
Subjects: LCSH: Marriage—History
Classification: LCC HQ515 .C668 2026 (print) | LCC HQ515 (ebook)
LC record available at https://lccn.loc.gov/2025047111
LC ebook record available at https://lccn.loc.gov/2025047112

Printed in the United States of America
1st Printing

The authorized representative in the EU for product safety and compliance is Penguin Random House Ireland, Morrison Chambers, 32 Nassau Street, Dublin D02 YH68, Ireland, https://eu-contact.penguin.ie.

For Jaz Aran Coontz

CONTENTS

FOR BETTER AND WORSE

INTRODUCTION

This isn't a book about why you *ought* to marry, or what you'll miss if you don't. Getting married won't transform an unhappy person into a happy one or an irresponsible person into a reliable one, at least not for long. And contrary to oft-repeated claims, getting more people married won't solve social problems such as poverty and crime. Furthermore, individuals who choose singlehood can lead very fulfilling lives, nurturing close relationships with friends and family and often maintaining broader social support networks than their married peers.[1]

But this is also not a book about why marriage is irrelevant or obsolete. Most Americans—like most Europeans—consider marriage the highest commitment a couple can make. Friends and coworkers extend extra respect and support to relationships when they know the couple is married. Parents are substantially more likely to approve of an adult child's romantic relationship with a partner, same sex or different sex, if the two are legally wed rather than cohabiting.[2]

And most Americans still marry, although they typically postpone doing so much longer today than they used to. In 1950, 87 percent of women aged twenty-five to twenty-nine had married.

By 2023, it wasn't until ages fifty to fifty-four that a comparable percentage of women had wed. But they did get there. And by that same year, a married couple's chance of divorce, which had been falling fairly steadily since peaking in 1980, was lower than at any time since the mid-1970s. Meanwhile, two-thirds of people who *do* divorce go on to remarry. The overwhelming majority of American women and men experience marriage.[3]

But they experience a very different kind of marriage, with very different demands, rewards, and risks, than people experienced just a few decades ago. One of the reasons I wrote this book was to explore how the rewards and risks of modern marriage are changing, and why new possibilities for achieving deep mutual satisfaction in marriage have been accompanied by serious new challenges to maintaining that satisfaction.

Very few unmarried young adults say they outright reject marriage. A 2024 poll by the Pew Research Center found that only 8 percent of unmarried adults aged eighteen to thirty-four said they didn't want to marry, while 69 percent said they did. Twenty-three percent, however, said they weren't sure.[4] In this book I explore how historically conditioned gender and marital patterns have interacted with contemporary economic and social trends to create such uncertainty and ambivalence, and why those sentiments now affect more women than men.

Young women's uncertainty about whether they will marry is a fairly recent development and can't be attributed simply to the rise of feminism. According to a national poll of high school seniors that has been taken for almost fifty years, female expectations to marry actually *increased* during the period when approval of feminist goals such as pursuing careers or running for political office was growing especially rapidly.[5]

Back in 1976, when University of Michigan researchers started asking high school seniors across the country about their intentions to marry, 73 percent of males and 84 percent of females said they expected to do so. From then until the mid-2000s, high school seniors' expectations to marry mostly stayed steady or increased, with women's hitting a high of 88 percent in 2002, 2005, and again in 2012.[6]

In 2019, however, the percentage of female high school seniors saying they expected to marry dropped to just 78 percent. By 2020, that had fallen to 74 percent and by 2021, to 69 percent. In 2023, it hit an all-time low of 64 percent. Male expectations to marry also decreased in these years, but by much smaller margins.

We don't yet know whether these trends foreshadow an accelerating trend toward higher rates of non-marriage or reflect a temporary reaction to the stresses of COVID and other recent social anxieties. Significantly, though, most of the fall in young women's stated expectations to marry was due to a surge in the numbers saying they had "no idea" if they would marry, rather than actually *expecting* or *preferring* not to. There was also a decline in the percentage of high schoolers of both sexes expressing confidence they'd be a "very good" as opposed to just a "good" spouse. This suggests that what's going on here is not an outright rejection of marriage so much as a growing worry that achieving or sustaining the *kind* of marriage most people now want might be especially difficult in today's social and economic climate.

I wrote this book to explore why so many people have become ambivalent about entering an institution that most still value, and I chose the subtitle to suggest that we have a better chance of helping individuals and society at large navigate the "challenging future" of marriage if we understand how people's rising expectations about the quality of marital relationships clash with the legacy of marriage's complicated past and the new socioeconomic insecurities of the present.

When I say "complicated past," I'm referring to the thousands of years in which marriage functioned to oppress the many people who were once compelled to marry, especially women, along with the many other people who were *not* allowed to marry or were born outside marriage. I'm not suggesting, however, that marriage is inherently or inevitably oppressive. Indeed, in chapter 1, I argue that for even *more* thousands of years, our earliest ancestors used marriage to organize peaceful cooperation and resource-sharing among different communities of hunters and gatherers and did so without forcing women into oppressive relationships or penalizing children born outside marriage.

Even after the institutionalization of repressive marital laws and exclusionary family practices, individual marriages have often served as sources of mutual support. That's why groups denied the right to marry have frequently invented their own marriage rules and rituals.

Enslaved African Americans, for example, defied their enslavers by "jumping the broom" to proclaim themselves married. A similar custom has been documented among several marginalized groups in Europe. Indeed, it was probably Welsh immigrants or indentured servants who introduced the custom to enslaved Africans, and they in turn introduced it to impoverished Whites in Appalachia and Louisiana, with each group tailoring the ritual to their own community values.[7]

More recently, gay and lesbian activists around the world have persevered against once seemingly huge odds to win the right to marry. There seems to be a halo effect attached to just having the *right* to marry. Prior to the national legalization of same-sex marriage in 2015, states that legalized gay marriage saw a 14 percent decline in suicide attempts by gay and lesbian high school students, while states that did not legalize same-sex marriage experienced no such reduction.[8]

Yet the same institution that can offer its members protection and respect from outsiders can also perpetuate the inequalities whose evolution and intensification I describe in chapter 1. Indeed, although I don't think marriage is inherently oppressive, historically inculcated patterns of husband dominance probably have something to do with the fact that whereas men and women in nonmarital heterosexual relationships in the US are equally likely to initiate a breakup, in heterosexual *marriages*, the majority of divorces are desired by the female.[9]

This book doesn't offer the kind of chronological or comprehensive history of marriage that I and other authors have laid out elsewhere.[10] Instead, I've selected five different periods in Anglo-American history in which the role of marriage in the larger socioeconomic and political order was changing, with formerly dominant ideas about gender, sexuality, love, and marriage being challenged, reworked, or repudiated in favor of new arrangements and ideals.

I chose these five periods in part to counter two extremes in thinking about the past that have recently led two different groups of people, for almost opposite reasons, to a similarly pessimistic place. At one extreme are people who romanticize one or another marriage and gender system in the past, leading them to claim that many contemporary relationship values and behaviors are harmful or even sinful and must be suppressed. At the other extreme are those who claim heterosexual marriage is inherently unfair to one sex—according to some, because of men's innate or historically ingrained flaws; according to others, because of women's recently acquired ones—and we should give up on it entirely. History supports neither of these beliefs. But I also chose these periods because each of them has bequeathed us patterns of thinking and behaving that undermine people's chances for building the mutualistic relationships most of us now want.

In chapter 1, I explore the role of marriage among our early human ancestors, back in the Paleolithic era. The idea that modern mate preferences and gender roles are somehow a genetic inheritance of a time when women needed husbands to protect and feed them and their children represents a serious misunderstanding of how hunting-and-gathering groups organized family and community life. Male-breadwinner families are a modern invention, and patriarchy, for all its staying power, is not a preordained, inevitable feature of human life.

Chapters 2 and 3 highlight the striking contrasts between the aristocratic patriarchal views about men, women, and marriage that prevailed in sixteenth- and seventeenth-century England and America and those that emerged in early capitalist democracy. Surprisingly, the ideology of aristocratic patriarchy, despite its strict controls over women, regarded women as more capable and strong-minded than did the emerging democratic ideology, which painted women as weak and vulnerable. Under patriarchy, men were considered more altruistic than women, who were said to put narrow family interests first. In some ways, though, the seemingly more flattering views of women's unselfishness that have proliferated in the twentieth century may today be more of an insidious threat, both to women wishing to succeed in the workplace and to women seeking security as what people mistakenly call a "tradwife," than straightforward misogyny.

Chapters 4 and 5 cover the transition from the officially strait-laced sexual morality of the Victorian era to a new celebration of heterosexual desire, alongside the emergence of an organized feminist movement. During the first two decades of the twentieth century, these changes provoked a backlash with striking similarities to the culture wars of our past few decades. Ironically, however, the eventual acceptance of heterosexual desire as "normal" came with trade-offs that still deform people's sexual expectations and behaviors.

The fifth historical period I discuss, before moving on to contemporary marriage issues in my final two chapters, saw the surprisingly short-lived triumph of the male-breadwinner family and near-universal marriage in the 1950s and 1960s. But beneath the seeming stability of marriage in that era, several forces were undermining working-class and middle-class security, creating new marital tensions even as people increasingly aspired to more egalitarian and mutually supportive family relationships. Chapter 7 describes the social and economic origins of recent changes in marital patterns, and in chapter 8 I examine some surprising reversals of the old "rules" that used to govern what predicts marital satisfaction.

Readers can skip to the final chapters if they wish, but I believe that understanding this history is important in helping us assess the new challenges and opportunities we face. For one thing, it reveals that there has been enormous variation in the official sexual, gender, and marital norms embedded in our nation's laws, political establishments, and economic institutions. The dominant values and practices promoted by political authorities and cultural elites and embraced by individuals aspiring to upward mobility have been remarkedly varied in successive periods, suggesting there is more leeway than we're often told in the kinds of social and gender arrangements that can work. But just because some very dissimilar behaviors and values about love, sex, gender, and marriage have been the norm at various times in our past, this doesn't mean people can easily discard the values they have grown up with and smoothly adopt new ones. We shouldn't underestimate the staying power of beliefs, behavior patterns, and validating myths that were once codified in law, inculcated by religious and educational authorities, and reiterated in everything from children's bedtime stories and popular literature to medical advice and political rhetoric.

Because the dominant ideas of previous eras were the ones most likely to be recorded and preserved, some of them continue to circulate through society even when they contradict the new ones. Over time we've accumulated a mishmash of different, often inconsistent, ideas about "traditional" gender roles, sexuality, love, and marriage, many of which we've absorbed at an unconscious level. They operate like earworms, intrusive refrains we can't drive out of our heads, telling us what we should and should not be doing or feeling. They reverberate in parts of our psyches that don't respond well to logic or even to proof that the behaviors they encourage have ceased to work, evoking reflexive responses and behaviors that persist long after people think they have repudiated the values they represent.

The result of this accumulated jumble of internalized messages and habits is that as new relationship values and priorities develop, they not only meet intense opposition from those determined to maintain the old gender and marital order. They also take a lot of time to be fully absorbed and put into practice even by those eager to dispense with the old ways.

That's especially true of the new values and behaviors that have emerged in the past few decades. For the first time in recorded history, people have begun trying to organize marriages that are free from coercion—coercion by the dictates of parents, the elder generation, or the state, by laws about who can or cannot marry or divorce, by men's power over their wives and children, by rigid rules about who plays what role in a marriage, and even by the biological facts that once made insemination, pregnancy, birth, and lactation a package deal.

I don't agree with commentators who say aspirations for new gender, sexual, and marital arrangements are unrealistic. The history I recount in this book shows that we have more latitude in how to organize healthy intimate relationships than most people realize. There is no such thing as the traditional marriage. The male provider family only became an ideal in the nineteenth century and a short-lived reality in the twentieth. Nor is there some universal template for what attracts men and women (or men and men, or women and women) to each other, or for what satisfies them in a relationship. Indeed, the astonishing variety of sexual beliefs, partner preferences, emotional priorities, and definitions of love that have flourished—or been considered shameful—in different time periods suggests that we have a lot of leeway in the relationship values, expectations, and practices we can successfully cultivate.

Nevertheless, creating and sustaining the voluntary, mutually supportive relationships that Americans increasingly desire is a serious challenge. It's made especially difficult both by the rapidly changing economic and social conditions that have produced the misdirected nostalgia I describe in chapters 6 and 7, and by stubbornly persistent habits and attitudes of earlier eras. Such habits once stabilized marriages, but many are now major risk factors for conflict and divorce, as I show in chapter 8.

Some of these self-defeating attitudes and habits are the results of earworms passed down from the era of the much-mythologized 1950s male-breadwinner family. Other earworms come from misinformation we've been fed about our evolutionary history or about our supposedly innate standards for what counts as sexual desirability and "true" masculinity or femininity.

Interestingly, scientists have recently identified the characteristics that make some songs likely to become earworms. The music and words are "simple, short, and repetitive." Their tunes are uncomplicated, with notes anyone can reach and phrases heard so often everyone can remember them.[11]

That's a pretty good description of the kind of ideas about love, sex, and marriage that have become earworms. I believe knowing the actual history of marriage can help people attune themselves to more complex melodies and become comfortable with a wider range of harmonies.

Still, it's not just historical misinformation and misplaced nostalgia that interfere with our quest to develop more rewarding and mutually satisfactory relations. External forces often prevent us from living up to our best intentions and goals. Individuals may now be legally free to wed anyone they choose, or to leave a marriage, or to remain single. But that doesn't mean they make such choices free from outside constraints.

Powerful outside forces affect how much we can hope to gain—or how much we risk losing—by getting married, as well as how successful we will be in managing relationships that require much more negotiation than when the "rules" of marriage were enforced by law. Economic and racial inequalities, employment opportunities, material resources, and social support systems all affect our access to desirable partners and our own desirability as partners. And when we do marry, these outside forces influence our behavior within marriage, again for better *and* worse.

We need to acknowledge the degree to which such forces impact our most intimate relationships so we can stop blaming ourselves or our partners—or less fortunate couples—for problems that often originate outside the relationship. Indeed, understanding what is *beyond* people's control as a couple can help them better manage what is *within* their control. This is where knowing the historical legacies that affect us can be helpful, because some things are harder to control than others. One of those is the set of various institutions and social policies we've inherited from these different periods and need either to work within or to change. More on those in later chapters.

Another is the array of socially conditioned habits and blind spots we've all inherited from long-standing cultural traditions and continuing childhood socialization. I've found that taking a historical perspective on bothersome behavior by others or myself—placing it in its socially conditioned context—helps me find more constructive ways to change it than just getting angry or feeling guilty. It creates compassion, which is not the same as acceptance, just a more effective way to work for change than denunciation.

For example, one of the surest signs of a healthy and trusting relationship, marital psychologists say, is "benevolent attribution." Relationships are more satisfying when partners generally interpret undesirable behavior by the other as an atypical and understandable lapse, perhaps due to exceptional stress or resulting from an external cause outside the individual's control. "Malevolent attribution," by contrast, is the tendency to see an offending behavior as yet another example of a partner's presumed irresponsibility, lack of commitment, or personality flaw.

In relationships that are fundamentally healthy, benevolent attribution is a strong predictor of long-term relationship satisfaction for both partners. But when a partner's undesirable behaviors occur often enough to have a negative effect on the other's well-being, failing to confront those behaviors because they may not have been intentionally hurtful never forces the partner to examine the effects of such behavior and take steps to reduce it. That's a strong predictor of escalating dissatisfaction or complete disengagement.[12]

I've come to believe that historical attribution offers a way to walk the fine line between the kind of forbearance that doesn't lead to change and the all-encompassing condemnation that increases the chance of estrangement. Understanding how socially conditioned reflexes and historical earworms can make any of us engage in behaviors that undermine our new standards for relationships allows us to express requests for change in ways that don't assume every failure is intentional but that encourage both partners to figure out how to move past negative patterns.

Being aware of these historical forces—which operate on same-sex couples and trans individuals as well as heterosexuals—can turn down the heat that is often generated when couples attempt the enormous task of fulfilling our new aspirations for family life while also meeting the demands of paid work in a country with the highest rates of economic insecurity and inequality among the world's wealthy nations and the most miserly support systems for families.

There is no way to completely resolve our marital and family stresses without better work policies and support systems. But as I show in chapters 6 and 7, there are lessons we can learn about what those might be when we examine the economic and legislative policies of the 1950s and 1960s instead of romanticizing the highly problematic marriage patterns and gender norms of those years. And in the meantime, there is compelling research about what we can do to move our relationships forward now, a point I elaborate in chapter 8 and Haley Swenson of the Better Life Lab lays out in more detail in her afterword.

In an attempt to keep this book short enough to interest the general reader, I have added extensive endnotes to support some of my assertions or to accommodate readers who may be interested in more specifics about historical events or sociological trends I mention in passing. If something seems unclear, you might check if there is a more detailed explanation in the notes.

We live in a world where language is evolving—and sometimes diverging—to reflect changing views and assessments of historical trends and current realities, so I want to explain a couple of choices I've made. Unless I am quoting someone else, I avoid the term *slave owners* in favor of the word *enslavers,* to remind people that the slave system in the Americas rested on the daily, violent renewal of subordination and punishment of attempts at escape. I also use the term *enslaved individuals* rather than *slaves* in my historical chapters, to emphasize the humanity that the institution denied them. In discussing ethnic identities, I use the word *Hispanic.* Many academics and some civil rights activists have adopted the term *Latinx* as a gender-neutral alternative to *Hispanic* or *Latino* (the letter *o* being a masculine identifier in the Spanish language, with *a* being a feminine one). However, some Indigenous people dislike use of the letter *x,* which colonists added to languages during conquest, while others object that the letter *x* doesn't coincide with Spanish pronunciation. As of 2021, only 3–5 percent of people of Spanish descent reported using the term *Latinx* to describe themselves. Almost 60 percent of the Spanish-language heritage population said they preferred *Hispanic* and almost 40 percent preferred *Latino.*[13]

In light of how rapidly language has been evolving, I would urge caution in jumping to conclusions about other people's use of terms. For example, many modern women object to being addressed as "ladies," a word often used in a patronizing way. Yet addressing women as "ladies" and men as "gentlemen" was once a democratic innovation. It accorded "commoners" the same polite mode of address formerly due only to elites. For most of the twentieth century, many Whites *refused* to call Black women "ladies," and throughout the country, people with conservative gender and sexual views made a point of saying that unconventional women didn't qualify as "ladies." So people from some backgrounds might believe that the term is courteous rather than condescending, and some "benevolent attribution" might be in order.

Chapter 1.

THE MANY AND MUCH MISUNDERSTOOD "TRADITIONAL" MARRIAGES

People's opinions about marriage tend to run to extremes. Writing for the majority in the 2015 Supreme Court decision legalizing same-sex marriage, Justice Anthony Kennedy described marriage as the "keystone of civilization," embodying humanity's "highest ideals of love, fidelity, devotion, sacrifice, and family." Throughout the ages, he declared, marriage has "always promised nobility and dignity to all persons, without regard to their station in life." In 2023, a book called *Get Married,* hailed as "vitally important" in *The New York Times,* claimed that the only way to "save civilization" in the twenty-first century is to convince more people to marry.[1]

Other people argue, though, in the words of a 2023 book titled *I Don't: The Case Against Marriage,* that marriage is an "inherently misogynistic institution . . . designed to keep women in service to patriarchy" and to reinforce an exclusionary "heteronormative" understanding of sexuality. In the author's view, society would be better off if marriage were "completely" destroyed.[2]

Such hostility toward marriage wasn't always a mark of radical feminists and queer liberation activists. The early Christian Church had an equally low opinion of marriage, though for a different reason: Lifelong celibacy was considered a morally superior choice. Toward the end of the fourth century AD, a monk named Jovinian began to preach that all baptized Christians were of equal moral status in the eyes of God, whether they remained virgins or got married. After all, he noted, St. Paul was quoted in the Bible as saying it is "better to marry than to burn" [with lust], which implied marriage was a worthy choice. But the most influential translator of the Bible, Jerome of Stridon, later pronounced a saint, vigorously denied that interpretation.

The only reason Paul said it was better to marry, explained St. Jerome, "is that it is worse to burn . . . It is as though he said, it is better to have one eye than neither, . . . [or] to stand on one foot and to support the rest of your body with a stick, than to crawl with broken legs." What God values most, Jerome continued, "is not a smaller evil, but a thing absolutely good."[3]

The debate was settled in 390, when a synod convened by the reigning Pope Siricius ruled it a heresy to claim marriage was as honorable a condition as celibacy. Jovinian and eight of his followers were excommunicated and exiled.

Throughout the Middle Ages, many Christian polemicists penned condemnations of marriage, wives, and sex that were occasionally so explicit they sound like pornographic marital aversion therapy. For example, St. Jerome told widows that remarrying instead of embracing celibacy would be "like a dog [returning] to his vomit." I doubt he would have held "childless cat ladies" in contempt.

Some Christian theologians did praise marriage, urging men to honor their wives. But not until 1215 was marriage elevated to the status of one of the Christian sacraments.

The problem with sweeping generalizations—pro or con—about marriage is that it's almost impossible to find any aspect of the institution that is "universal." The gender arrangements, sexual norms, interpersonal dynamics, and acceptable numbers of partners allowed in marriage have all varied enormously over the ages, not just across cultures but also within them. The medieval Church may have preached the need for sexual abstinence, for example, but in popular culture during the same time period, and even in some medical circles, celibacy was considered a serious threat to health. One French poet claimed that one hundred thousand pilgrims had died on the Crusades "because from women they abstained." In the sixteenth and seventeenth centuries, women who remained virgins too long were said to be at risk of contracting or even dying of "green sickness."[4]

In his dissent to the Supreme Court ruling legalizing same-sex marriage, Chief Justice John Roberts claimed that for "thousands of years of human history, in every society known to have populated the planet," the word "marriage" "referred to only one relationship: the union of a man and a woman." In fact, however, polygyny—the marriage of one man to several women—was common throughout the ancient world. It is the type of marriage mentioned most often in the first five books of the Bible. Anthropologists have also identified more than fifty societies that permitted polyandry—marriage between one woman and more than one man. Some societies even accorded legal recognition to marriages between a living person and the ghost of someone already deceased.[5]

And marriages of the past did not always enforce "heteronormativity." Every past society we know of has used the categories of male and female to assign people to different work activities, ritualized duties, and modes of dress. But in many cultures, individuals born with one set of sex organs could choose the kind of work, clothes, duties, and/or sex partners typically associated with someone born with different sex organs. For example, more than one hundred different traditional Native American societies included men who dressed and lived as women, while perhaps one-third of that number accepted women who dressed and lived as men. Several groups recognized a third gender that was neither man nor woman, or was both. Some "two-spirit" individuals, as they are now termed by contemporary Native American activists, married a person of the same biological sex. Others married a different-sex partner.[6]

Such societies would probably not have been shocked by someone changing their sex organs as well as their clothing, had that been possible, although some disapproved of individuals who tried to *combine* the occupations and social roles of both genders. Others, however, revered "two-spirit" individuals for their ability to fuse male and female roles and capabilities.[7]

Despite the tremendous variety of marital arrangements around the world, I find it useful to distinguish between three overarching marriage systems that arose successively in history (although at many times and in many places, they overlapped), and a fourth system that's still in the process of construction. What differentiates these systems is not the form marriage took, which has always varied from one society to another and within subgroups of the same society, but the role marriage played in the larger social and economic order.

The first system, to which most of this chapter is devoted, is the one that characterized the band-level foraging societies of the Stone Age. Marriage among our Paleolithic ancestors played a very different role than it did in the patriarchal, class-stratified kingdoms and states that began to appear approximately twelve thousand years ago. In chapter 2, I describe the patriarchal marriage system that characterized premodern England and colonial America, and how that gave way to a third model of marriage based on a new ideal of male breadwinning and female domesticity. The male-breadwinner model, which many people mistakenly view as "traditional marriage," was still novel in the late eighteenth century and didn't describe the reality of most American families until the twentieth century. Since the 1970s it has begun to give way to a still-evolving form of marriage in which new opportunities for gender, racial, and sexual equality coexist in tension with growing economic inequality, outdated institutional arrangements, and cultural backlash. But vestiges of those old systems—along with misunderstandings about how they actually worked—hamper our ability to meet the new challenges facing married couples.

Many of the conflicts within and about marriages that we're experiencing today are the legacy of social norms and conditioned reflexes inherited from the male-breadwinner-female-homemaker marital system, along with some leftovers from the autocratic patriarchal one. But our understanding of the options we have for constructing marriages and gender relationships that meet contemporary needs is limited by widespread misunderstandings about the evolutionary legacy of the first, and earliest, marriage system I describe here—misunderstandings that lead some people to believe our present-day gender, sexual, and romantic habits are hardwired and should not or cannot be changed.

MYTHS ABOUT STONE AGE MARRIAGE

For the first two million years of humanity's existence, our ancestors lived in small bands or camps, ranging in size from about fifteen to fifty people. They moved with the seasons and with fluctuations in food sources, using simple tools to gather, scavenge, fish, and hunt for food.[8] Many people erroneously think these societies were based on a gendered division of labor that continues to shape our sexual preferences and social arrangements today. The sociobiologist Edward Wilson summed up that view succinctly: "In hunter-gatherer societies, men hunt and women stay at home. This strong bias persists in most agricultural and industrial societies and . . . appears to have a genetic origin."[9]

Women, according to this story, didn't go out hunting, partly because of their lesser strength and partly because they were tied down by pregnancy, nursing, and round-the-clock childcare. A woman supposedly needed a mate agile enough to hunt food for her and her children and "manly" enough to protect them from predators. A man, in turn, was said to want a woman fertile enough to bear him children and compliant enough to remain monogamous so his hunting efforts wouldn't be wasted on feeding children who would perpetuate some other man's genes.

Those mate selection preferences, many believe, were bred into us over time because they led to reproductive success. Stone Age women who preferred tall, well-muscled, somewhat older and more experienced men were supposedly more likely than women attracted to less "masculine" men to end up paired with a good provider and protector. They could raise more healthy, well-fed children who in turn would inherit their parents' genetic preferences.[10]

Men, according to this theory, had the best chance of passing along their genes if they were attracted to younger women with good reproductive potential, clues to which supposedly include full lips (since lips tend to thin as people age), clear, smooth skin and glossy hair (both indicators of good health), and a small waist combined with large hips. Some evolutionary psychologists have even calculated the ideal waist-to-hip ratio (WHR) for a prime baby-making candidate: 0.70. That is a waist 70 percent as large as her hips.

Why should this shape be a good signal of fertility? Before puberty, boys and girls have waists that are about 90 percent the size of their hips. During puberty, however, the release of estrogen causes fat to accumulate around a woman's hips, decreasing the *relative* size of a healthy woman's waist from about 90 percent of her hips to just 70 percent. After a woman starts to bear children, however, or as she ages, body fat begins to accumulate in the waist, increasing the waist-to-hip ratio again.

Therefore, the reasoning goes, a WHR of about 0.70 signals a woman at the peak of her reproductive potential—ready to have a baby but not yet started down the road toward an aging ovary. Men who preferred such women supposedly had more children and passed that preference on to the sons they sired.

America's most famous sex symbols have generally approached this bodily ideal. Marilyn Monroe's waist was 23.5 inches and her hips were 33.25, a ratio of 0.71. Kim Kardashian's waist and hips, as of 2022, were 26.5 and 39 inches, respectively, a ratio of 0.68.

But is this preference really a legacy of our Paleolithic past? When researchers showed pictures of a female with a 0.70 WHR to isolated groups of Indigenous hunter-gathers in Peru and Tanzania, the men thought the woman was not only unattractive but unhealthy. One speculated that the poor thing was suffering from severe diarrhea! In general, women in foraging and horticultural societies tend to have higher waist-to-hip ratios than in societies where women do less physically demanding work. And men in those societies consistently report finding such sturdy female bodies more attractive than thin or hourglass figures.[11]

Cross-cultural research also calls into question the idea that some Paleolithic division of labor explains each sex's preference for what we now see as stereotypically "feminine" and "masculine" features. In a 2014 study, researchers went to twelve cultures at very different levels of economic development and social complexity and showed individual men and women in each society three pictures of a person of the other sex. One picture was unaltered, one had been manipulated to exaggerate the average facial features generally associated with females, and one had been manipulated to exaggerate the features of an average male face.

Women in foraging and horticultural societies preferred pictures of men whose features had been digitally altered to appear more feminine than average. Men in nomadic herding cultures and hunting-and-gathering societies tended to prefer women with masculinized faces. Only in more complex urbanized environments did male subjects report strong preferences for exaggeratedly "feminine" faces. And even there, other studies show, people's actual choices don't always match the stereotyped ideals they report holding.[12]

Aside from looks, what were our Stone Age ancestors seeking in a mate? When we examine how people likely organized their lives during the Paleolithic period, it makes no sense to claim that our success as a species derived either from women's ability to snag mates who would feed their children or from men's ability to ensure they only fed children who would perpetuate their genes.

Heterosexual pair bonding seems to have been pretty ubiquitous in foraging societies, past and present. But that's not because marriage was the only way, or even the main way, women and children got fed. Most archaeologists believe our Stone Age ancestors subsisted in ways much like those practiced in more recently recorded hunting-and-gathering societies, where women typically provide about half the calories people consume. Most of what women contribute consists of plants and tubers, although they also net fish, dig shellfish, and catch small animals. They walk for miles gathering food, often carrying a child at the same time.[13]

Women are perfectly capable of hunting for bigger game. Among the Agta people of the Philippines, women, hunting with dogs, provide a substantial percentage of the wild pigs and deer consumed by the group. Women of the Copper Inuit often hunt reindeer and seals. And burial sites in the Americas from the Late Pleistocene and Early Holocene periods yield evidence of females who were almost certainly big-game hunters.[14]

But the larger and more dangerous the animals, or the farther they must be pursued, the less common it is for women to join the hunt. This makes perfect sense given women's reproductive value and the exigencies of pregnancy and nursing before the availability of contraception, tampons, and bottled baby formula.

Still, even when hunting is done by all-male groups, women in foraging societies don't need to be married to a skilled hunter—or even to be married at all—to get highly valued protein for themselves and their children. Meat from a hunt is typically distributed among all band members rather than taken home by the hunter who happens to make the kill. He doesn't even get the first helping, and his children don't get a larger share.[15]

The eminent evolutionary anthropologist Sarah Blaffer Hrdy points out that ethnographers working with the Hadza and the Ju/'hoansi (often referred to as the Bushmen or !Kung) foragers report finding no "significant weight differences between the children of exceptional hunters and those whose fathers never killed anything. . . . Children whose fathers had died or decamped still got fed."[16]

Furthermore, Hrdy points out, women in band-level societies are not as tied down by childcare as wives became in the nuclear male-breadwinner families of 1950s American suburbs. Grandmothers, fathers, other nursing moms, older children, and unrelated band members all participate in feeding and tending to children. Among the Hadza, babies up to age four are in the care of people other than their mother, on average, for about 40 percent of daylight hours. Among the Efe of Eastern Congo, that rises to 60 percent of the day. Mothers often nurse each other's children. Among the Yora of Peru, children who have been weaned spend, on average, 40 percent of their time eating in households other than their own.[17]

Researchers used to think that the distinctive human practice of collaborating in food procurement and sharing its products emerged in small, stable groups of *closely related* kin, whose descendants inherited their survival-enhancing propensity to share with each other. But it turns out that members of bands are not especially closely related, and band membership fluctuates significantly, since individuals and families frequently change camps. One study of thirty-two band-level societies found that primary kin typically make up less than 10 percent of a residential band. Yet members routinely share highly valued resources such as meat and honey with everyone present at the camp, including members of other groups who are just visiting—and back-and-forth visiting is extremely common among foraging bands. Experts now believe that because sharing helped band-level societies survive temporary food shortages and other emergencies, it became an inherited capacity and socially reinforced habit not restricted to blood relatives.[18]

Kinship obligations do organize many kinds of work and food sharing in such societies, but what counts as kinship is sometimes socially rather than biologically determined. The Inupiat of the Alaskan North Slope sometimes name children or rename adults after a dead person, thereby creating obligations between them and their namesake's family. Among some groups of Inuit, people born on the same day are considered kin, while children born to a man and woman who at one time had a sexual relationship are viewed as siblings even if neither child was born of that union. In matrilineal societies, children are considered more closely related to their uncles—their mothers' brothers—than to their fathers, their mothers' husbands.

It's even possible that in some cases individuals came to consider themselves related *because* they shared, rather than sharing because they were related. Among the Malays of Langkawi and some other groups around the world, eating and living together are thought to *create* kinship. Among several New Guinea groups, kinship is thought to be generated through the transmission of the "fat" or "grease" found not only in fathers' semen and mothers' breast milk, but also in sweet potatoes, a vital subsistence food. As social glue, blood may *not* actually be thicker than water, or at least not thicker than *shared* water and food.

Archaeologists believe that, like contemporary foragers, our Paleolithic ancestors promoted social cooperation and reciprocity through frequent informal visiting, special friendship ceremonies, periodic large gatherings involving feasting, storytelling, singing, and dancing, and even collective work efforts on large monuments or other structures used for ceremonial or spiritual purposes.

Ongoing cooperation between unrelated individuals in different groups is often established through rituals such as the gift-exchange partnerships that Ju/'hoansi individuals enter into in Southern Africa's Kalahari Desert. These create long-term relationships between people who live more than one hundred miles apart, and there is evidence of similar exchange partnerships in Africa dating back to the Middle Stone Age.[19]

All this isn't to say that mate selection and marriage weren't critical to the cooperative practices that contributed to the evolutionary success of *Homo sapiens*. They were indeed, but this was as much a result of the *social* relationships marriages created as of the *genetic* ones. Rather than marriage being invented to enable a woman to get food and protection and a man to maximize the chances of passing down his own genetic material, it would be closer to the truth to say that marriage was invented to turn strangers into relatives.

REVISITING STONE AGE MARRIAGE

Band-level foragers almost invariably practice what anthropologists call exogamous marriage—taking a partner from outside the band and the kin group—and they tend not to have strict residence rules about who moves where at marriage. Such practices spread individuals and social obligations widely, increasing the number of in-laws, cousins, nephews, and nieces who are not biologically related to one of the partners but are part of a network of reciprocity. In the thirty-two foraging societies studied by Kim Hill and his colleagues, for example, people commonly recognize and interact with such fictive "kin" through many degrees of separation—not just your spouse's brother, for example, but your spouse's brother's *wife's* brother and sister are considered in-laws.[20]

Unlike the marriage patterns that became common in societies as kin groups developed hereditary inequalities in access to resources and wealth, exogamous marriages circulate people, resources, and obligations across geographic boundaries and among genetically unrelated individuals. Such marriages create extensive social networks that unite and reunite different groups across space and over time. New connections are passed down across generations, producing in-laws, nieces, nephews, grandchildren, and a widening circle of cousins spread among disparate bands.

In fact, the acquisition of in-laws is so important in creating and perpetuating reciprocity that elders in contemporary band-level societies don't leave mating decisions entirely to individual choice—and neither, researchers believe, did our ancestors. One study of 190 hunter-gatherer societies found that 85 percent of them relied primarily on parents or close kin to arrange young people's marriages. Anthropologists who recently examined the relatedness patterns of members of contemporary foraging groups have concluded that "arranged marriages probably have an evolutionary history going back at least 50,000 years," possibly as far back as the first human migrations out of Africa.[21]

Yet because band-level societies have next to no inheritable private property or status distinctions, they rarely enforce arranged marriages as strictly as parents and authorities started doing in the kingdoms and states that eventually emerged in many parts of the world. In most foraging societies, elders organize matches, but husbands and wives are free to part.[22]

There is no way of knowing for sure the interpersonal dynamics of marriage and male-female relationships among our ancient ancestors. But on one thing most researchers agree: There is no evidence in either the ethnographic or the archaeological record of band-level societies that they practiced the systematic oppression of women or the punitive attitudes toward children born out of wedlock characteristic of the stratified societies that arose later.[23]

Overall, each sex generally organizes and controls whatever work and ritual responsibilities their cultural traditions assign to their gender rather than working under the direction of the other sex. And individuals of both sexes have considerable personal autonomy. Most band-level societies are remarkably accepting of premarital sex by women as well as men. Some even tolerate extramarital liaisons. Sexual jealousy does occur, and ethnographers report cases of men beating their wives. But such behavior is disapproved.

Women are free to leave their husbands. And children born outside marriage, whether as a result of premarital or extramarital sex, have a full claim on the group's resources.

One of the best-documented examples of the difference between band-level marriage values and those that developed in patriarchal societies is found in the records of the Jesuit missionaries who arrived in what is now Canada in 1625, aiming to convert the native peoples. The Jesuits were horrified by the degree of gender equality they encountered, along with the casual acceptance of premarital and extramarital sexuality and divorce. One missionary recorded his attempts to convince the native men that they should "rule" their wives. He pointed out to one man that in such a permissive atmosphere, he couldn't be sure his son was his own flesh and blood. The Jesuit incredulously recorded that the man replied: "Thou hast no sense. You French people love only your own children; but we love all the children of the tribe." Scandalized though he was, the Jesuit commented that the answer was so "absurd" it actually made him laugh.[24]

THE RISE OF PATRIARCHAL MARRIAGE

There are many competing explanations for why—after millennia of egalitarian band life—economic, social, and gender inequality developed in many places around the globe. I'm not rash enough to try to choose between them.[25] But the development of inequality *among* families almost invariably exacerbated inequalities *within* families, transforming the social functions of marriage and elevating the prestige and power of men over women and children.

Wherever people began to domesticate animals, intensify agriculture, or develop regular surpluses they could store for the future, sharing became less advantageous and protection against outsiders more necessary. This encouraged patrilocal residence and patrilineal descent, keeping related males together to defend property or conduct raids against the property of groups in other territories.

As some families and lineages accumulated more surpluses or acquired new resources, they gained prestige and influence. Less successful families and individuals had to offer extra incentives to intermarry with more successful ones. If unable to secure a marital connection, they might solicit loans or favors they could repay only by offering tribute or even becoming debt-slaves. The stage was set for the emergence of kingdoms and states in which rulers could recruit or conscript armed followers to impose their will on lower-class individuals and raid or conquer other territories and peoples.

This didn't happen overnight, and in some places it didn't happen at all. But wherever inequality of resources accelerated, this created new opportunities for elites—and aspiring elites—to enhance their power and wealth by plundering other societies' land, enslaving their people, or demanding tribute. All this made the remaining peaceful, egalitarian societies especially vulnerable to conquest, colonization, or outright extinction.[26] And these new ways of acquiring and protecting wealth fundamentally changed the function and dynamics of marriage.

MARRIAGE IN ANCIENT CLASS SOCIETIES, KINGDOMS, AND STATES

As families and lineages accumulated resources unevenly, marriage arrangements ceased to circulate people, goods, and obligations. Instead, they concentrated resources and obligations within restricted social circles, excluding other groups from these networks.

In contrast to the exogamous marriage practices of foragers, stratified societies typically practiced endogamy, or marriage within in-groups, reinforcing obligations based on blood ties and co-residence rather than reaching out to construct new cooperative relationships. Cousin marriage, almost unheard of among foraging bands, became a preferred way of amplifying a kin group's resources.

Elite parents exerted stricter control over young people's marriage choices, allowing their children to make marital alliances only with families of equal or greater status or wealth, and preventing them from marrying a member of a lineage or social class with whom they wanted no connection. As Sarah Blaffer Hrdy points out, women were increasingly obliged to marry men who could provide economic resources, political alliances, or armed service to their lineage or clan. They were "less able to prioritize criteria like 'generosity,' 'tolerance,' or 'good sense'" in choosing a marriage partner, or to consider how gentle he would be as a mate and how helpful as a co-parent. Furthermore, the rise of patriarchy, Hrdy notes, not only placed men *above* women but also placed them *apart* from babies.[27] And that had lasting repercussions, given the research I describe in chapter 8 on how caring for babies affects people's brains.

Meanwhile, the invention of "illegitimacy" allowed elites to deny any obligations to offspring born from a relationship they didn't approve. In some societies, parents or authorities could dissolve a match made without their consent, thus rendering "illegitimate" any children born to the offending couple. And in many stratified societies, an "illegitimate" child was what the legal system in patriarchal England called a filius nullius—a child of no one, entitled to nothing.

Fathers and husbands carefully monitored women's sexual behavior in order to safeguard the patrilineal inheritance of property and ensure that a wife or daughter would not introduce unwanted blood lines and allegiances into their families. As late as 1838, we can see the legacy of such patriarchal motives in a ruling by the New Jersey Supreme Court that the "harm" of adultery lay not in "the alienation of the wife's affections, and loss of comfort in her company," but in "its tendency to adulterate the issue of an innocent husband," forcing him "to maintain another man's children" and turning "the inheritance away from his own blood, to that of a stranger."[28]

By the Bronze Age, dominant clans and lineages had developed into hereditary aristocracies in many areas of the world. As elite families and ambitious individuals competed for power and resources, getting the right marriage partner became increasingly important for forging political and military alliances or bolstering claims to hereditary rank. Conversely, preventing rivals from achieving a desired marriage became a way to block them from acquiring advantageous allies. Questions about who could marry whom and whether someone could divorce and remarry came to involve enormous amounts of negotiation, maneuvering, and duplicity. Sometimes they even led to the murder of an inconvenient spouse, a potential rival for a ruler's choice of mate, or children from a previous marriage.[29]

After the Fall of the Roman Empire, in what is now Western Europe, the Christian Church became a major political and economic power, as well as a spiritual one, in part because of its ability to bestow or withhold religious sanctification to a marriage or an annulment. Monarchs and great nobles lobbied, bribed, and threatened various arms of the Church to get their own marriages sanctified, even when a proposed match violated the Church's complicated rules about what constituted incest. But they eagerly offered military aid to help Church officials force a rival to abandon plans for an advantageous marriage that violated those rules. They pressured the Church to annul their own childless marriages, but to refuse annulment and remarriage to a childless rival. After all, an estate or kingdom without an heir was just asking to be taken over.

In the following chapter, I describe the differing forms of social and gender inequalities that developed in the aristocratic patriarchal regimes of premodern England and America and in the nominally democratic market societies that gradually replaced them. But more inclusive notions of social solidarity and more flexible sexual, gender, and marital patterns than those sanctioned by elites continued to exist in many peasant communities and marginalized subcultures. And throughout the ages, spiritual leaders and philosophers drafted manifestos designed to foster wider circles of social cooperation and sharing.

Centuries before the Christian Church became cozy with aristocrats and kings, and in defiant opposition to the principles of the Roman Empire under which he lived, for example, Jesus insisted over and over upon the moral obligation to share with others beyond one's own family, echoing—whether consciously or not—the principles of hospitality practiced by band-level societies. In Matthew 25:35–37, for example, Jesus suggests that anyone who feeds and clothes the hungry, cares for the sick, or shows compassion to the imprisoned is actually doing it to him: "For I was hungry and you gave me something to eat, I was thirsty and you gave me something to drink, I was a stranger and you invited me in, I needed clothes and you clothed me, I was sick and you looked after me, I was in prison and you came to visit me."

When the Gospels quote Jesus directly on the subject of family, it often has him urging his followers to subordinate family obligations to the task of building a more inclusive brotherhood (some of the Gospels imply a sisterhood as well) of true believers.[30] Christ commands people to "Honor your father and mother," but he also tells them to leave their nuclear families to build that wider Christian community—even if they must "hate" them in order to forsake them. Do not even stop, Jesus tells one follower, to bury your own father.

Interestingly, several passages suggest that Jesus endorsed an understanding of social obligations closer to that of our hunting-and-gathering ancestors or today's "chosen families" than to the narrow "family values" we sometimes hear preached today. In one scene, reported in each of the synoptic gospels (Matthew, Mark, and Luke), Jesus refuses to grant members of his own family a special audience, declaring that his *real* family is the community of believers (Luke 8:9–21).

And when Jesus is dying on the cross and sees his mother in the crowd with her sister and brother-in-law, he does not commend her to the care of those biological relatives or in-laws. Instead, he creates a fictive family for her. Calling forth his disciple John, he says to his mother, "Woman, behold your son," and to the disciple, "Behold your mother" (John 19:25–27).

Such expansive definitions of family and inclusive ideals of social solidarity never disappeared. Nor did the idea that individuals should be able to choose their own marriage partner or divorce an unsatisfactory mate. But over the following centuries, religious, economic, and political elites strove to impose the marital rules and social practices that benefited themselves on individuals and communities that were more tolerant of different forms of romantic and sexual arrangements. The political institutions, legal principles, cultural norms, historical myths, psychological habits, and gender anxieties they bequeathed us continue to frustrate people's attempts to build more egalitarian marriages and more inclusive family support systems today.

Chapter 2.

THE PARADOX OF PATRIARCHY AND THE DARK SIDE OF DEMOCRACY

PROLOGUE: The Mystery of the Mrs.

A few years ago, a *New York Times* reporter called me after reviewing the paper's archives and noticing that well into the 1970s, every married woman in a news story, no matter how well-known in her own right, was identified by her husband's first as well as last name, with a "Mrs." in front. The renowned Mexican painter Frida Kahlo was called Mrs. Diego Rivera. Pictures of singer and songwriter June Carter Cash were filed under "Cash, Johnny & Mrs." Coretta Scott King was Mrs. Martin Luther King Jr.

The *Times* wasn't alone. Until 1970 *The Washington Post*'s style manuals mandated that "Mrs." was never to be used with a woman's first name, only with that of her husband.[1]

This wasn't just a journalistic peculiarity. In the late 1960s, my husband worked at a gas company in Seattle, Washington. As part of an increasingly informal youth culture, he was puzzled by the fact that when women called to report a gas leak or inquire about service, they almost invariably identified themselves in this "Mrs. John Smith" way. He said he was always tempted to ask, "May I call you John?"

Many people assume that the "Mrs. Man" naming custom was inherited from the patriarchal English law of "coverture," which held that upon marriage a woman's legal identity and rights became submerged in her husband's. But this practice actually originated only in the 1800s, and it illustrates an intriguing difference between the social norms of aristocratic patriarchy and early capitalist democracy.

Five hundred years ago, the prefix "Mrs." indicated a woman's *social* status, not her marital status. It was a contraction of Mistress, which was typically pronounced "mizzus." A "Master" or "Mistress" was someone of wealth and rank, entitled to deference from individuals lower down the social scale. Taylor Swift would have been called Mrs. Taylor Swift from the moment she gained her current fame and fortune and for the rest of her life, whether or not she eventually married.

Using Mrs. to indicate a woman's *marital* status didn't become the norm until the nineteenth century. And not until the last half of that century did it become typical to identify a wife by her husband's first as well as last name. Far from being a holdover from the days of aristocratic patriarchy, subsuming a wife's name into her husband's was part of a new set of gender arrangements that celebrated the *brotherhood* of men and the marital status—along with the *motherhood*—of women.

HOW THE MISTRESS BECAME "MRS. MAN"[2]

In the patriarchal era, royalty and great aristocrats were typically identified by the house from which they were descended or the territory they ruled. Eleanor of Aquitaine didn't change her name when she married King Louis VII of France, nor when that marriage was annulled and she wed the Duke of Normandy, who became Henry II of England. The first wife of Henry VIII was Catherine of Aragon; his fourth wife, Anne of Cleves. Among the three highest ranks of the British nobility, women—married or unmarried—were (and still are) addressed as Lady plus their first name.[3]

Surnames developed only gradually, from the eleventh century onward, usually as a way of identifying people by their occupation or personal characteristics, as in Harry (the) Baker, Edmund (the) Miller, Mary (from the) Bridges. Not all surnames derived from men. Madison means "son of Maddy," the nickname for Maud.[4]

Among English commoners, unlike elsewhere in Europe, married women typically took their husbands' last names. But even in England, Chief Justice Edward Coke ruled in 1628, this wasn't a legal requirement. Coke's own wife never took his name, and her choice didn't cause any of the outrage that ensued in 1855 when American feminist Lucy Stone announced she wouldn't assume her husband's last name. Indeed, when a man married an heiress in feudal times, he sometimes took *her* last name.[5]

As England developed a class of affluent merchants, businessmen, and professionals, the prefix Mister or Mr. became a way of distinguishing high-status male "commoners" from ordinary ones. The term "Mrs." was originally the equivalent female honorific. In tax records and business directories of the seventeenth and eighteenth centuries, as well as in private correspondence, female business proprietors, estate owners, heiresses, and prominent authors, whether married or not, were typically identified with the prefix Mrs.

Only a minority of women qualified as a Mrs. But only a minority of men qualified as a Mr. In 1620, when the *Mayflower* landed in Massachusetts, just 11 of the 41 men recorded as signing the Mayflower Compact had a "Mr." in front of their names. In 1793, when city officials compiled a list of householders for the market town of Bocking, England, only 9 percent of the 545 men heading households were listed as "Mr."*

As more men were accorded the prefix of Mr., the prefix Mrs. was extended to their wives. Yet socially prominent unmarried women continued to be addressed as Mrs. on their own account. At lower levels of society, the term was sometimes used to indicate a woman with authority over others. On great estates in Britain in the eighteenth and nineteenth centuries, the main housekeeper, single or married, was called Mrs. to distinguish her from the underservants. In the 1854 British novel *North and South,* the clergyman's wife employs a housekeeper who is called Dixon by her employers, but "Mrs. Dixon" by the housemaids she supervises.

Even after Mrs. began to designate a woman's marital status, it was not at first customary to drop a woman's first name in favor of her husband's. In 1832, *Godey's Lady's Book,* the most widely read women's magazine in America, gave its annual writing award to a story ridiculing a woman who pretentiously introduced herself as Mrs. Washington Potts. As late as 1860, a Texas Supreme Court judge claimed that the practice of calling a woman by her husband's first as well as last name was a fad confined to "polite soci-

* In a society where inequality was accepted as a matter of course, people didn't see the denial of a prefix before one's name as the insult it had become by the late nineteenth century in America, when even low-status Whites qualified for the title of Mrs., Miss, or Mr., but all Black men and women were typically called by their first name. Not until 1964 did the Supreme Court rule that Southern courts must extend the same courtesy titles to Black men and women that they did to Whites.

ety." Not until the late nineteenth century did the "Mrs. Man" form of identification became standard.[6]

So how did we get from a practice initially derided as pretentious by early nineteenth-century Americans (and immediately denounced as insulting by nineteenth-century feminists) to a situation where most women were routinely identified—and usually identified themselves—by their husband's first and last name?

That was a complicated journey, but it reflected a major change in marriage and gender norms connected to the expansion of political democracy and the spread of a competitive market economy.

THE PARADOX OF PATRIARCHY: Hierarchies of Gender and Rank in Premodern Europe and America

The formal subordination of wives in premodern England and colonial America was harsh. All property a woman independently brought to marriage and anything she inherited or earned afterward belonged to the husband. Wives weren't legally entitled to make contracts in their own name or sue in court. Husbands had the right to physically discipline their wives.

Yet the patriarchal hierarchy of premodern Western Europe and the American colonies was not as monolithic as people often assume. In a period when landed wealth and inherited rank were the source of political and social power, very few men qualified as "patriarchs"—and some women could become, in effect, honorary ones. Seventeenth-century Swedish courts used the word *husbonde*, or master, to describe both male and female property owners. Authorities would often declare a married woman who ran her own business a "feme sole," officially granting her an independent legal existence. Even without such a designation, married women frequently conducted business transactions and initiated court actions.[7]

Other things being equal, a man took precedence over a woman. But other things were seldom equal. A wife was supposed to defer to her husband, but her husband was supposed to defer to women of higher rank, which is why advice books of that era warned men not to marry above their station. A study of the correspondence of Scottish gentry between the years 1650 and 1850 found that the only woman who married a man of lower rank, the Duchess of Hamilton, was also the only wife who never ended letters to her husband by describing herself as "obedient."[8]

Social "inferiors"—the word then referred to a person's position in the social hierarchy—were expected to defer to masters and mistresses, regardless of sex or age. A "stable boy" might be a man in his fifties, but he and other low-ranking men bowed their heads, stepped aside, and lowered their eyes when greeting a "superior" woman or man.

Today, female supervisors who oversee large numbers of employees tend to experience *greater* harassment from male underlings than women lower down the chain of authority,[9] and powerful female politicians are often subjected to vitriolic abuse by less powerful men. But back then, no low-ranking man would dare insult a high-ranking woman. As historian Mary Beth Norton writes, "the notion that a hierarchy based on rank might give way to one resting on gender—with the consequence that a lower-ranking man would take precedence over a higher-status woman—was literally unthinkable" in the seventeenth century.[10]

Women were certainly subordinate to men of equal or superior status. But when we look beyond the misogynistic rhetoric of Christian anti-marriage polemicists, we often find a surprising respect for women's competence. Paradoxically, the very ideology that justified women's subordination made it less necessary to rationalize that subordination on the basis of supposed female incapacities.

Today, we value the ideal of equality. When we deny rights to an individual or group, we feel a need to justify why they don't deserve or could not handle equality. But in the sixteenth and seventeenth centuries, most Europeans and Americans believed that inequality in society was both a political necessity and a social good. Equality, in the words of a seventeenth-century American minister, would create "confusion . . . and every evil work."[11]

In this belief system, there was no need to construct elaborate justifications for the subordination of women—or of serfs and slaves. In 1700, a Boston trader, responding to a fellow merchant who questioned the morality of slavery, summarized the traditional view: "God . . . hath ordained . . . some to be Monarchs Kings Princes and Governours, Masters and Commanders, others to be subjects . . . bound to obey; yea, some born to be slaves."[12]

Likewise, God had ordained wives to obey husbands. Sixteenth- and seventeenth-century advice books conceded that many a wife was wiser or more virtuous than her husband, but insisted that she must nevertheless obey him, "whether he be . . . simple" or even "evil." God had appointed him head of the family, and it would be "monstrous" for the body to control the head. The American preacher Benjamin Wadsworth, describing "The Well-Ordered Family" in a 1712 sermon, admitted matter-of-factly to wives that "possibly thou hast greater abilities of mind than he has . . . yet since he is thy Husband, God has made him the Head, and set him above thee."[13]

Such nonchalant admissions that a woman could be smarter than her husband are absent from nineteenth-century advice books, where women's need to "submit" was rephrased as a need "to be taken care of."

Patriarchal ideology of the sixteenth and seventeenth centuries didn't sugarcoat female subordination. Women weren't assured that their morals were higher or their duties more important than men's. But neither were they told they were too weak or too naïve to exercise political and economic initiative. Indeed, women were considered more prone to ambition, greed, and sexual excess than men. They needed to be controlled not so much for their own protection as for the protection of men.

Although men believed wives *should* subordinate themselves to their husbands, few were confident most *would* do so. Local officials were fully aware of the capabilities that led some women to defy husbands and preachers and occasionally band together to physically attack men who'd wronged them. To combat such behavior, authorities passed regulations *requiring* male heads of households to discipline willful wives and wayward servant girls. Legal records reveal that they frequently had to punish men for *failing* to do so.[14]

It was taken for granted that a woman could act with the same resolve and success as a man. That's what made her dangerous. But when a woman behaved like a man in order to accomplish an acceptable goal, such conduct brought admiration rather than disgrace. Many seventeenth- and eighteenth-century ballads recount admiring tales of cross-dressing women who joined the army or navy in male disguise and fought as skillfully as any man.[15]

TRADITIONAL CO-PROVIDER MARRIAGES

Few marriages in premodern England and colonial America resembled the male-breadwinner families we mistakenly call "traditional."

Like their Stone Age ancestors, although without their autonomy, wives were essential family co-providers. Running a farm or business was generally a two-person career, with both partners producing goods and services for barter or sale and household use.[16]

Nor did having children cause a wife to withdraw from economic production and exchange. Single women in their teens and early twenties tended to work as servants in other households, saving up to help establish their own. These servants—and the householders' own children as they aged—handled cleaning and infant care, freeing wives to focus on their co-provider duties.

Indeed, prior to the nineteenth century, when a man referred to himself as his family's sole provider, he was not bragging but requesting leniency because his "yoke-mate" was unable or unwilling to pull her own weight. The word "breadwinner" as a term for a husband only came into use in the 1820s.[17]

In what was perhaps the greatest difference with the wage labor system that triumphed in the nineteenth century, husbands and wives had similar rhythms of labor and leisure. Economic historian Jonathan Levy points out that people didn't typically make "any distinction between the family and the market, home and work."[18] Husbands and wives jointly supervised servants, apprentices, and hired workers. Production for the market was put on hold as needed to haul water, tend to children, feed the fire, harvest food, and take meals.

In case of illness or absence, moreover, each partner had to know how to do the tasks the other might typically do. One fifteenth-century conduct book even noted that a wife must know how to command the estate's men and defend her lands if attacked.[19]

Family life back then was far from egalitarian. Gender and age hierarchies were strictly enforced. But it's hard to imagine a woman in those days describing herself as "just a housewife." Indeed,

English legal records of the sixteenth and seventeenth centuries reveal that married women typically described themselves much as men did—as individuals who lived by their "owne labor" or "industrye." They jealously guarded their reputation as reliable workers and helpful neighbors.[20]

A farm wife didn't wait for her husband to "bring home the bacon." She helped raise, kill, and dress the pig, salted the pork, cured the bacon, and frequently took it to market. Paintings of the era depict women driving cows to market and freely mixing with men there. "Milk-wives" traveled to regional markets to sell butter and cream. "Fishwives" were described by a seventeenth-century observer as returning from a day's trading, "their heads full of wine, and their purses full of coin," then stopping at an alehouse before heading to their separate homes.[21]

During the sixteenth and seventeenth centuries, the "putting out" system increased people's opportunities to earn cash at home. Merchants gave raw materials to individuals who then processed them on their own schedule and got paid when the agent came to pick the products up for resale in larger markets. Women spun wool or cotton into yarn or cloth. Men made parts of shoes. This kind of work, where people sold not their time but their products, allowed individuals to combine paid work with family duties or put that work aside during planting and harvest seasons.

Overall, then, the marital division of labor didn't draw husbands and wives into qualitatively different spheres of activity. In a world where economic, personal, neighborly, and familial relationships were all intertwined, it wasn't possible or desirable for men to specialize in detached, impersonal business interactions and wives in personal relationships. Women had to have a good head for business. Men had to keep track of family and friendship obligations. Indeed, men rather than women wrote the bulk of family correspondence, passing on news about baptisms, weddings, funerals, illnesses, the comings and goings of mutual friends, and other "domestick concerns" that later became seen as feminine "gossip." Both sexes had to "make nice" to social superiors and *be* nice to neighbors and kin whose cooperation they depended on.[22]

A frequent complaint of women in contemporary heterosexual marriages (and also in many paid jobs) is that they are expected to manage the emotional work of relationships. Under aristocratic patriarchy, emotion work was more connected to rank than to gender. Men as well as women had to read and try to massage the emotions of social superiors, flattering or placating as needed. Neither men nor women bothered to do so with social inferiors.

Nor, aside from Parliament, did men and women inhabit separate political spheres. Among elites, most political negotiations were conducted through familial and personal networks and patron-client relationships, where women played important roles. The only way the lower classes could express opinions about policies and leaders was through public demonstrations, sometimes including violent riots. Women participated in and occasionally initiated these.[23]

THE EMERGENCE OF "SEPARATE SPHERES"

Rapid economic and social change during the seventeenth century disrupted old ways of making a living but also made England a world power. London became an international trading center, supporting a wealthy financial elite and a growing layer of bureaucrats, lawyers, and "self-made" businessmen.

Some women found new entrepreneurial opportunities in this expanding consumer society. By the eighteenth century, a thriving community of self-made "mistresses"—shopkeepers, ribbon weavers, brick-makers, and fan-makers—served London's seven hundred thousand residents. Women invested in the London Stock Exchange and engaged in moneylending.[24]

But traditional patterns of inheritance and power left men better positioned to take advantage of expanding commercial opportunities. Few female entrepreneurs could leverage the assets and political networks needed to build highly capitalized industries or international trading firms. Such companies clustered in new business districts, where men increasingly conducted business and discussed politics in offices, men's clubs, and coffeehouses some distance from home. Wives had fewer occasions to act as deputy husbands or deputy diplomats.

As the putting-out system gave way to wage labor in centralized workshops and factories, the lower levels of society also saw an increase in the percentage of husbands routinely working away from home. Well into the nineteenth century, the term "male breadwinner" was a misnomer for most such families, because daughters as well as sons often contributed wages to the household. But the activities, responsibilities, and schedules of *wives* increasingly diverged from those of husbands.

Economic historians Sara Horrell and Jane Humphries argue that there were two different routes to male-breadwinning families in the middle and lower classes. The "detrimental" route involved a decrease in locally available work that wives and mothers could combine with household responsibilities. As forests and commons were converted to enclosed pastures, traditional ways of provisioning the family while remaining close to home—gleaning richer neighbors' fields for leftover crops and vegetables, collecting firewood, foraging for edibles—disappeared. Dairying, once a female-run occupation conducted from home, was taken over by highly capitalized industries employing full-time wage workers. By 1790, centralized factories with efficient spinning machines were providing full-time work for young unmarried women while depriving a much larger number of housewives of paid work they had formerly done at home. When men's work didn't pay enough to compensate for the loss of women's contributions to the family economy, destitution often ensued.[25]

There was also, however, a "beneficial" route to male-breadwinner families, when increases in men's real wages or business earnings allowed wives to spend more time improving the household's food, clothing, comfort, and sanitation through careful shopping, food processing, sewing, and laundering. Many things a family required could still be produced or finished off at home more cheaply than purchased ready-made, so even lower-class families often kept wives at home if they had children who could join the husband doing wage labor. In a reversal of today's patterns, working-class women tended to work outside the home when their children were young and withdraw from the labor force when their children became old enough to replace them as paid workers.[26]

These rearrangements of family responsibilities gradually produced a new view of marital roles and relationships. Men's activities and schedules, which had to be prioritized, came to be seen as "productive" work. Women's activities made men's earnings go further, producing a home more comfortable than a working farmhouse or shop could ever be. But though it took a lot of unpaid effort to make a home appear to be a place of tranquility, that effort was increasingly seen as a "labor of love."

During the late seventeenth century, Englishmen began to refer to women as "the fair sex," a phrase unknown before the 1660s. Among urban elites in the American colonies, marital portraits of sturdy "yoke-mates" gave way to paintings emphasizing wives' slender waists, graceful necks, and flowing locks.[27] It became a marker of successful masculinity to have a wife—and a status symbol to *be* a wife—who looked as if she didn't have to do hard labor and might even be too delicate to do so.

At the same time, such wives and mothers, secluded in the home, were increasingly described as the emotional center of gravity in a changing world. Their home was said to be an "Empire" from which they exerted moral sway over men bound to them by the "silver cord" of mother love and the "silken bond" of marriage. As wives and mothers, they supposedly wielded a "power," as one woman claimed, explaining why she declined to work for women's voting rights, with "which no king or conqueror can cope."[28]

When I first began studying family history, I saw these nineteenth-century celebrations of women's "power" as naïve or openly cynical rationalizations of women's second-class citizenship. I was focused on what women lost when they were denied access to the expanding economic and political rights that White men gained in the late eighteenth and early nineteenth centuries. Since then, however, I've become more aware of what *men* lost when they became immersed in a sphere of economic and political interactions disconnected from interpersonal obligations and interdependencies.

THE APPEAL OF DOMESTIC IDEOLOGY FOR MEN

Many men were troubled by the impersonality, competitiveness, and "soullessness" that characterized economic relationships in the new order, where take-it-or-leave-it bargaining replaced past favors or desire for future goodwill in determining the availability of goods and labor. Politics had once been an elite family affair, with offices passed down from parents to sons and sinecures distributed to clients. Now influential men had to compete for the votes of commoners. Thomas Jefferson described America's emerging system of party politics as a place where "all the worst passions of men are marshalled to make one another as miserable as possible."[29]

In the older system of household production and local markets, economic transactions were inextricably intertwined with social obligations and neighborly relationships. When economic historian Arthur Cole studied the diaries of colonial merchants, he was struck by how much of their "business day" involved conversations in coffeehouses, attendance at "Town Affairs," and excursions to shop, go fishing, or do little favors for friends.[30]

By the late eighteenth century, however, the pressure to be more "businesslike" was taking its toll. Diaries, letters, and public writings of nineteenth-century middle-class men overflow with expressions of longing to find "refuge" from "the vexations and embarrassments of business," the "sacrifice of good" for "advancement of personal interest," and the "heartlessness of strangers."[31]

Many people came to see the family, as one man wrote in 1827, as an oasis "of pure disinterested love, such as is seldom found in the busy walks of a selfish and calculating world." Only at home, mused another, can we "cease the struggle in the race of the world, and give our hearts leave and leisure to love."[32]

Tracing changing views about marriage and family life among middle-class businessmen in nineteenth-century New England, historian Catherine Kelly found that men's views shifted from respecting their wives' business savvy toward idealizing their seclusion within the family circle. They revered mothers and wives for protecting their "sanctuary" from the "contamination" of "pecuniary" calculations. And there was an increasing tendency to see women—or at least "true" women—as untouched by the passions of men, whether sexual or self-seeking.[33]

Idealization of private family life crossed class and color boundaries. Middle-class African Americans in the antebellum North also lauded women for preserving "the sanctities of domestic life." Antislavery activists used domestic ideology to indict enslavers for violating the purity of womanhood and the sacredness of family. And White working-class men wrote wistfully about the "calm and quiet retreat" domesticity offered from the "unjust and tyrannical" factory system.[34]

The veneration so many men expressed for the "virtue" of their mothers and wives was not just for show. Many men *wanted* their womenfolk to do what twentieth-century men often complained about women doing—to act as their moral "mentor," reminding them of social responsibilities and moral obligations; to counter "the utilitarianism, the money-loving spirit of the day"; to make them "more virtuous, more useful, more honorable."[35]

The future president Ulysses S. Grant wrote to his fiancée that whenever he felt tempted to do something morally questionable, he asked himself, "Well now if Julia saw me would I do so." In 1852, another man wrote to his wife, "I hope you will 'preach' to me whenever you feel prompted to do so, that you may instill some of your goodness into me."[36]

Contemporary individuals who scornfully offer a Tampax to a man who weeps from emotion completely misunderstand the tenets of "traditional masculinity." Perhaps it's just because male dominance was still so solidly entrenched in law and custom, but few of our founding fathers felt any need to "keep a stiff upper lip" to prove their "manliness." Rejection of intense emotional expressiveness as "girlie" only took hold in the last third of the nineteenth century, as I explain in chapter 4. Historian Richard Godbeer's study of diaries and letters from the early Republic reveals male friends sentimentally commemorating the anniversaries of their first meeting, reproaching one another for failing to answer letters, weeping with joy or loneliness, gushing about the pleasure of their reunions, and confiding their anxieties about whether their feelings for a special woman were reciprocated. Reading the letters Godbeer found, I sometimes felt I was hearing echoes of the earnest conversations I had with girlfriends during my teenage years.[37]

THE ADVANTAGES OF DOMESTIC IDEOLOGY FOR WOMEN

To the extent it was accepted by men, the new gender ideology softened the strictness of patriarchal marriage. The acerbic English intellectual Harriet Martineau complained that America's domestic ideology offered women "indulgence . . . as a substitute for justice." Compared to patriarchal discipline, however, indulgence probably seemed like a pretty good deal to many women.

Domesticity gave women who wouldn't have qualified as a "Mrs." in the old social order an alternative source of respect and influence. Instead of being "deputies," valued for their productive contributions to the household but bound to obey their husbands, wives could become experts in a world of family rituals and neighborly interactions in which men played a more marginal role than in the past. Women's enhanced reputation for morality and compassion even allowed some women to enter teaching and nursing jobs before marriage and after marriage to take a larger role in religious and charitable work.

And in a change that must have felt especially gratifying to women aspiring to middle-class status, women who met the standards of "respectable womanhood" were now offered courtesies once reserved for social superiors. Men bowed, doffed their hats, opened doors, and yielded the right-of-way to "ladies," even ones of lower social status than they, although they no longer did so to "gentlemen," even ones of higher status. Such deference, however, was not a tribute to the recipient's power, but instead to her presumed defenselessness.

Overall, the theory of separate spheres, with its concern to protect women's delicacy, led to a marked improvement in the lives of women whose families, husbands, and communities put it into practice. But the rewards it offered were explicitly understood as a substitute for the new rights being claimed by men. And the contradictions between extending rights to (some) men while denying them to other humans encouraged the invention of novel justifications for inequality that still plague our gender, race, and religious relationships.

The burgeoning world market economy accelerated European conquest and colonization, greatly expanding the preexisting slave trade and spurring a more intensive and brutal form of slavery, centered on the production of profits rather than comforts for slave "owners." But it also created new economic opportunities and new scientific discoveries, while the spread of literacy and new humanist ideals fanned discontent with long-standing aristocratic hierarchies. Many of the people who began demanding "liberty" and "natural rights" intended them only for "freeborn," White, Christian European men with enough property to have a stake in a class-divided society. But other people adopted more expansive definitions.

In the seventeenth century, English rebels beheaded one king and deposed another before restoring a monarchy that made new concessions to Parliament. In the eighteenth century, French revolutionaries beheaded another king and declared their commitment to "Liberty, Equality, Fraternity." The American Declaration of Independence claimed "all men are created equal." Such ideas had a dynamic that was hard to contain.

In 1706, the British author Mary Astell demanded, "If all men are born free, how is it that all women are born slaves?" People increasingly asked the same question about Africans and Native peoples in the Americas. Shortly after the American Revolution, a Massachusetts court abolished slavery, ruling that it violated the state constitution's declaration that all men are born "free and equal." Vermont and Rhode Island followed suit. In 1790, New Jersey extended voting rights to "all inhabitants"—including females and free Blacks—who had assets of at least fifty pounds. Antislavery activists took the lead in expanding demands for the "rights of man" into a quest for "human rights."[38]

Individuals whose only goal was to share in the commercial and political privileges formerly monopolized by aristocratic elites were horrified by calls to extend rights to "people of all sexes, colors, tongues, characters, and conditions."[39] But how could they resolve the apparent contradiction between fighting for their own liberty while denying "liberty" to women and enslaved individuals?

The old view had been that the social order depended on everyone from the lowliest peasant to the richest prince submitting to the authority of those above them. Marriage was seen as a microcosm of this larger political hierarchy. "The wife submits to the husband as the husband submits to the Crown" was a typical justification for wifely subordination. But with two kings recently beheaded by their subjects, that analogy now raised uncomfortable possibilities.

The right to enslave and dispossess other peoples was also something that was once either taken for granted or justified by their "heathen" religions and supposedly "inferior civilizations." But when members of those groups began to convert to Christianity, acquire education, and learn "civilized" ways, that could backfire.

How could people reconcile defending slavery and opposing women's rights while demanding liberty for White men? The answer increasingly favored by conservatives was that some groups were excluded from liberty not by man's laws but by some trait with which nature had endowed them—or failed to endow them. This was the great paradox of the Enlightenment and the Age of Revolution: They simultaneously popularized the historically exceptional idea that all human beings have universal moral rights and impelled people who denied such rights to others to justify it on grounds that those others were somehow less than fully human.

When it came to Africans and Native Americans, for example, it became increasingly common to rationalize their oppression by a feature that neither education nor even "right religion" could change: the color of their skin. Blackness and redness were declared "nature's sign" of inborn inferiority or savagery. One British defender of slavery concisely explained why such racism was essential in a world where talk of "human rights" was taking hold: "A negro must be divested of his Humanity . . . before he can become *private property*."[40]

Women's exclusion from political and economic liberties was also said to be imposed by nature, although women's nature supposedly required them to be protected *from* society rather than for society to be protected from *them*. "Dame Nature," it was said, had made women too fragile to venture into the aggressive world of commerce and politics.[41]

Patriarchy had painted women as industrious but insubordinate, competent but conniving, and self-reliant but selfish. Democracy, by contrast, described women as delightful but delicate, virtuous but vulnerable, and "wonderful but weak."[42] They were said to need a different Bill of Rights than men, guaranteeing them "tenderness, delicate treatment, and refined consideration," rights to which men were *not* entitled.[43] Only occasionally was the ominous implication made explicit: When women "assume the character and rights of men, they relinquish [those female] rights," and can be treated as brutally as men.[44]

BECOMING MRS. MAN

The reverence for womanhood that many men professed, then, was conditional on women's abstention from the aspirations and competitive achievements of men. As the guardian of home, "pure disinterested love," and unselfish "devotion to others," a woman was expected to be self-effacing. Her "dignity," the philosopher Jean-Jacques Rousseau declared, "consists in being unknown to the world." During the nineteenth century, a common saying in England and America was that a woman's name should appear in print on only three occasions—her birth, her marriage, and her death. In 1899, one newspaper suggested that the feminist Susan B. Anthony might actually be a man, given her "well-developed desire to see her name in print."[45]

Advice books that had once instructed women to obey their husband no matter how onerous his demands now assured them they would find their greatest happiness by anticipating their husband's wishes and adopting his tastes and interests as her own. Even the philosopher John Stuart Mill, who supported women's right to vote and to work outside the home, declared in 1832 that a woman's "natural impulse . . . [is] to associate her existence with him she loves, and to share *his* occupations." As one publication put it in 1868, a wife is a "living satellite," moving "through life in the orbit to which her husband draws her."[46]

No wonder many women concluded that the only way to gain social acknowledgment was to bask in the reflected glow of their husband. Consider the example of Isabel Arundell, who married the British explorer Richard Burton in 1861. "I worship ambition," she wrote in her diary when she first met him. "Imagine," she continued, the thrill of "making your name a national name!" She then confessed: "I wish I were a man: if I were, I would be Richard Burton. But as I am a woman, I would be Richard Burton's wife."

Isabel went on to become Lady Burton when her husband was knighted in 1886. In America, where becoming Lady Someone-or-other wasn't possible, women with similar ambitions sometimes insisted on being identified by their husband's profession or political position rather than his first name. To use a few real-life examples: Mrs. Governor Robinson, Mrs. Senator Ingalls, Mrs. Judge Humphrey, and Mrs. Professor Cosby. Julia Gardiner, the widow of former President John Tyler, used to sign her letters "Mrs. Ex-President Tyler."[47]

Chapter 3.

HOW THE GENDER LEGACY OF DEMOCRACY HOLDS WOMEN BACK

We've come a long way from the restricted roles prescribed for women in nineteenth-century Anglo-American culture. Yet in the early twenty-first century, researchers began reporting on two puzzling political and occupational patterns they labeled the "gender equality paradox."

First, they noted, several strongly patriarchal countries around the world have accrued a much better record of female political leadership than has the United States. In the past seventy-five years, more than a dozen women have exercised political power at the highest levels of such states. The list includes Prime Minister Indira Gandhi of India, President Corazon Aquino of the Philippines, Prime Minister Benazir Bhutto of Pakistan, and State Counsellor Aung San Suu Kyi of Myanmar. As of 2023, by contrast, the US ranked seventy-first in a worldwide survey of the extent of female representation in national legislatures. Mexico, our supposedly "macho" neighbor, ranked fourth.[1]

Second, even though modern economies that continue to enforce patriarchal norms have a lower percentage of full-time female workers than more democratic systems, women who *do* work for pay in such societies are much better represented in typically male-dominated STEM (science, technology, engineering, and math) occupations than women in more gender-egalitarian nations. In fact, according to the World Economic Forum's Global Gender Gap Index, the more gender-equal a society's laws and social programs are, the *less* likely girls and women are to enter these traditionally male-dominated and generally higher-paying occupations.[2]

Some analysts claim these patterns prove that men and women really *do* have different natures and preferences. They point out that most female leaders in patriarchal societies didn't seek power on their own initiative, but were pressed into service as the wives, widows, daughters, or sisters of men who headed powerful dynasties. They were furthering their lineage's interests. Similarly, they say, such societies offer women few opportunities for decent-paying jobs and have limited social safety-net programs for women and children. This leaves women who need or want secure paid employment little choice but to enter male-dominated fields that offer financial security even if those jobs don't conform to their "real" interests or personality.

In societies where women are free to "follow their heart," this updated version of separate spheres thinking goes, they generally don't pursue power or choose impersonal, analytical, and "cold" professions like math and science. "In the pursuit of happiness," argues Christina Hoff Sommers of the American Enterprise Institute, "men and women take somewhat different paths." Women, she argues, prefer jobs that let them exercise their aesthetic tastes and caregiving impulses. And sure enough, women occupy only 15 percent of America's engineering jobs, while accounting for 84 percent of interior designers and occupational therapists and 87 percent of registered nurses and nurse practitioners.

Furthermore, because women prioritize personal relationships, says Sommers, they tend to avoid or quit jobs that interfere with family obligations. These choices may not offer great opportunities for advancement, she concludes, but women are "self-determining human beings."[3]

The problem with this argument is that the democratizing market societies of the eighteenth and nineteenth centuries didn't just *allow* "self-determining" women to follow preexisting "feminine" interests and aptitudes. They helped *create* those interests and aptitudes, praising and rewarding some activities when done by women and denigrating or penalizing different choices.

A recent examination of international data reveals that gender stereotypes about what people want to do and are capable of doing are not universal, as one would expect if they reflected innate preferences. Men and women in hierarchical and patriarchal societies actually exhibit *smaller* differences in their self-reported personalities, capabilities, and preferences than do people in most modern democracies.[4]

Consider the claim that women are "naturally" less interested in or good at "cold" skills like math as men are. It turns out this may be more a result of internalized stereotypes rather than intrinsic disinterest or inability. In 2014, experimenters in the US randomly assigned several male and female participants either a male or female avatar in a virtual reality game, then placed each in a virtual math competition with two supposedly opposite-gender avatars. Participants who were assigned a male avatar and then put into competition with two supposedly female avatars consistently turned in the strongest performance, regardless of their actual offline gender. In this case, not only did the women assigned a male avatar live *up* to stereotypes about men and math, but the men assigned a female avatar lived *down* to feminine stereotypes![5]

The same unconscious adjustment to gender stereotypes can occur in people's interpretation of their own emotions. In one study, a bunch of volunteers were put into teams that played against each other. Some volunteers were asked immediately after the game to report their emotions while playing. Others were only asked this question after a week had passed.

Among individuals asked to recall their feelings immediately after the game, there was no difference in the kinds of emotions males and females reported having experienced. But after a week had passed, the females in the experiment reported feeling more stereotypically feminine emotions, such as sympathy and guilt, while the males "remembered" having more "masculine" feelings, such as anger or pride.[6]

Yet another study found that when one group of volunteers was asked to recall how they'd felt during a period a few months earlier, the male and female subjects reported equally intense (or not intense) emotions. But a different group of volunteers was asked to do this right after being prompted to think about gender. In this group, the females "recalled" having more intense emotions and the males "recalled" less intense ones.

In other words, when we think about what's supposedly "normal" for people of our gender to feel, it can actually change our memory or interpretation of our feelings.

How about the way gender stereotypes affect the way we feel about people of the "other" sex? Overall, the gender stereotypes we've inherited about women's nature from the democratic ideology of separate spheres tend to produce in many men what researchers call "benevolent sexism"—helpful and protective behavior based on the assumption that women aren't strong enough or knowledgeable enough to do some things for themselves. It's "benevolent" because it can be as kind as offering to change a flat tire and as heroic as leaping forward to deflect an attack or stepping aside to let a woman be rescued first in an emergency. But it's "sexism" to the extent it assumes in advance that a woman won't be able to do something for herself.

Some researchers see benevolent sexism as simply a kindly mask for hostile sexism, and it's true that benevolent sexists sometimes turn antagonistic when a woman rejects proffered protection or violates feminine stereotypes. Countries whose citizens score highest in benevolently sexist attitudes also score high in measures of hostile sexism.[7]

But at least in small doses, I don't think benevolent sexism is necessarily cover for hostility. It often makes a woman's everyday life easier, and many women welcome its inoffensive forms, not to mention its heroic ones. For years, many well-intentioned men have honestly believed this is the best way to show respect and regard for women and have gone to considerable trouble to do so.

Still, even in its most benign forms, this kind of behavior comes with costs. Managers who hold benevolent views of women are pleasant to work for, but they're less likely to assign women the challenging tasks that bring promotion, even when women express interest in those. Men who offer benevolent assistance often take over a task rather than sharing it. Girls and women accustomed to receiving such assistance get into the habit of asking people to do things *for* them rather than learning how to do things themselves—something that can leave them out of luck if no benevolent sexist happens to be around when needed.[8]

Furthermore, experimental studies show that instructions and assistance couched in benevolent or protective terms can actually undermine women's performance by reminding them they might fail. When experimenters exposed undergraduate women to either a benevolent, hostile, or neutral comment in a mock job interview, the women who heard the benevolently sexist comment reported more doubts about their own competence afterward and exhibited impaired problem-solving. The hostile sexism, while offensive, didn't trigger similar declines in self-confidence or performance.[9]* Until very recently, moreover, benevolent views of women tended to be extremely condescending. In 1973, a study exploring what people considered to be typically masculine and feminine characteristics found that while women were credited with many warm fuzzies, such as compassion and emotional sensitivity, they were also described as "gullible, childlike, flatterable." As late as 1977, more than half of Americans polled said women were less "emotionally suited" for politics than men.[10]

THE PITFALLS OF BEING PRAISEWORTHY

In recent years, confidence in women's intellectual and practical capabilities has steadily increased. Analyzing fifteen nationally representative polls from 1946 to 2018, social psychologist Alice Eagly and her colleagues found growing respect for women's intelligence, creativity, and competence, starting in the 1980s. By

* "Benevolent" racism is less common than benevolent sexism, but in racial interactions, too, receiving subtle indications that someone lacks confidence in your abilities, without any show of animus, seems to create more self-doubt than does open hostility. When Black and Hispanic subjects engage in face-to-face interaction with a White subject who expresses attitudes and behaviors characterized by either blatant, subtle, or no racial bias, they display impaired cognitive functioning after being exposed to the subtle bias, but not after hearing the blatant comment or having the unbiased interaction. See Mary Murphy et al., "Cognitive Costs of Contemporary Prejudice," *Group Processes & Intergroup Relations* 16, no. 5 (2013): 560–71, https://doi.org/10.1177/1368430212468170.

2018, 86 percent of respondents said men and women were equally intelligent. Of the 14 percent who thought there was a difference, twice as many credited women rather than men with the intellectual advantage! Almost half (46 percent) said women were more organized than men, while fewer than 5 percent believed men were more organized than women.[11]

This is a significant comedown in men's reputation for competence and an impressive improvement for women compared to the stereotypes of nineteenth-century domesticity and the 1950s "feminine mystique." But it does raise a version of the old schoolyard taunt: "If we're so smart, why ain't we rich?"

Part of the answer, paradoxically, may lie in the very fact that the increase in benevolent views of women—and in views of women as benevolent to *others*—has been so huge, especially in comparison to people's less favorable views of men. Eagly and her colleagues found that over the past several decades people have become increasingly likely to describe women as more ethical, compassionate, sociable, altruistic, and ready to sacrifice for others than men.

When Eagly's team combined all the "expressive" (or emotionally insightful) traits and the "communal" (or prosocial) traits that various polls had asked people about over the years, they calculated that in 1946 only 54 percent of respondents, a bare majority, thought women had more such traits than men. By 1989, 83 percent of respondents gave the advantage to women. And as of 2018, a whopping 97 percent agreed that women were more likely than men to prioritize the good of others and of society. This is a huge change from older patriarchal views of men as the altruistic, self-sacrificing sex and women as more likely to put personal ties and nuclear family interests ahead of the common welfare.[12]

But women's heightened reputation for intelligence, competence, and altruism doesn't mean women are now on an equal footing with men when it comes to opportunities outside the home, much less pulling ahead as some people now claim. When the researchers separated out what they termed "agentic" qualities—traits associated with goal attainment, competitiveness, decisiveness, potency, and the ability to take command in emergencies—from other intellectual and practical traits, they found that men are still much more likely to be credited with such attributes than women.

This may explain some of the antisocial features of today's so-called "manosphere." To the extent that being a man is defined as the opposite of being a *woman,* rather than the opposite of being a *boy,* as was once the case, the fact that women have increasingly adopted social roles and personality traits formerly considered male prerogatives leaves some men anxious about how to assert a distinctly "masculine" identity. One response is to highlight their aggressive and domineering capacities and to denigrate expressive, altruistic, and conciliatory behaviors as unmanly.[13]

Even among individuals who don't reject empathetic and communal traits, the widespread assumption that men are more forceful than women undermines confidence in women's leadership skills. "Agentic" traits often lead to aggressive, self-serving, and domineering behaviors that are seen as unlikable or even "toxic," but also as sometimes necessary in competitive situations. So when it comes to being thought capable of handling high-stakes leadership positions, it is an advantage for men to be seen as capable of toxicity—or even prone to it—and a disadvantage for women to be seen as too generous to be poisonous when needed.[14]

In other words, going back to that schoolyard taunt, a lot of Americans believe that females are smart enough and competent enough that we *could* be rich and powerful, but we're way too nice to *want* to be.

And yet in a classic double bind, it's a big disadvantage for a woman to be seen as *not* too nice to be noxious, because that undermines the points she normally gets for being "communal" and "expressive." When a job is advertised as requiring good communication skills, for example, female applicants have a big advantage over males. Indeed, a good part of women's recent upward occupational mobility is connected to that niceness advantage. Women's supposed knack for combining competence and intelligence with superior expressive and caregiving skills surely helps explain why women account for three-fourths of all human-resources managers and 70 percent of managers in medical and health services.[15]

Stereotypes about women vary by race, ethnicity, and sexual identity. White women get the most credit for communal, empathetic qualities. Black women who have overcome discrimination to attain positions of authority don't face the same penalties for engaging in agentic behaviors as do White women and Black men, but elsewhere, stereotypes of "angry Black women" are widespread. Among White and Asian tech workers, women who identify as LGBTQ and don't conform to conventional feminine norms in appearance or behavior are viewed as more competent by their male colleagues than more traditionally "feminine" women. In other fields of work, however, such women experience additional harassment. Among scientists, Asian American women report the greatest backlash for assertive behavior.[16]

Despite these variations, the overall association of agency with men and empathy with women is strong across racial and ethnic categories. In general, as psychologists Laurie Rudman and Peter Glick note, "women are held to a higher standard of niceness than men" and penalized when they fail to meet it.[17] And the pressure to "be nice" gets internalized surprisingly early.

In a 2017 project, researchers followed four hundred children, aged five to seven, from a middle-class community in Illinois. For one study, children were told one story about a "really, really smart" person and another about a "really, really nice" person. Afterward, the children were shown pictures of males and females and asked to guess which ones might be the persons in the stories.

Typically, when asked to describe a generic character, about 70 percent of young children describe someone of their own sex. And sure enough, at age five, both boys and girls were likely to choose a person of their own gender as the "really, really smart" character *and* as the "really, really nice" one. By age six, however, a significantly lower percentage of girls picked a female as the "really, really smart" character, while boys became less likely to believe that the "really, really nice" person was a boy.[18]

Other studies reveal that by the time girls have reached adolescence, most have regained the sense that they can be smart. They actually report feeling less compulsion to conform to gendered norms of behavior than do their male counterparts—with one notable exception. Females aged fourteen to nineteen report feeling "a lot" of pressure to manage people's emotions, even at the expense of their own, while boys feel an equal amount of pressure to hide their softer emotions.[19]

The expectation that women will take responsibility for the invisible labor of anticipating people's needs and managing, fine-tuning, or repairing emotions—and that because they are more empathetic and better organized than men, they *need* to do so—has become a source of particular inequality and tension in contemporary heterosexual marriages.[20] But that expectation is not a result of inherent gender differences. It is the legacy of separate spheres ideology—something that has been with us long enough to have created habits that are hard to break, but not long enough to doom us to keep replicating them.

Chapter 4.

SEPARATE SPHERES, SOULMATE LOVE & SEXUAL TENSION

The Contradictory Legacy of Nineteenth-Century Courtship

Over the past few decades, somewhere between 60 and 75 percent of American adults have consistently told pollsters they believe in "soulmates"—that everyone has someone, somewhere, with whom they are "meant" to be, an "other half" who will complete them.[1]

Marriage researchers worry about the popularity of such views, because individuals who believe marriage involves finding your "perfect match" are more likely to abandon a relationship when problems arise than people who see love as a process that evolves over time.[2] Personally, I think many people simply use the term to indicate their deep mutual understanding. Either way, though, it's notable that while something akin to "soulmate" love was often celebrated in romance stories across the ages, it was almost never recommended as the basis of marriage.

Not until the nineteenth century, and then only in a few countries, did people come to believe they should marry a "soulmate."

And once they did, they meant something very different from either the instant passion described in premodern love stories or the "best friend plus good sex" relationships valued by so many people today.

Premodern stories about soulmates typically began with two people falling in love at first sight, sometimes against their own wishes, but then never wavering in their commitment, despite being forbidden to marry or becoming separated and facing all manner of obstacles to reuniting. Stories about such electrifying, undying love have always appealed to people's longings for romance. But they were often also cautionary tales, ending in tragedy, because at least for ordinary mortals, such love wasn't what marriage was supposed to be about. The Italian humanist Alessandro Piccolomini declared in 1540 that "love is a reciprocity of soul." For that reason, he argued, it "has a different end and obeys different laws from marriage. Hence one should not take the loved one to wife."[3]

This was a common belief throughout the ages. In premodern Europe and America, people generally agreed that romantic passion interfered with the sober judgment required to choose the most appropriate partner for the family enterprise a couple would need to manage, whether that be a great estate, a modest farm, or a small business. Across the social spectrum, the ideal was to marry someone who would be an asset to the family economy and whom you could learn to love. And in the upper classes, even believing you'd *never* love your partner didn't necessarily prevent an advantageous match.

Many premodern married couples clearly did love each other, and scattered references in letters and diaries suggest that some shared a strong sexual bond. But most people believed such feelings to be a fortunate outcome of marriage. Indeed, too much married ardor was considered unseemly. Tranquil affection, coupled with wifely obedience and husbandly self-restraint, was considered the best guarantee of a successful marriage.[4]

Rather than falling in love and then deciding to marry, people in premodern England and America typically decided it was time to marry, or for their child to marry, and then looked for someone suitable, often asking friends and family to help them find someone with the required material resources or social connections. England's first matrimonial ad, published in 1695, read simply: "A Gentleman about 30 years of Age, that says he had a Very Good Estate, would willingly Match himself to some Good Young Gentlewoman that has a Fortune of 3000 £, or thereabout, and he will make Settlement to Content."[5]

During the eighteenth century, however, what had once been a wistful fantasy—the idea of falling in love before marriage, and marrying *because* you were in love—became increasingly attainable. The expansion of wage labor meant a couple could earn a living without having to depend on parents' willingness to offer a dowry or grant them land. It also made it less necessary for a man to pick a wife on the basis of her ability to help run a farm or business.

Yet despite the growing popularity of "marriage by fascination," as the French disapprovingly called the love match, many people considered it risky. Parents worried that the new emphasis on marrying for love would lead young people to choose their partners on the basis of physical attraction or personal charm rather than on the practical considerations that made marriage work. Worse yet, a woman who fell in love with a man before marrying might have sex with him before the wedding, ruining her life should the man leave her unwed and pregnant.

Such worries account for the popularity of the "seduction" novels that were all the rage in eighteenth- and early-nineteenth-century

England and America. In William Hill Brown's *The Power of Sympathy* (1789), a young man attempts to seduce Harriot, a woman from a lower social class. Her virtuous resistance convinces him she's worthy of marriage, but just before their wedding, the lovers discover that Harriot is the illegitimate child of her fiancée's father. She dies of grief and he takes his own life.

In Hannah Webster Foster's *The Coquette* (1797), Eliza flirts with two potential suitors—one a respectable but boring clergyman; the other an aristocratic libertine. By the time she realizes she loves the clergyman, he has tired of her frivolity and is pledged to another. Despondent, Eliza allows the aristocrat—who by then has married another woman for her money—to seduce her. "Polluted," Eliza goes off to die alone, leaving her seducer to belatedly repent his "black catalogue of vices."[6]

Susannah Rowson's *Charlotte Temple* (1794) was supposedly based on the true story of a fifteen-year-old girl who ran off to America with a British army officer who abandoned her after she became pregnant. The number of villains who contribute to Charlotte's seduction and tragic death defies credibility, yet *Charlotte Temple* was the biggest bestseller in America until the publication of *Uncle Tom's Cabin* in 1852. Crowds made pilgrimages to the church where she was supposedly buried.[7]

Real-life failures of the love-based courting system might not have been so dramatic, but they were not rare, especially in the heady decades following the American Revolution, when premarital and nonmarital births shot up. In Philadelphia, unwed birth rates doubled in the late eighteenth century. "Every town and village" in America, lamented *Massachusetts* magazine in 1791, "affords some instance of a ruined female fallen from the heights of purity to the lowest grade of humanity."[8]

Even as novels celebrating romantic love proliferated, so did warnings about its dangers. Advice books urged women to focus on the spiritual qualities and moral character of a potential suitor rather than being seduced by his charm. Men were told to ignore a woman's looks or social "accomplishments" and focus on "her character as a woman."[9]

Not everyone accepted the idea that premarital sex "polluted" a woman. But the nineteenth-century purity-until-marriage campaign had a real impact. Premarital conceptions, calculated by the percent of postmarital births that occurred awkwardly soon after the wedding, fell from a high of about 30 percent during the second half of the eighteenth century to a low of approximately 10 percent by the mid-nineteenth century, well before widespread access to reliable contraception.

Letters and diaries confirm that many men as well as women subscribed to the idea that they must "save themselves" for marriage. In 1880, on the eve of his marriage at age twenty-two, the future president Theodore Roosevelt wrote triumphantly in his diary that he could go to his wedding bed "absolutely pure. I can tell Alice everything I have ever done."[10]

DILEMMAS OF THE LOVE MATCH

But the very success of the purity campaign posed a dilemma for people seeking to follow the middle-class marriage script. Love was now generally accepted as the impetus for marriage. However, since love occasioned by "fascination" or "mere attraction" was dangerous, how could you know when and with whom it was safe to begin a romantic journey? On the other hand, how could "playing it safe" nurture the intense love that was supposed to differentiate "modern" marriages from the pragmatic matches of the past?

The emergence of the male-breadwinner marriage and the doctrine of separate male and female spheres described in chapter 2 offered a starting place for redefining love. In the older household economy, husbands and wives had overlapping responsibilities and skill sets. In the male-breadwinner family, by contrast, marriage was a relationship between two people who specialized in entirely different responsibilities and skills.

Their *differences*, rather than their shared duties of provisioning the household and sustaining relationships with kin and community, were now said to be the basis of love and marriage. The British philosopher John Ruskin explained in an 1865 essay: "Each [sex] has what the other has not: each completes the other, and is completed by the other: they are in nothing alike, and the happiness and perfection of both depends on each asking and receiving from the other what the other only can give."[11]

The most desirable partner was no longer someone who could work alongside you or take over your duties if need be. Rather, it was someone who would bring to the relationship characteristics and skills you didn't possess—along with *inabilities* that made them dependent on the skills and traits you did possess. You would neither need nor want that person to help out in your tasks, nor would you expect to be asked to share theirs.

For the nineteenth-century middle class, writes historian E. Anthony Rotundo, "the highest ideal of marriage was the union of opposites," a union many believed to be literally magnetic. As the popular lecturer and author Orson Fowler declared, "*attraction or affinity* for . . . the opposite . . . constitutes the very *embodiment and heart's core* of true love."[12]

But how can two people with completely opposite experiences, tasks, activities, skills, and assignments in life find the deep intimacy that leads to true love? Nineteenth-century marital guides counseled one sure way. Love was said to flow from the partners' mutual understanding and appreciation of each other's souls. Despite its emphasis on the differences between male and female capacities and roles, the new middle-class love script insisted that "manly" men and "true" women shared a *class* similarity of soul and character that differentiated them from their upper- and lower-class counterparts. They could bond over their mutual commitment to moral rectitude and their disdain for self-indulgence.[13]

Most premodern stories about "soulmate" love had involved couples falling in love at first sight, but the Victorian idea of soulmate love was quite different. It was not something you recognized immediately. You could only know you'd found your "other half" when you became absolutely sure that your souls and characters—rather than your skills and interests—were perfectly matched. Achieving that "communion of souls" became the goal of middle-class courtship.

Despite their "opposite" responsibilities and abilities, men and women could find common ground in their veneration for religion, virtue, home, and family. And unlike later drafts of the middle-class gender script, emotional expressiveness about these topics was equally essential for both sexes. Men as well as women began any serious relationship by "laying bare" their souls, freely disclosing their moral aspirations, their longing for the other's love, and their doubts about being "worthy" of that love.

People who subscribed to these values created a distinctive style of courtship, far more emotionally expressive and sentimental than in either medieval or modern times. Diaries and letters of courting couples in the middle classes overflow with expressions of their longing to examine "all the recesses" of each other's hearts, to become certain of their "similitude of thought & feeling," to reach "the sweet communion of souls."[14]

Rural and working-class Americans, both Black and White, were slower to accept romantic ideas about courtship. More often, they continued older patterns, deciding it was time to marry and then seeking help from friends or relatives to find an eligible partner. When such couples exchanged letters about the possibility of marriage, they seldom expressed passionate devotion, even though letters and diaries after marriage often reveal strong affection. As one woman wrote to a suitor, "you said if I was willing you was . . . I think more of you than any other Jentlemen and I recon you are the one as you say you are willing."[15]

Reading middle-class courtship letters from this era, on the other hand, always leaves me with the sense that these couples are trying to reassure themselves that they will be as morally and emotionally indispensable to each other as earlier generations were indispensable to each other in practical matters. The letters contain an almost obsessive quest for ever-higher levels of mutual "sympathy," "candor," and "trust."[16] Their desire to be "worthy" of the other, their fears that they might not be, and their pleas to be reassured about how "perfectly" their souls are matched are expressed with a fervor foreign to most modern ears.

When I've given students such letters to read, what surprises them most is the ardor expressed by the men. It was not unusual for a nineteenth-century suitor to express sentiments such as those of one man who wrote that "to love with all one's soul" is to blend "all things that are high, ardent and pure. . . . I have no word for it but worship." Another told his intended "I cannot have a separate existence from you, I breathe by you; I live by you."[17]

As historians Peter Stearns and Mark Knapp note, these men not only accepted but actually "gloried in the idea that love required full emotional disclosure," with "no holding back" of feelings. They admitted to insecurities about their loved one's devotion and spoke of weeping from loneliness when absent from her. Nathaniel Hawthorne, writing to Sophia Peabody in 1840, declared: "Where thou art not, there it is a sort of death."[18]

To highlight the differences between the emotional language of middle-class love then and now, I sometimes asked students to read the letters aloud to each other. The first reaction of most males was to adopt a sarcastic tone, distancing themselves from the emotion. When I urged them to read as if they meant it, they would often shift uncomfortably and sometimes even blush. Almost invariably, some woman would demand to know why today's supposedly enlightened men were so freaked out by such emotionalism.

In some ways, though, the letters strike me as a form of premarital bargaining analogous to that of traditional arranged marriages. In this case, the negotiations were over the emotional rather than the material assets each partner would bring to the match.

In the male-breadwinner family, unlike the co-provider family economy, a woman's security in marriage depended more on her husband's love than on his practical need for her help. So women were especially anxious to make sure a suitor had sufficient funds in his emotional bank account. Historian Karen Lystra reports that women frequently subjected their fiancé to "elaborate emotional tests," expressing doubts about the man's sincerity or the depth of their mutual understanding and sometimes actually breaking off the engagement before allowing themselves to be persuaded by an eager beau that his love was ample enough to see them through.

Of course, the letters and diaries that provide most of our information about courtship and marriage in this era are not representative of the population as a whole. Most were written by literate, White, middle-class Northerners who moved in the same social circles, although middle-class Black Americans expressed similar sentiments. Historians of sexuality point out that many of what we now label "Victorian" sexual and courtship norms reflect the systematic exclusion of many alternative sexual subcultures and mores from the historical record.[19]

Some rural and working-class communities maintained a tradition of ribald sexual expression and tolerated premarital sex. Many idealistic individuals and groups advocated "free love," by which they typically meant not "open" relationships, but rather voluntary commitments based on a higher morality than that of a marriage system in which most women had few options if their husbands were abusive or unfaithful.

Even among people who ostensibly promoted middle-class morality, there were plenty who practiced something quite different than what they preached. Prostitution was one of the fastest-growing occupations of the era, flourishing not only in port cities and "disreputable" sections of towns but middle- and upper-class ones. By the 1820s, clients could buy "brothel guides" indicating which houses were "genteel" enough to satisfy "gentlemen of distinguished rank, education, and conduct."[20]

In the 1880s, moral reformers, trying to protect young girls from exploitation, campaigned to raise the legal age of consent, which was between ages ten and twelve in most states and just seven in Delaware. Many legislators and "respectable" businessmen opposed these reforms, and their objections reveal the pervasiveness of sexual hypocrisy. Several complained that such laws would allow "working girls" to "blackmail their employers" (presumably after a ten-year-old had "freely" consented to sex). And in an example of the racial exceptions to many men's supposed reverence for women's purity, a Kentucky legislator claimed that criminalizing sex with all twelve-year-olds would put a Black female "on the same plane" as a White one.[21]

But I focus here on publicly approved middle-class values, aspirations, and behavior patterns, not only as reflected in diaries and letters that have been preserved but also as promoted in didactic literature and official histories, enforced in public institutions, endlessly repeated in sermons, marital advice books, and children's literature, and passed down to future generations as how "normal" people felt and behaved. They have become part of the "earworms" that many Americans have trouble driving out of their heads.

Despite what we now know about the underside of Victorian morality, it's impossible to doubt the sincerity of the emotional and moral sentiments expressed in many of the love letters and diaries that have survived. These give us a picture of Victorian soulmate courtship and marriage at its best. And its best is often very moving.

Still, even the "best case scenarios" reveal the limitations inherent in the notion of love as a union of opposites. For one thing, separate spheres were not equal spheres. Nathaniel Hawthorne assured Sophia that he desired "to toil for thee, and to make thee a happy wife." And yet, he said, he still felt "that my Dove is to follow my guidance and do my bidding. . . . My love gives me the right, and your love consents to it." This idea is expressed in scores of letters from nineteenth-century men to their fiancées and wives.[22]

Sophia wrote that she "gratefully submit[ted] to the inconveniences of his needs and demands," but her choice of words does not suggest unadulterated delight. Indeed, studies of New England women's diaries in this era reveal that many women felt very ambivalent about assuming the wifely duty of becoming "responsible for the happiness and virtue of others."[23]

Anxiety about such issues may help explain the frequency with which many women, having accepted a proposal, postponed the actual wedding as long as possible, prolonging the relative freedom they had during courtship and would legally lose once wed. But apprehension about the wedding night was almost certainly another factor, given the sexual inexperience of these women and the mixed messages about sex they received from moral and medical advice books.[24]

SEX BETWEEN SOULMATES

I say "mixed messages" because the "rules" for middle-class marriage might have been easier to follow if cultural arbiters had been as thoroughly disapproving of sexual pleasure and as confident in women's lack of sexual desire as is often claimed. But Victorian teachings about sexuality were more complicated and ambivalent than many people realize.

To be sure, the British physician William Acton's opinion that "the majority of women (happily for society) are not much troubled with sexual feeling" was liberally quoted by experts on both sides of the Atlantic Ocean. One American author even claimed that most wives never felt "the faintest ray of sexual pleasure." Another rather creepily suggested that women's feelings when submitting to their husbands' embraces were "more of the motherly nature than the conjugal."[25]

Yet nineteenth-century moralists didn't think women were incapable of lust. Indeed, they continually emphasized how easily girls—even White, Protestant, "well-bred" girls—could slide into sexual depravity. Females were considered just as susceptible as males to "the solitary vice" of masturbation. Reading poetry, attending ballroom dances, or drinking stimulants such as tea or coffee were all said to produce "excessive excitement" that led girls into "vicious habits." The stimulation caused by dancing, claimed bestselling author Dr. John Kellogg, inventor of Corn Flakes, is what had led three-quarters of the "debased" and "degenerate" female prostitutes in New York City to their ruin.*

Girls and young women were warned to zealously guard their purity of thought, appearance, and behavior. Yet after marriage, even Acton conceded that "moderate gratification of the sex-passion" was important for wives' as well as husbands' happiness and that "physical attraction" (a polite word for sex) enhanced domestic harmony. At least one other author went further, declaring it a woman's "duty"—to herself as well as her husband—"to heartily enjoy" her marital relations.

Despite condemning "animal" passion, most Victorian moralists regarded the "sex instinct" as something bestowed on humans by God so that we would follow his command to procreate. Having sex with the intention *not* to procreate was sinful, but spiritually motivated marital sex could be healthy and holy.[26]

Still, experts cautioned that the "sex instinct" could be dangerously addictive, even within marriage. It should be indulged only infrequently, in small doses. Having sexual intercourse too often or enjoying it too much could damage the entire nervous system, leading to impaired vision, memory loss, insanity, and even suicide. If sex had come in a bottle of tablets, the label would have warned: "Take only the smallest dose necessary. Do not mistake this medicine for candy."

Opinions differed, though, as to what constituted an appropriate dose. At one extreme was Dr. John Cowan's widely read *The*

---

* In a book titled *Plain Facts for Old and Young*, Kellogg warned that in addition to the risk of insanity and death, "self abuse" posed females with an additional gender-specific hazard: ulceration of their fingernails from touching the "acrid, irritating secretions of the vagina."

Science of a New Life, which urged couples to abstain from sex for three years after each successful impregnation. At the other extreme, a few experts believed once or twice a week was acceptable so long as the man could withstand the depletion of his "vital fluids" and didn't force himself upon his wife if she was not amenable to such frequency.

As for treating sex like candy, most authors agreed that while pleasure was a desirable accompaniment of sex, sex for pleasure *alone* was indeed unacceptable. Orson Fowler, whose 238-page tome on *Love and Parentage* went through thirteen editions between 1844 and 1850, declared: "In exact proportion as the love of any individual tends to sexual gratification as such, it is debasing and brutal: because unguided by intellect, and unsanctified by moral purity." In 1882, Dr. Henry Guernsey warned readers of his *Plain Talks on Avoided Subjects* that although "well-regulated sexual intercourse is necessary to the married," pursuing sex for "mere carnal pleasure" violated its "high and holy" purpose of encouraging procreation. Couples must rise "above sensualism."

It was theoretically possible to achieve a marital sex life that was both mutually pleasurable and morally commendable. And when men fully embraced the love ideal and women had the opportunity to unhurriedly explore their sexual feelings, many couples were able to achieve sexual harmony. Some letters of middle-class couples explicitly refer to their erotic pleasures (though historians note that individuals frequently inked these passages out before saving their letters).

But even without the insensitive behavior that so many wives complained of, it was hard for women and men to escape the social messages about the evils of desire or to find accurate information about how to attain sexual satisfaction. Most Americans remained woefully ignorant of female sexuality. As one doctor complained bitterly in 1880, there was practically an "army" of "pseudo-moralists" who "defrauded" women by preaching frigidity "as a virtue to be cultivated" rather than educating couples about the importance of clitoral stimulation during sex.[27]

As late as 1921, more than a decade into the sexual revolution I describe in the next chapter, a survey of predominantly well-educated, middle-class women found that the majority had entered marriage with almost no exposure to sex education. Nearly 60 percent claimed they had "never" experienced sexual desire prior to marriage. Although 43 percent reported being "attracted" by their first experience of sex, almost a quarter described being "repelled." Twenty-two percent said "neither," elaborating on that with words such as "frightened," "disappointed," "indifferent," or "relieved" that it wasn't worse. And even women who reported enjoying sex often expressed ambivalence about their feelings of pleasure.[28]

One obstacle to enjoying sex was the very thing that supposedly *justified* enjoying it: the possibility of procreation. In 1850, the typical American woman in her forties had raised five or six children, often experiencing several other pregnancies that ended in miscarriages or infant deaths. Almost everyone knew someone who had died in childbirth or been left with debilitating conditions by the birthing experience. Couples spent most of their lives, as contemporaries often put it, "under the shadow of maternity," and many women dreaded sex because of that shadow.[29]

Yet over the course of the nineteenth century, the average number of children among Whites fell from seven per woman in 1810 to about four in 1895, with the sharpest declines in the urban middle classes. Some of this seems to have been the result of more sexual restraint among men who'd internalized the new emphasis on women's asexuality. But there's evidence that couples were avoiding procreation in other ways, including contraception and abortion.[30]

While using contraception relieved the dread of pregnancy, it created a different source of ambivalence about sex. In the 1921 survey, many women reported feeling guilty when they had sex without intending to procreate. And even women eager to use contraception often felt nervous about seeking it out. On the one hand, an expanding urban, commercial society was making it easier than ever to prevent or end a pregnancy. Urban shops and itinerant peddlers offered a growing array of "rubber goods" for sale. Newspapers openly advertised birth control devices and abortion services. On the other hand, self-appointed purity police were organizing campaigns to penalize and even jail individuals who sold or purchased such "indecent" objects and services.

In light of current battles over abortion law and policy, it's important to note that the late nineteenth-century campaign against birth control and abortion was new in American history. When the Supreme Court repealed abortion rights in 2022, Justice Alito, writing for the majority, claimed that "an unbroken tradition of prohibiting abortion on pain of criminal punishment [had] persisted from the earliest days of the common law until 1973." But that is demonstrably false.

In fact, from colonial times onward, midwives routinely supplied patients with herbs and other medicines supposed to abort a pregnancy. When Benjamin Franklin adapted and published a popular British "How to" manual for Americans in 1748, among the instructions he added was one on how to induce an abortion. The manual was popular enough to go through at least twenty editions.[31]

Until the 1840s and 1850s, abortion was completely legal in many jurisdictions until quickening. In others it was merely a misdemeanor. "Quickening" is the term for when a pregnant woman first feels her fetus move, something that typically occurs between the fourth and fifth months. That left women up to twenty-one weeks to legally arrange an abortion—more time than currently allowed in many American states.[32]

As of July 2025, for example, abortion was entirely banned in Alabama, Arkansas, Idaho, Indiana, Kentucky, Louisiana, Mississippi, Oklahoma, South Dakota, Tennessee, Texas, and West Virginia. In Florida, Georgia, Iowa, and South Carolina it was only allowed up to six weeks, a date at which many women don't even suspect they are pregnant. North Carolina and Utah set the cutoff date for a legal abortion at twelve and eighteen weeks, respectively.[33]

Legal prohibitions against birth control and abortion mounted in the 1840s and 1850s, but only in 1873, after Congress passed the Comstock Act, did they start being rigorously enforced. This act, named for Anthony Comstock, the legislation's most zealous advocate and enforcer,* made it a crime to mail, sell, give away, or even merely possess "obscene, lewd or lascivious," "immoral," or "indecent" pictures, publications, and articles, including contraceptive information and devices.[34] Over the next decades, thousands of Americans were arrested and even jailed for such "crimes."[35]

Comstock boasted that he had driven fifteen abortion providers to suicide, but throughout the nineteenth and early twentieth centuries, licensed physicians were actually allowed more latitude in deciding whether an abortion was "therapeutically" necessary than they are in much of America today. Commonly accepted reasons included not just imminent threat of maternal death, but excessive nausea, suicide ideation, or even extreme anxiety.

No such latitude was offered to people who assisted women with birth control. Even those who simply provided contraceptive

* Comstock's vicious persecution of birth control providers seems almost pathological in light of the fact that his own mother had bled to death after delivering her tenth child!

information or sex education risked prosecution. In 1904, for example, Dr. Charles Malchow, a professor at Hamline University's medical school in St. Paul, Minnesota, published *The Sexual Life*, a book based on an article he'd written for a medical journal on "sexual ignorance" as "The Great Cause of Domestic Infelicity." Malchow explained how physicians could help their married patients achieve "sexual passion," emphasizing the importance of foreplay for a woman's satisfaction.

The Sexual Life eventually sold one hundred thousand copies, but all Malchow got from it was a federal obscenity conviction and a year in prison. In 1906, President Theodore Roosevelt refused a request to pardon him, declaring he "would as soon see poison circulated in the household" as that "hideous and loathsome" book.[36]

DESIRE AND DANGER

For many women, the debates, sex scandals, and prosecutions of that era highlighted both the possibilities and the perils of pursuing sexual pleasure, especially as other social changes were undermining the safeguards and predictability that Victorian courtship rituals had provided.

For most of the nineteenth century, successful soulmate courtship depended on two preconditions. First, it worked best for women who moved in social circles where people's reputation for propriety was well-known and they needed to maintain that reputation to protect their social standing and economic prospects.

As one middle-class man from that era explained, any female a male was likely to meet in these social settings came from a family that was part of his *own* family's community. She "carried with her the sanctions and refusals of society"[37] and was therefore not *per-*

sonally responsible for enforcing the rules of gentlemanly behavior prevalent in her class or community. The *man* was personally responsible for not violating them.

Second, it was vital that a man be willing to disclose his feelings early in the relationship, admit his vulnerabilities, and reassure the woman about his intentions. That's what made it safe for her to admit the growing intensity of her own feelings.

During the last quarter of the nineteenth century, however, two changes began to undermine the protections, along with the restrictions, of a courtship system based on the notion of love as the magnetic attraction of people with opposite duties and capacities but linked by emotional and spiritual communion. One change made it easier for men and women to enjoy similar activities and explore mutual interests. But the other made it harder for them to identify with each other's emotions, and especially for a woman to see into a man's "soul."

The first change was the decrease in gender segregation that accompanied the growth of educational institutions, urbanization, and industrialization. Increasing numbers of males and females attended high school, and although only a small percentage went on to college, women constituted a third of college students by 1880 and almost half by 1919. By 1890, more than a third of all unmarried White women and half of unmarried Black women aged fifteen to twenty-four were in the paid labor force.[38]

At most levels of society during the nineteenth century, the usual way for a young male and female to start "keeping company" had been for the man to call upon the woman at her home and socialize with her on the porch or in the parlor. But the cramped housing conditions of the growing urban working class made it difficult for young people to entertain at home. Instead, young men and women socialized on apartment stoops, walked in the parks, or arranged to meet at a dance hall. Historians have traced the first uses of the word "date" to lower-class slang in the 1880s, referring to such arranged meetings. At the time, that word had unsavory connotations for middle-class Americans.

Not until the twentieth century did the practice of dating spread to middle-class youth still living at home. But the amusement parks that sprang up around the country after 1880 created new places for people to meet, as did the dance halls, saloons, theaters, and eating establishments that multiplied in business districts of the nation's cities. By the late nineteenth century, young women and men who attended school or worked outside the home had more opportunities to meet and interact with people from a wider range of backgrounds and occupations than before.

The erosion of gender segregation raised the possibility that courtship and marriage could be based on real-world companionship and shared activities, not just spiritual communion. But it also made it more likely for a woman to meet potential partners who did not feel bound by the "sanctions and refusals" of her community or family. So for a woman of any class who welcomed her new freedoms but still hoped to end up in a "respectable" marriage, it was more essential than ever to be able to interrogate a man's feelings and explore his soul.

And therein lay a problem. Because a second change during the last decades of the nineteenth century actually heightened the difference between men and women in one critical area. Middle-class men began to reject the habits of emotional expressiveness and self-disclosure they had formerly shared with women.

Part of this change probably reflected men's psychological and moral accommodation to the realities of a market dominated by robber barons and a world order driven by imperialist rivalries. Another part stemmed from the need some men felt to shore up their sense of identity and entitlement as women began to enter formerly all-male enclaves. Clerical work, for example, had originally been a desirable entry-level job for middle-class men. As late as 1880, only 4 percent of clerical jobs were held by women. By 1900, women comprised more than a quarter of the clerical work force.[39]

The late nineteenth century witnessed a growing cultural redefinition of manliness in the middle classes. In the eighteenth and early nineteenth centuries, traits such as ambition, competitiveness, and aggressiveness had been seen as needful but potentially antisocial male *capabilities*, not commendable in and of themselves. Women's role was to help men contain, or at least channel, those aptitudes in morally acceptable ways. But by the last third of the century, such traits had begun to be seen as healthy masculinity and women's efforts to soften or redirect them were increasingly resented.

Psychologists and physical education advocates now declared that mothers stunted the development of boys when they emphasized being "good" and acting "nice." In the 1890s, the word "sissy," once slang for little sister, became a taunt directed at boys and men who were gentle. The original middle-class ideal of "manliness" was conceptualized as the opposite of childishness—and also the opposite of what middle-class men viewed as lower-class belligerence and upper-class arrogance. But in the late nineteenth century that gave way to a new and very different model of "manliness" or "masculinity" as the opposite of femininity.[40] The resultant pressure on males to demonstrate their *manhood* instead of their *adulthood* has been good for neither sex.

Given women's economic dependence on men, however, it's not surprising that as male success in the world became seen as the result of forcefulness, ambition, and occasional ruthlessness, women began to view those traits as desirable in men. Women's letters and diaries from the late nineteenth century are markedly less effusive than in earlier decades about the appeal of male vulnerability, and more approving of ambition. Women sometimes expressed concern that a potential suitor was not "masterful" enough. One woman even described a suitor as "too soulful."

For women attracted by this new magnetism of opposites—by men who were powerful, stoical, and forceful—attraction involved both fascination and fear. The sort of man best able to protect and provide for a woman, to offer her a secure or even luxurious life, was a being whose motives and emotions were largely inaccessible to her and whose actions she couldn't control.

Conversely, though, the things that made a man unreadable and even risky also made him desirable. And by the late nineteenth century, most women understood that desire had a sexual element, not just a soulful one, even if they were not supposed to surrender to it.

Hence the appeal of what has been the classic plot of romance novels since the mid-nineteenth century. From *Jane Eyre* (1847) to the *Fifty Shades of Grey* novels and movies (2011–2018), women have devoured stories about male heroes who are older, richer, more powerful, and/or more knowledgeable than the heroines, but also unpredictable and intimidating. The fantasy is about finding a man so formidable that he could (and sometimes does) overpower you, but who will then find you womanly enough, charming enough, and just feisty enough that he will instead use his power to protect you, eventually revealing his vulnerabilities to you alone.[41]

In this revised version of love as the attraction of "opposites," a woman doesn't fall in love with a man *because* he has revealed his soul to her. He reveals his soul to her only after he has commanded—or commandeered—her desire and then yielded to the power of her love. In some recent versions, the woman agrees or even asks to be hurt, and this very different kind of mutual exploration leads to self-disclosure, eventually ending with the man surrendering himself to love.[42]

The eroticization of such kinds of gender difference has left a legacy that is increasingly problematic for heterosexual partnerships. For more than one hundred years, women learned to associate attraction with uncertainty, desire with risk. Men, meanwhile, were taught that the way to attract a woman's admiration is to be powerful, the way to overcome her reserve is to take charge, and the way to express love is to provide, protect, and instruct.

The result is that women sometimes confuse apprehension or intimidation with infatuation. And men often confuse showing off with showing love. Knowing the historical origins of that habit is one reason I'm a bit more forgiving of "mansplaining" than some of my friends. (Another is that I am uncomfortably aware of how much "momsplaining" we women tend to do in what we've been taught to see as our own sphere of expertise.)

It's true that many heterosexual men and women find sexual pleasure and romantic satisfaction in acting out gender differences. Even ardent feminists often expect men to initiate or escalate relationships and to come up with a charming "surprise" proposal when things get serious. And I don't condemn such playfulness.

But there is a dark side to expecting men to initiate, as we see in some of the ambiguities about what constitutes an inappropriate advance. And even in its most innocuous forms, the eroticization of gender dissimilarities hinders us from tackling one of the big challenges in contemporary heterosexual relationships that I discuss in chapter 8—how to make our similarities sexy.

There is one final irony to the history I describe in this chapter. As emotional intimacy with men became more difficult to achieve, emotional intimacy with other women changed shape. Heterosexual women started bonding with each other over their attempts to decipher men's intentions and hidden motivations and to validate each other's feelings, producing a hyper-introspective, intensely self-revelatory, female subculture that we don't see in earlier historical periods. For many women, this has created a contradiction between the strength and decisiveness they find erotic and the disclosure of inner feelings that makes them feel loved—the first only obtainable from a certain kind of male lover, but the second often completely absent from his repertoire.[43]

Chapter 5.

FROM SPIRITUAL SOULMATES TO SEXUAL PLAYMATES

The Culture Wars of a Century Ago

During the first two decades of the twentieth century, America experienced a revolution in sexual and gender mores as shocking to people raised on mid-nineteenth-century social conventions as our current sexual and gender rearrangements are to people raised on mid-twentieth-century ones. And it triggered a culture war remarkably similar to the one we've been experiencing one hundred years later.

To understand just *how* shocking that revolution in sexual mores was, consider that "respectable" nineteenth-century Americans thought it immodest to refer to a specific body part, such as a leg, in mixed-sex conversations. People were supposed to instead use the word "limb." As late as 1887 this view was still widespread enough to spur an irreverent writer in *The Popular Science Monthly* to bemoan the "ritual of modesty . . . making us say stomach instead of belly, limb instead of leg, retire instead of go to bed, and forbidding us to call a female dog by name."[1]

Less than three decades later, such decorum had been shattered.

A 1913 editorial in the literary magazine *Current Opinion* observed that Americans had begun discussing sex with "a frankness that would even startle Paris." A 1914 *Atlantic* article titled "The Repeal of Reticence" lamented the new "obsession" that had set people "all a-babbling about matters once excluded from the amenities of conversation." In the words of a St. Louis newspaper editor, it was now "Sex O'Clock" in America.[2]

Many people, of course, continued to subscribe to older moral conventions. A good illustration of the gulf between old and new mores can be seen in the May 10, 1918, issue of the American military newspaper *Stars and Stripes*, which featured poetry written by soldiers on the battlefields of Europe during World War I. One poem described a soldier's "burning" longing for the woman he had left behind:

How I long for your smiles of gladness
That are haunting my mem'ry still,
And the love in your eyes beseeching
Even now makes my pulses thrill.
How you held me with hands so gently,
Closely pressed to your throbbing breast;
In that last fond embrace . . . I promised
To live true through the crucial test.

The poem went on to describe how the soldier yearned to feel the "caress" of his loved one's hair against his skin and to kiss her "soft as roses" lips.[3]

It would be easy to read this as an example of the "repeal of reticence" in American courtship. But I left out the first lines, which reveal that the thrilling pulses, beseeching eyes, throbbing breasts, caressing touches, and soft lips were not those of the soldier's sweetheart or wife but of his mother. "I am writing this little poem / to the mother I left behind, / And it tells of my longing for her / Over here in the daily grind."

When I read excerpts from this poem aloud, people often gasp when they discover the object of the soldier's longing. Psychologist Joshua Coleman tells me that most family professionals shown such a poem today "would assume the existence of an underlying family pathology, suspect a real possibility of incest, and worry about the man's ability to construct a healthy heterosexual relationship with a woman his own age."[4]

These reactions reflect our modern assumption that sensual language and touch suggest the existence of a sexual relationship or the desire for one. But in the first two decades of the twentieth century that was a novel assumption. If it had indeed struck "Sex O'Clock" in America in 1913, many Americans had not yet reset their watches. They were still operating on "Sexual Silence Time," where sensual language was considered fully appropriate in public when used about presumably *asexual* relationships, but *only* about such relationships.

Throughout the nineteenth century and into the first decade or two of the twentieth, most people thought it perfectly normal for a son to call his mother his "best girl" or "darling" and to kiss her on the lips, and for a mother to call her son "lover" or "lover boy." When one woman wrote in her memoir about being grateful her son's last gaze as he left for World War I had been directed at her rather than his wife, her feelings could still be described in a 1925 *Washington Post* book review as "a testimonial to the enduring love which abides between mother and son" rather than a sign of an unhealthy rivalry for her son's attention.[5]

The same assumption of normalcy extended to same-sex physical affection in the nineteenth century. People weren't shocked that male friends embraced in public, professed deep mutual love, shared the same bed, or wept from loneliness when separated. No one blinked when female friends sent each other letters filled with "a thousand kisses" or a wife banished her husband to the parlor so a visiting friend could spend the night in bed with her.[6]

What *would* have shocked people schooled in Victorian notions of sexuality would have been to hear someone like Joshua Coleman pair the words "healthy" and "heterosexual." When the word "heterosexuality" first appeared in mainstream dictionaries in the early twentieth century, it was defined as "an abnormal or perverted sexual appetite toward the opposite sex" and a "depraved" or "morbid" passion for the opposite sex.[7]

Mass-market dictionaries began to define heterosexuality as a "normal" desire only in the 1930s. But well before that, many Americans had begun to adopt ideas about sex, gender, courtship, and marriage that contradicted the most deeply held convictions of middle-class Victorians about what feelings, behaviors, and topics of conversation were psychologically healthy and morally virtuous and which were abnormal or degenerate. In the space of just two decades, heterosexual desire went from being something you concealed to something you boasted about if you were a man and sought to inspire if you were a woman. Conversely, the "silver cord" binding a man to his mother went from being celebrated as the epitome of wholesome love to being considered a sign of serious maladjustment.

THE COLLAPSE OF TRADITIONAL COURTING AND RISE OF MIDDLE-CLASS DATING

Today many Americans see dating as a healthy alternative to contemporary practices such as "hooking up" and "swiping right." But dating was a suspect innovation in the nineteenth century. Not only were young men and women "keeping company" without proper introductions or supervision, they often dated a series of partners they had no intention of marrying. Dating also gave young people a freedom from parental and neighborly oversight that allowed for more physical intimacy than the older practice of "calling."[8]

In chapter 4 I noted that dating first arose among urban working-class youth whose living quarters were too cramped to allow for socializing at home. But once middle- and upper-class youngsters were exposed to the amusement parks, movie palaces, vaudeville theaters, and dance halls of the burgeoning leisure and entertainment industries, they quickly determined there were more enjoyable places to hang out than home. And it was hard to keep young people in the parlor once they had access to trolleys, streetcars, and automobiles. By 1916, there were more than three and a half million cars registered in America.[9]

As early as 1910, the nationally syndicated advice columnist Dorothy Dix was complaining that "the average father does not know, by name or sight, the young man who visits his daughter and who takes her out to places of amusement." In 1924, a writer in *Harper's Monthly* ruefully labeled the death of parental supervision a done deal: "So far as the young girl was concerned, the duenna had long since disappeared. The chaperone, after becoming a non-intrusive joke, was finally forgotten. The automobile took her place as the third party."[10]

One coed coolly reported in the early 1920s that her generation was "happily" drinking, smoking, and necking—doing "all the things that our mothers, fathers, aunts and uncles do not sanction." In small towns as well as big cities, high school and college students held "petting parties," with couples pairing off in various parts of a room. These were hardly orgies, historian Paula Fass points out: The presence of other couples restrained people from having intercourse and made it easier for young women to set limits. Still, it's difficult to overstate the challenge such activities posed to Victorian sensibilities.[11]

When young people socialized in their own neighborhoods, it was generally with people of their own class, race, religion, and ethnic group. But with the spread of amusement parks, cabarets, dance halls, and especially the speakeasies that sprang up after the implementation of Prohibition in 1920, they had more opportunities to interact with people from other backgrounds. The resulting "cultural appropriation" went in several different directions.

In dance pavilions, working-class youths introduced their middle-class counterparts to the "tough dancing" that inspired moralistic jeremiads in books like *Dangers of the Dance* (1922). Black Americans invented the music that earned the era the title of "the Jazz Age." Affluent White women pioneered the bobbed hair and short dresses that became the uniform of "flappers," styles quickly adopted by youngsters of other classes and colors.

La Pelona ("short-haired girl") was the term for the Hispanic flapper. African American flappers were numerous enough to make Black elites worry they were hurting the "reputation of the race." Asian flappers were in shorter supply, but Anna May Wong, the first Chinese American film star and an international fashion icon, adopted the flapper look and cigarette-smoking persona early in her career.[12]

Most flappers moved on to marriage. And although they were more likely than their mothers to have premarital sex, it was usually with the man they eventually married. Still, social conservatives lumped flappers together with "free love" advocates, feminists, and birth-control activists as threats to marriage and the moral order. They even condemned social hygiene reformers, who advocated strict sexual purity but believed in educating youths about the realities of venereal disease and prostitution. Much like modern opponents of sex education, defenders of nineteenth-century middle-class morality countered that such knowledge acted as an "artificial stimulus" to sexual exploration: Youths needed not more education but more "religion and discipline."[13]

The newfangled practice of using scientific surveys to investigate sexual attitudes also outraged social conservatives, who claimed the survey questions themselves introduced youth to evil temptations. In 1925, for example, when the all-female Smith College circulated a questionnaire about views on sex and marriage, this triggered an avalanche of furious letters and editorials—and even a "patriotic mass meeting"—to protest such a "filthy-minded" effort "to promote the disintegration of the family by bringing shamelessly into the open consideration of illegitimate childbirth."[14]

To be fair, Victorian moralists faced challenges that were more radical than knee-length dresses, petting parties, and sex education. The well-known Judge Benjamin Lindsey promoted the "horrifying" idea that young couples should be issued licenses to live together for up to two years if they agreed to use birth control for the duration, after which they could either divorce by mutual consent (not then an option in a standard marriage) or convert to a conventional marriage. And in urban enclaves such as Greenwich Village in New York City, a mélange of sex radicals, bohemians, and feminists advocated much freer forms of "free love" than their nineteenth-century forerunners.[15]

Consider the challenge to conventional morality posed by two of Broadway's most popular plays in 1926. One was the highly praised drama *The Silver Cord*, which depicted the intense mother-son love described in that World War I poem as a perversion. During the dramatic final clash between one son's wife and his controlling mother, who has tried to sabotage both her two sons' marriages, the daughter-in-law tells her husband that his jealous mother can't "bear the thought of our loving one another as we do . . . because, down, down in the depths of her, grown man that you are, she still wants to suckle you at her breast!"[16]

When I first read *The Silver Cord*, I wondered how many people might have bought tickets to a play whose title misled them into thinking it would celebrate the "sacred bond" between mother and son. But no one would have gone to the other huge hit of 1926 by mistake. Actress-director Mae West's production, *SEX*, told the story of a prostitute courted by a Royal Navy lieutenant who wants to be more than her occasional paying client and also by a wealthy young man who is infatuated with her but unaware of her occupation. Completely dispensing with the tragic finale that traditionally accompanied any fictional violation of the Victorian moral order, *SEX* ends with the prostitute cheerfully announcing she is one of the "wretches" the young man has earlier scorned, derisively telling his mother she can have him "back," and happily departing for Australia with her navy officer.[17]

Reviewers called the play "nasty," "vulgar," "degenerate," and "sewage," but audiences snapped up tickets. In February of 1927, *SEX* was shut down by the police, in part, some historians think, to prevent West from also opening *The Drag*, a "homosexual comedy-drama" centered around a flamboyant cast of gay men, whose off-Broadway previews were already playing to sellout crowds.

The Drag never did open on Broadway, but real-life drag balls occurred regularly between the 1890s and the late 1920s, attracting thousands of spectators and participants. Female and male impersonators performed in fancy Manhattan venues as well as in run-down working-class saloons and small-town theaters across the country. Gay clubs operated openly.[18]

As for Mae West, after serving ten days in prison, where she was invited to dine with the prison warden and his wife, she went on to become one of America's most popular movie stars.

Small wonder the guardians of "traditional" Anglo-American Protestant moral values felt frustrated. In enforcing the "anti-obscenity" Comstock Act of 1873, parts of which remain in effect to this day, Anthony Comstock reportedly destroyed 50 tons of "obscene" books, 28,400 pounds of printing plates, and nearly 4 million pictures, and he got more than 3,000 persons arrested for morals violations.[19] Yet by the early 1920s, "salacious" dances were a national craze, America had the highest divorce rate in the Western world, the movie industry had turned Theda Bara into its first full-fledged "sex goddess," and juries and judges were increasingly nullifying obscenity prosecutions brought under the Comstock Act. And now here was mother-love being defamed, prostitution romanticized, drag shows glorified, and "pornographic" actresses fêted.[20]

Outraged conservatives mobilized to fight "rampant sexual immorality" and "contempt for marriage and motherhood." At stake, in the words of one prominent Baptist pastor, was the survival of a society "where women are still honored, where men are still chivalric, where laws are still respected, where home life is still sweet, where the marriage vow is still sacred."[21]

Then as now, deeply felt moral anxieties were often intertwined with racial and religious prejudices. For example, although some Christians' opposition to birth control was driven by adherence to God's command to procreate, many middle- and upper-class White Protestants were more concerned about the prospect of "race suicide," the early twentieth-century version of today's "great replacement" theory. The difference between then and now was that in the 1910s and 1920s they feared being replaced not only by African Americans, Jews, and immigrants but also by Catholics and lower-class fellow Whites.

"MAKE AMERICA DECENT AGAIN"

By World War I, moral anxieties had merged with racial, ethnic, and religious antagonisms to ignite a culture war strikingly similar to that of the early twenty-first century. Almost one hundred years before Donald Trump launched his first campaign for the presidency by calling Mexican migrants "killers and rapists," America-firsters were accusing European immigrants to America of coming to "plunder, pillage, rape, and murder." During the 1920 election, both major parties promised mass deportations of immigrant "criminals."[22]

Membership in the Ku Klux Klan surged in the aftermath of World War I, reaching more than two million in 1925, far larger than in its terrorist heyday during the 1870s. KKK chapters targeted Black Americans with particular viciousness, but also went after Catholics and Jews, along with individuals of any gender, color, or creed who violated their version of Victorian morality. They horse-whipped "sinners" such as "loose" women, abortion providers, bootleggers, and adulterers of both sexes. In some towns, they burned buildings that hosted youth dances. Elsewhere they patrolled backroad parking spots to "clear the highway of spooners."[23]

Twentieth-century culture warriors advanced conspiracy theories that foreshadowed those of their twenty-first-century counterparts. Like contemporary right-wingers who believe financial and political elites clandestinely run the country through a "deep state," they claimed Jewish financiers were building "a government within our government." In 1920, more than one hundred years before Tesla CEO Elon Musk was assigned the task of crippling today's supposed "deep state," another auto magnate, Henry Ford, published a sensational series of newspaper articles about the nefarious aims of this alleged secret Jewish government, instructing all his auto dealerships to distribute copies to customers.[24]

Contemporary conspiracy theorists claim Democratic politicians and Hollywood celebrities are Satan-worshiping pedophiles operating a global sex trafficking ring and killing children in order to harvest a supposed antiaging chemical derived from their adrenal glands. The corresponding fantasy one hundred years ago was that a secret Catholic society had required its members to take a solemn oath to "burn, waste, boil, flay, strangle and bury alive" Protestants and Masons, "rip open the stomachs and wombs of their women and crash their infants' heads against the walls."[25]

In 1910, in response to fears about Jewish "cartels" trafficking women, Congress passed the Mann Act, originally called the White-Slave Traffic Act, making it a crime to transport, arrange transportation, or even just "persuade" a woman to travel across state lines for "sexually immoral" purposes. Today, claiming that "abortion cartels" are taking women across state lines to get abortions, legislators in several states that have outlawed abortion have introduced laws making it a crime to assist people in obtaining out-of-state abortions or acquiring abortion medication by mail. Some measures would actually criminalize abortion *patients* for "trafficking" their fetus, often referred to as a "preborn child."[26]

In the 1920s, defenders of "traditionalism" sought to ban German philosophical theory and fire the "oligarchy" of professors who were promoting the "lie" of evolution. Between 1922 and 1929, seven states and scores of school districts banned any teaching of evolution. When legislators in other states failed to pass such measures, well-organized countrywide boycotts intimidated publishers into deleting mentions of evolution from national textbooks.[27]

In the 2020s, their counterparts prohibit teaching about critical race theory, gender identity research, and global warming. On April 25, 2025, Mississippi Governor Tate Reeves signed into law a bill forbidding "any formal or informal education, seminars, workshops or institutional program that focus on increasing awareness or understanding of issues related to race, sex, color, gender identity, sexual orientation or national origin."[28]

TAKING SEX MAINSTREAM

Despite the 1919–1920 Palmer Raids, the jailing of thousands of dissidents, and frequent vigilante attacks, dedicated organizers continued to combat lynching, defend civil liberties, expand women's rights, and work to legalize birth control. And in the late 1920s the culture wars began to abate. People could see that dating and sex education were not destroying marriage. Indeed, rather than abandoning marriage as they gained new freedoms, youths married at higher rates and younger ages in the first decades of the twentieth century than they had in the 1880s and 1890s.[29]

Birth control, sex education, jazz clubs, and dancing were now so common that individuals who still railed about their sinfulness were increasingly ignored. Amusement park entrepreneurs such as Frederic Thompson had largely succeeded in their efforts to convince middle-class Americans that "gaiety," thrill-seeking, and "a carnival spirit" were compatible with "decency." And the film industry had accustomed people to expect sexual titillation even in mainstream movies.[30]

In this context, the most militant moral crusaders came to be seen as extremists. "Comstockery" became a mocking word for prudery. The KKK experienced a sharp drop in influence and membership in the late 1920s.

Another calming factor was that many early twentieth-century critics of Victorian moralism gradually retreated from some of their radical stances. By 1930, for example, the Greenwich Village feminist, socialist, and World War I protestor Floyd Dell was explaining away his earlier views as a temporary "ideological overcompensation" for the repression of the past. He assured people that in calling for the "destruction of the patriarchal family and its accompanying social sexual institutions," he hadn't intended to endorse free love or undermine women's "natural" roles as homemakers. He'd simply wanted to help young people live "happily ever after in heterosexual matehood."[31]

The onset of the Great Depression of the 1930s, followed by America's entry into World War II in 1941, put debates about sexuality and feminism on the back burner. Marriage and birth rates fell during the Depression, but the outbreak of war triggered a rash of marriages. Some of these were literally rash: In 1946, the divorce rate soared to a high not reached again until the 1970s. However, divorce rates then fell while marriage rates, along with childbearing, rose sharply.

Up through the 1960s, dating continued to be the primary way that young men and women explored relationships on the way toward marriage, although its conventions changed over time. In the 1930s, the big thing was to date lots of different people. During the 1950s, "going steady" became the teenage fad.[32]

In the 1960s, as an "anti-establishment" youth movement gathered steam, premarital sex became more common. Still, as late as 1968 unmarried cohabitation was rare enough to cause a national stir when a Barnard College student was caught violating campus rules by living with her boyfriend.[33] Dating remained the primary path to marriage, and few people dawdled along the way.

Despite the initial outrage they triggered, the sexual and marital norms that evolved between the early and the mid-twentieth century culminated in what many people now consider a postwar "Golden Age" of marriage, which I discuss in the next chapter. But the new mores had decidedly mixed consequences, whose legacy still shapes and often deforms contemporary sexual and romantic relationships.

NORMALIZING HETEROSEXUAL DESIRE—AT A PRICE

The gradual acceptance of sexual desire as a basic human drive and of sexual satisfaction as essential to well-being reduced the guilt produced by nineteenth-century strictures against "carnal indulgence," encouraging men and women to experiment with ways of heightening their pleasure. Elated diary entries and grateful letters to the authors of the increasingly explicit advice manuals that proliferated in this period leave no doubt about how many individuals embraced the normalization of heterosexual desire and pleasure.

Some people even concluded that if sexual desire is so strong and sexual satisfaction so essential, same-sex attraction and love should also be accepted as legitimate. But others reasoned that if heterosexual desire was "normal," same-sex desire must be "abnormal," and since sexual desire was so powerful, same-sex affection could easily escalate into "perversion." Thus, even as the sexual revolution of the early twentieth century inspired some people to demand recognition and legitimation of a same-sex identity, it led others to become preoccupied with identifying signs of sexual "abnormality" and "correcting" any behavior that might encourage "homosexual tendencies."

This was a relatively new preoccupation. Historian Richard Godbeer argues that American men of the Revolutionary Era were capable of an "intensely physical yet nonsexual love" that is foreign to most contemporary men. Through most of the nineteenth century, it was common for male friends or roommates to share a bed. Writing to a fiancée, a man could nonchalantly mention the pleasure of "sink[ing] peacefully to sleep" in the arms of a male friend. "Sodomy" was a crime that if discovered could be harshly punished. But sleeping together was not cause to suspect it. In 1846, when New York policeman Edward McCosker was accused of "lewdly" touching another man, a colleague testified in his defense that he had "been in the habit of sleeping with said McCosker for the last three months," and he'd never "acted indecent."[34]

The very reticence about sex that "free thinkers" mocked had sometimes protected discreet same-sex couples from stigma. Historians have discovered a surprising number of small-town communities where same-sex couples who behaved as if married were accepted, so long as they followed community norms, avoided any display of sexuality, and were "good neighbors."[35]

But in the early twentieth century, the emerging sense of homosexuality as a *condition* or *identity*, rather than just another "sinful" behavior like masturbation, triggered attempts to either "cure" or quarantine gay men and lesbians and to inoculate youths against "infection." Preventive measures included discouraging the physical affection and passionate expressions of love that had once been an accepted part of friendship. By the 1910s, even very young girls were being warned against "snuggling," while psychologists and educators labeled the high school crushes and college "smashes" that had never before raised eyebrows as threats to "normal" heterosexual development and marriage.

The pressure on men to avoid affectionate physical contact was especially strong. By the 1930s, it had created a striking transformation in men's behavior that can be traced in historian John Ibson's fascinating collection of American photographs over the decades. From the mid-nineteenth century into the 1920s, male friends often had photographs taken of themselves unselfconsciously holding hands, embracing, or sitting on one another's laps. Early portraits of sports teams and work crews show boys and men with arms around each other's shoulders, leaning against each other's chests, or casually touching each other's legs. But such poses gradually disappeared over the course of the 1920s.[36]

By the early 1930s, the initial curiosity and humor inspired by the shake-up of older sexual and gender norms had faded in the face of heightened attempts to reinforce the boundaries of "modern" gender and sexual identity. Drag shows began to be regarded with suspicion rather than amusement. Historian George Chauncey has described the stepped-up campaign by authorities to marginalize gay subcultures during the late 1920s and the 1930s, a project that continued throughout the postwar era.[37]

The new tendency to interpret physical displays of affection as stemming from sexual desire forced many gay, lesbian, bisexual, and transsexual individuals to police their behavior in public. But it also impoverished heterosexuals' experience, making them uncomfortable with physical intimacy outside an explicitly sexual relationship and uneasy about expressing loving feelings toward people who were not potential sexual partners.

In recent years, for example, Americans' growing (and long overdue) disapproval of nonconsensual sexual relationships has led to a campaign against "unwanted" touching. When it comes to sexual advances, that's a vitally important issue. But a side effect of the twentieth-century rediscovery of the power of sexual desire may have been to pathologize nonsexual touching.

Contemporary Anglo-Americans are far less physically affectionate with our friends—and even with our partners and children—than most other cultures. A 1999 comparison of French and American adolescents interacting at fast-food restaurants, for example, found that French teens touched each other much more than their American counterparts, while American teens quite literally kept their hands to themselves—engaging in more self-stimulation (rubbing their arms, fingering their hair, etc.) than their French counterparts.[38]

Nonsexual touching is an extremely important part of social bonding, eliciting more positive feelings and interactions than simple verbal exchanges. People respond more favorably to a request if they are touched at the time the request is made. And a notable anthropological finding is that individuals in cultures that encourage friendly touching are less aggressive than people in cultures that discourage it. So we miss out on some important forms of connection when we become afraid to touch anyone without prior permission or regard a spontaneous touch from another as "intrusive."

Of course, unwanted sexual touching, or an unwanted sexual response to a friendly touch, is a different matter. But some of today's tension over unwanted sexual overtures may stem from another feature of the sex, gender, and courtship system that triumphed in the early twentieth century—men's increased responsibility for initiating and escalating romantic relationships and women's increased responsibility for setting sexual boundaries.

ENCOURAGING MALE "INITIATIVE"

In the nineteenth-century courtship script, it was up to the girl and her mother to invite a boy to call. They provided the meeting place, the refreshments, and the entertainment, whether that be a walk, a parlor game, or a song at the piano. Etiquette advisors cautioned young men not to ask permission to call, but to wait for the woman to issue the invitation.

But going on a date meant paying for commercial refreshment and entertainment. So as the moneymaker in society, the male was expected to pick up the tab. Accordingly, etiquette advisors now insisted that a female could never ask a male for a date, even if they had gone out before.[39] She must always wait to be asked.

Even today, men still initiate most dates and follow-up invitations, not to mention the overwhelming majority of marriage proposals. This forces the man to risk a rejection, while inhibiting the woman from initiating or accelerating the relationship.

In conjunction with the new endorsement of masculine forcefulness I described in chapter 4, the heightened emphasis on male initiative undermined the Victorian insistence on men's responsibility for respecting sexual boundaries. Whatever its other inequities, nineteenth-century gender ideology had advocated a single standard of sexual behavior for males as well as females, expecting men as well as women to summon the strength of character to practice self-restraint. Plenty of men never accepted the Victorian ideology of male purity, and there was considerable tolerance for hypocrisy. Still, the diaries and letters of nineteenth-century middle-class Americans reveal that many men tried to live up to it, if only because they believed that otherwise they would be rejected by the kind of woman they wanted to marry.

But the (re)discovery that most women—even "respectable" women—have a sex drive and might *welcome* a sexual overture undercut the idea that a virtuous man was morally obliged to restrain his desire. Since a woman had her own sex urges, it was up to her to say no. And since she might want to have sex but feel inhibited by social convention, there was no reason for a man to prematurely take no for an answer.

By the end of the 1920s it was no longer bad character for a man to try to go as far as he could sexually, even with a woman of his own class, color, and social circle. It was seen as his masculine *nature,* and it did not disqualify him in a woman's eyes as a potential husband. If a woman yielded to her own desire and let him go "too far," however, *her* character—at least as a potential wife—came into question.

Yet with "sex appeal" now viewed as a key component of a woman's attractiveness and mutual sexual enjoyment as a critical part of marriage, setting limits and saying no became trickier. One woman I interviewed described the fine line she and her friends thought they had to tread in the late 1940s: "A guy wouldn't want to marry someone who was 'easy,' but he also wouldn't want to marry 'a prude.'"

The key was to be a "good sport" while remaining a "good girl." In contrast to Victorian advice manuals that admonished girls to shut down the first hint of a sexual overture and cold-shoulder any boys who did not immediately desist, girls and women in the mid-twentieth century were advised to indicate they were flattered rather than offended by a male's sexual interest, even if they felt compelled to say no. Indeed, by that time, many people—including many women—believed that saying no was often just a ritualized pause before saying yes. As the Pointer Sisters sang in their 1978 hit: I say no when you pull me close, "I say I don't like it, but you know I'm a liar."[40] That song, though written by a man, continues to be performed and recorded by female singers to this day.

Chapter 6.

NOSTALGIA FOR THE 1950s

What We're Told We've Lost vs. What We've Actually Lost

Nearly half of Americans believe our country's cultural values have changed for the worse since the 1950s. That includes 51 percent of Whites, but also, despite the oppressive legalized segregation in that era, 48 percent of Blacks, 44 percent of Hispanics, and 41 percent of multiracial individuals.[1]

My own attitude toward nostalgia has evolved since the late 1980s and early 1990s, when I wrote a book I now think was too dismissive of people who fell into what I then called "the Nostalgia Trap."[2] Some types of nostalgia are actually healthy. And when it comes to dealing with *unhealthy* nostalgia, I've come to believe that the only thing worse than pandering to it is failing to acknowledge the genuine injuries or anxieties that produce it.

Healthy nostalgia is typically triggered by memories of specific experiences involving friends, family members, or favorite occasions. These memories are usually quite selective, but selective memory can be an asset in personal life. How many women would choose to have a second child if the pain of childbirth didn't fade from their memory?

Personal nostalgia doesn't involve a longing to re-create a whole past way of life. Rather, it's a half-pleasurable, half-poignant yearning to recapture a *feeling* associated with past experiences with friends and family. Reminiscing about such things actually makes people more optimistic about the possibility of making *new* friends.[3]

A BRIEF HISTORY OF NOSTALGIA

But some forms of nostalgia are not so benign. Indeed, the word "nostalgia" was first coined in 1688 to describe a severe pathology that had emerged earlier in the century and that went on to infect tens of thousands of people. Because the disease produced an "obsessive" and "debilitating" longing in people to return to the place they'd been raised, a Swiss medical student, Johannes Hofer, combined two Greek words—*nostos*, or homeward journey, and *algos*, or pain—to name the malady "nostalgia." For the next 150 years, medical practitioners confirmed that "homesickness" could trigger despair, delusion, dementia, and even death.[4]

Outbreaks of nostalgia were first recorded among Swiss mercenary soldiers serving in foreign lands but were soon observed in almost every European country and colony, along with the United States. The disease was highly contagious. In the 1790s, whole companies of French soldiers were afflicted by it. During the American Civil War, doctors reported that 5,213 White and 324 Black soldiers in the Union army came down with the illness. Seventy-four of them died.

Aside from sending people back home, there were few effective treatments. During the American Civil War, some commanders tried shaming homesick soldiers with ridicule. Others prohibited army bands from playing "Home, Sweet Home" for fear the song would trigger a new outbreak of the contagion.

Soldiers were especially susceptible to the disease, but it also afflicted immigrants, domestic servants living far from home, seasonal migrant laborers, exiles, and chattel slaves. Travel per se was not the cause, because nostalgia was rarely seen in peddlers who roamed from town to town to make a living or in people who traveled for pleasure, so long as they knew they were free to return home.

Historian Thomas Dodman argues that the nostalgia epidemics of those days were not medical fads or misdiagnoses but "real" illnesses that arose in a period when many people were being uprooted from "the localized, dense network of social relations" that gave people in premodern communities their sense of identity. In that era, different localities maintained very distinctive customs, laws, institutions, and even dialects. Work, commerce, and other parts of life were organized locally on the basis of long-standing interpersonal networks and shared rituals. As a result, people often had a severe emotional and physical reaction when they ended up in a place where they could not rely on familiar customs and relationships. They became literally homesick.

Remarkably, though, by the late nineteenth century, most Europeans and Americans had developed an immunity to the more debilitating symptoms of the illness, although those continued to plague enslaved individuals, exiles, and displaced Indigenous peoples. In 1884, the French army recorded its last official death due to "nostalgia." Even before then, "forward looking" Americans—especially those who had *bettered* themselves by moving—had begun to view homesickness as a passing anxiety of childhood and to label adults who suffered from it as "backward."[5]

What brought the epidemic to an end? As more individuals discovered that geographic mobility could generate upward economic and social mobility, as advances in technology and transportation allowed movers to keep in closer touch with those they left behind, and as the emergence of standardized economic and political institutions meant they encountered familiar practices and rules in new settings, people began to accept change as an essential part of the human condition. Nostalgic feelings mellowed into a wistful affection for past experiences and places that had happy memories, allowing people to appreciate the past without rejecting the present.

MODERN-DAY NOSTALGIA

In recent decades, however, many parts of the world have seen a revival of the more pernicious form of nostalgia, what we might call *past-sickness*—the longing to re-create not a pleasant *feeling* or specific *experience* from their past, but rather a bygone *way of life.* While personal nostalgia leads people to idealize some of their own experiences, past-sickness leads them to idealize a whole, and often wholly misremembered, set of social arrangements and political institutions from another era.

Societal and personal nostalgia have opposite effects. Researchers have demonstrated that in a cold room, indulging in personal nostalgia makes people feel physically warmer. It also tends to make them *act* more warmly. After engaging in nostalgic thoughts or conversations about good times with friends or family, individuals feel more generous toward others.

But societal nostalgia has a different dynamic. When people think nostalgically about an entire *era* or *community* rather than about particular experiences, they start identifying more intensely with the kind of people they associated with in the past and judging members of other groups more negatively. They become *less* optimistic about their ability to forge new connections and more hostile to strangers. They reject ideas, policies, or even—as we see in debates about climate change—scientific findings that don't fit their vision of the way the world used to be and ought to be again.

There's one important difference between the societal nostalgia epidemics of the seventeenth to the nineteenth century and those of more recent times. Back then, serious nostalgia attacks usually afflicted people who'd left the locales in which they'd been raised and were feeling disoriented or disadvantaged in their new surroundings. Today, the condition is most common among people who remain in communities or social networks that have missed out on or feel marginalized by recent societal and economic trends.

Instead of leaving their homes behind, such people are left behind in neighborhoods, community networks, and regions that no longer deliver the benefits they once did. Their traditional sources of identity, security, influence, and social status have been undermined. New technologies, occupational patterns, and cultural values seem to threaten their future livelihoods or disrespect their way of life.[6]

Such people aren't wrong to feel a sense of loss. But just as an injury to one part of the body can produce "referred pain" in a different part, social and economic disruptions in one part of society can produce symptoms that lead people to misdiagnose where their pain actually originates. Today, for example, many individuals have come to believe the problems they face are caused by other people's abandonment of "traditional" postwar gender roles, marital arrangements, and cultural mores. In fact, however, much of their distress results from politicians' and corporations' abandonment of postwar policies that once curbed the excesses of Wall Street and the ultrarich.

WAS THE 1950S A "GOLDEN AGE" OF MARRIAGE AND FAMILY LIFE?

The 1950s was the closest America has ever come to a system of universal marriage. Between 1950 and 1970, the typical age at first marriage hit an all-time low—just twenty for women and twenty-three for men. Only 6 percent of people who came of age in the 1950s reached age thirty-five without already having married. Just 5 percent never married. This was half the percentage of lifelong singles in the late nineteenth century.[7]

Unlike the decades since the early 1970s, for most of the twentieth century marriage rates were basically the same for Black and White Americans. In fact, until 1970, Black women were more likely than White women to be married by age thirty-five.[8]

Although families were not as homogeneous as portrayed in the mass media of the day, diversity in family forms was arguably at an all-time low. By 1960, two-thirds of children under age fifteen lived in male-breadwinner families, a higher figure than ever before or since. Only 18 percent lived in families where both parents were employed. Unmarried cohabitation was extremely rare, and just 1 child in 350 lived with a never-married mother. Same-sex marriage was illegal (as was interracial marriage in thirty-one states). Many gay men and lesbians felt obliged to hide their sexual orientation or even to marry an opposite-sex partner to avoid social stigma.[9]

The cultural approval of marriage was overwhelming. Two-thirds of Americans told pollsters that women who didn't want to wed were "neurotic" or "selfish." Bachelors were labeled "infantile," "narcissistic," and "deviant."[10]

The ubiquity of this marriage system, however, rested on two pillars, both of which were essential to its stability and neither of which survived intact into the 1980s. One pillar was an economic system in which the average young man could get a living-wage job upon leaving high school or the military and expect his wages to rise steadily in tandem with his experience. The other pillar was a legal system and social environment in which a woman had little chance to participate in the prosperity of the era except by getting married.

Never before or since have opportunities for upward mobility risen faster for a larger segment of the male wage-earning population. From 1947 to 1973, each cohort of twenty-five- to twenty-nine-year-old men earned, on average, three times as much in constant dollars as their fathers had at the same age. A man's real wages typically doubled from age twenty-five to age thirty-five and rose by another 30 percent between age forty and age fifty.[11]

Job opportunities and wage rates were very unevenly divided by race, as they had been for all of American history. Yet unlike the decades before World War II and since the mid-1970s, every economic expansion that occurred between 1949 and 1969 saw at least two-thirds of the income growth go to the bottom 90 percent of the working population. And every section of the population, including low-wage workers in general and Black workers in particular, saw their income increase at a rate commensurate with the general rate of economic growth.[12]

That steady improvement in living standards, in conjunction with the confidence inspired by the recovery from the Great Depression and the defeat of the fascist powers in World War II, gave people a confidence in their children's and grandchildren's future that many cannot muster in today's economic and political environment.

THE TWO PILLARS SUPPORTING THE POSTWAR MARRIAGE REGIME

The first pillar of the postwar marriage regime, then, was a male-breadwinner wage system in which a woman could marry almost any employed, minimally responsible man and expect to live in a home of her own, modest though it might be, and see her family's standard of living rise over time. As of 1960, the median price of a house in America was only a bit more than twice as much as the annual median income, compared to almost six times as much today.[13]

But the second pillar of the postwar marriage regime was an economic and legal system in which a woman could seldom *get* a home on her own or keep it after a divorce. Women were excluded from most of the new employment and educational opportunities open to men, confined instead to the low-paid jobs advertised in the "Help Wanted: Female" sections of newspapers. The average college-educated woman working full-time year-round earned less than the average high-school educated man. Even when a woman earned a decent wage, she couldn't normally get a loan to buy a home or start a business unless her husband or father guaranteed it. No wonder most women accepted the cultural pressures to marry early and to stay married even if unhappy.[14]

The sexual and gender patterns of that era were neither as innocent nor as idyllic as portrayed on television sitcoms. It should have been easier to postpone pregnancy until marriage in the 1950s and early 1960s, when the average age of marriage for a woman was just twenty. But researchers estimate that nearly one woman in four was pregnant before marriage.[15]

A young woman who got pregnant and could not or would not marry was often sent away to a "home" for unwed mothers, where she was pressured into giving up her baby. Four million babies were put up for adoption in the United States between 1945 and 1973. That's an average of almost 143,000 per year, compared to fewer than 18,000 per year as of 2021, despite roughly equal numbers of total births per year in both eras.[16]

The realities of 1950s and 1960s marriages would come as a shock to any contemporary woman who dreams of emulating the tradwife influencers she sees on social media. During the entire postwar era, rape was illegal only if a man forced a woman *other than his wife* to have sex. As one legal scholar explained in 1957: "A man does not commit rape by having sexual intercourse with his lawful wife, even if he does so by force and against her will." Not until the mid-1970s did states start repealing the marital exemptions to their rape laws. Only in 1993 did the last states make marital rape illegal.[17]

Outright wife-beating was technically illegal, but by today's standards the tolerance for domestic violence back then is quite astonishing. In 1958, for example, *The New York Mirror,* then the nation's second-largest circulation newspaper, conducted "man-in-the-street" interviews asking the question "If a woman needs it, should she be spanked?" Every respondent they quoted replied in the affirmative. One man argued that spanking was okay even when a woman *didn't* need it. "Most . . . have it coming to them anyway. If they don't it will remind them how well off they are."[18]

Even many prominent "family experts" agreed that "most" victims of abuse "had it coming." In 1964, a national medical journal published the results of three psychiatrists' in-depth analysis of thirty-seven domestic violence cases. The report noted that the wife-beating had gone on for years and was typically only discovered when a teenage boy intervened to protect his mom. Astonishingly, however, the psychiatrists argued that the son's intervention destroyed a "more or less" satisfactory "marital equilibrium." Most battered wives, the psychiatrists explained, were "aggressive, efficient, masculine, and sexually frigid." When a husband beat such a wife, it helped him to "re-establish his masculine identity" and her to feel less guilty about "her controlling, castrating behavior."[19]

Child abuse was not recognized as a social problem in 1950s medical journals, despite much higher rates of unexplained childhood injuries than are seen today. Incest was largely ignored or denied—and in some cases described as female "sex delinquency" rather than adult predation.[20]

Stringent legal restrictions on divorce made it hard to terminate an unhappy marriage. The law not only forbade divorce on grounds of mutual consent; it also forbade divorce on grounds of mutual maltreatment. Most state laws held that any party seeking to end a marriage had to be free from any "suspicion that he has contributed to the injury of which he complains." If neither party came to court "with clean hands," neither was entitled to a divorce.

Even when a woman could meet the grounds for a fault-based divorce, she was seldom entitled to a fair division of the family assets. Throughout the 1950s and into the 1960s, forty-two states and the District of Columbia held that earnings acquired during marriage were the sole property of the person who earned them, so a divorcing homemaker wasn't entitled to share what her husband had accumulated while she'd raised their children and kept their house. And as of 1957, only 19 percent of divorced women were legally entitled to alimony.[21]

Police records, psychologists' accounts, oral histories, and marital surveys from the 1950s and 1960s reveal that many seemingly "stable" marriages of the postwar era were marked by substance abuse, domestic violence, infidelity, or simple day-to-day misery. Couples stayed together not because they were better partners but because they had fewer alternatives—as well as lower expectations. As one thirty-two-year-old woman who married in the early 1960s and was interviewed by Lillian Rubin in the early 1970s described a satisfactory marriage: "Any woman who's got a man who hardly ever gets violent and who doesn't drink much hasn't got a lot to complain about."[22]

This was also a period of heightened repression of gay men and lesbians. In 1952, the American Psychiatric Association categorized homosexuality as a mental disorder and psychiatrists sanctioned "cures" such as electroshock therapy. In what now seems like a dress rehearsal for 2025, the federal government barred gay and lesbian people from civil service jobs in 1953, while the military went on a campaign to fine and dishonorably discharge gay men and lesbians.

WHAT FAMILIES SHOULD REALLY MISS ABOUT POSTWAR AMERICA

Despite the limited options for people who didn't want to marry or were stuck in miserable marriages, the increasing security of the postwar economy made it easier for heterosexual men and women to start a family and, when both partners were loving and committed, to sustain supportive relationships. But the rising living standards and economic stability of that era had a different source than we're often led to believe.

Contrary to claims we hear from contemporary nostalgia

purveyors, the postwar era was not a time where "free enterprise" reigned supreme, unfettered by government "interference." Rather, it was a time of much more extensive government-funded job creation, stricter regulation of businesses and banks, higher tax rates on the wealthy than today, and stronger guardrails against financial piracy, such as the now-common practice of speculators engineering hostile takeovers of healthy companies to strip their assets and run them into the ground.[23]

In the 1930s and 1940s, while government regulators reined in the financial speculation and stock market chicanery that had triggered the Great Depression, Congress put millions of Americans to work building the nation's infrastructure and implementing rural-electrification programs that transformed the lives of American farmers. The federal government stopped auctioning off public lands to private investors and spearheaded a massive expansion and improvement of our national parks. The feds also reorganized the banking system, overruling "free market" principles to make home down payments more affordable and establish thirty-year fixed-rate mortgages. The 1935 Wagner Act made it easier for workers to organize unions and bargain collectively.

Racism limited the reach of many New Deal reforms. Southern legislators insisted that domestic and agricultural workers, disproportionately Black and Brown, be excluded from the Minimum Wage Act and other fair-labor standards. The Federal Housing Authority's practice of "redlining" Black and Hispanic neighborhoods as being "at risk" of deterioration over time disqualified residents of these areas from government-guaranteed housing loans, depriving them of the rise in housing values that was the main source of security for working-class Americans in the second half of the twentieth century. Together with restrictive covenants in many urban and suburban neighborhoods, this perpetuated a housing-based wealth gap that continues to disadvantage Black families generations later.[24]

Yet despite that ongoing discrimination, working people of all racial and ethnic groups benefited from the investment government made in jobs and education and the restrictions it imposed on the prerogatives of industrialists and financiers. By 1955, one-third of all workers were in unions, five times more than at the beginning of the 1930s and three times more than in 2023. And although most unions only gradually opened their doors to Black men and to women, the expansion of higher-paid union jobs raised the wage floor for nonunion workers as well. The greatest reductions in wage inequality among all workers during that era were in regions where unions grew the most.[25]

Compared to today, it's surprising how widely the principles of the New Deal were accepted in elite political and business circles back then. No less a staunch anti-communist than Dwight Eisenhower, supreme commander of the allied forces in Europe during World War II and president of the United States from 1953 to 1961, assured a correspondent in 1954 that if "any political party attempt[ed] to abolish social security, unemployment insurance, and eliminate labor laws and farm programs, you would not hear of that party again in our political history." Only a "tiny splinter group," he continued, hoped to turn the clock back, and he listed its membership: "H. L. Hunt (you possibly know his background),* a few other Texas oil millionaires, and an occasional politician or business man from other areas. Their number is negligible and they are stupid."[26]

---

* H. L. Hunt was an oil tycoon who was one of the world's richest men at his death in 1974. Today the Hunt family's holdings in oil, real estate, and sports make it worth just shy of $25 billion as of February 8, 2024, according to *Forbes* magazine.

Eisenhower continued the job-creation initiatives of Presidents Roosevelt and Truman, funding a massive interstate highway building project that provided living-wage jobs to at least three generations of blue-collar workers while opening new land for suburban development and recreational use. Investment in higher education also soared during Eisenhower's tenure, including tuition coverage and living stipends for veterans while in school.

And contrary to the myth that the internet was invented in a teenager's garage, it was government funding in 1960s universities that created the protocols allowing separated computer networks to communicate with each other: Not until 1995 was the main transmission line of the internet turned over to private commercial providers.[27]

Finally, the postwar economic expansion was financed by a much more progressive tax system than we have seen in the past several decades. A 2019 analysis by *The New York Times* found that in the 1950s and 1960s, the super wealthy paid "vastly higher tax rates" than they have since. Unlike today, their total income sources were taxed at higher rates than the rest of the population.[28] This makes sense to me, since the wealthy make more use of tax-funded infrastructure such as airports, roads, and property protection services than the rest of us. They also consume more energy and raw materials and often run enterprises that generate pollution whose cleanup comes from public funds.[29]

And contrary to the claims of those who say taxing the rich discourages investment, real US gross domestic product grew faster in the 1950s and 1960s than in more recent decades.[30]

Most business leaders of that era accepted the idea that company profits should be reinvested in productive capacity rather than diverted to stock buybacks and bonuses for chief executive officers.[31] In 1965, the average compensation for a CEO in the largest US companies was 21 times the wage of a typical worker in that company. In 2023, it was 290 *times as much*.[32]

To get a sense of what that means, the CEO of Carnival Cruise Lines, who is far from the highest-paid executive among Fortune 500 companies, makes more than $23 million a year, according to paperwork issued by that company on February 28, 2025. That works out to $65,750 *per day* (including holidays and weekend days), more than the median *annual* earnings for full-time wage and salary workers in the United States, which as of 2024 were $59,228.[33]

Taken together, the prevailing practices of the postwar era led to rising wages for workers on all rungs of the income ladder. Looking at the overall trends in wages between 1945 and 1974, Rand Corporation economists Carter Price and Kathryn Edwards estimate that if the equitable income growth of that period had continued, by 2018 the bottom 90 percent of the population, Black as well as White, would have ended up with incomes 67 percent higher than they actually did.[34]

RISING SOCIAL AS WELL AS ECONOMIC EXPECTATIONS

By the mid-1970s, however, both pillars of the 1950s marriage system—the social restrictions on women and on premarital sex and the economic progress for working-class men—were being undermined. One factor undercutting the social restrictions was the booming consumer economy's rediscovery of the early twentieth-century marketing insight that "sex sells." The sexual revolution of the 1920s had made recreational sex central to its definition of a successful marriage. But the temptation to engage in recreational sex *before* marriage was always built into the model, and it became more prominent as sexual titillation became mainstream, contraception more reliable, little girls were given Barbie dolls instead of baby dolls, and adolescents of the postwar baby boom pioneered a mass youth culture.[35]

Prosperity awakened new aspirations for personal growth as well as personal pleasure. Many young women, often encouraged by mothers who'd warned them "not to be just a housewife like me," decided to pursue higher education or a career before marriage.[36]

Rising expectations also revived demands for greater social justice. The civil rights movement exposed the hypocrisy of those claiming America was the "leader of the free world" while sanctioning legal segregation. A revitalized feminist movement, its ranks swelled by growing numbers of female college students, critiqued the sexual double standard, decried inequalities in marriage, demanded easier access to divorce, and agitated against restrictions on birth control and abortion rights. And the formerly discreet gay rights movement became "loud and proud," especially after six days of clashes between police and protesters in 1969, sparked when patrons at the Stonewall Inn, a gay bar in Manhattan, fought back after maltreatment during a police raid.

Like the changes in gender and sexual mores that had shocked so many Americans in the 1910s and 1920s, those of the 1960s and early 1970s challenged mainstream values and behavior patterns. But a 1920s-style backlash to these changes took a bit more time to gain steam.

For a while, in fact, some of the new ideas seemed uncontentious. In 1969, the Republican governor of California, future president Ronald Reagan, signed the first no-fault divorce law in the nation. In 1971, both houses of Congress passed the Comprehensive Child Care Act to accommodate the needs of working mothers. President Nixon vetoed the act in an early concession to right-wing complaints about government usurping family functions, but both he and his Republican successor Gerald Ford endorsed the Equal Rights Amendment. The ERA was approved for ratification by the House of Representatives in 1971 and by the Senate in 1972. By 1977, it seemed destined to pass, having gained thirty-five of the thirty-eight state ratifications needed to become law.

SOCIAL AND ECONOMIC BACKLASH

Meanwhile, however, many corporate executives and wealthy families had grown concerned that the other mainstay of the 1950s marriage system—the New Deal's expanded protections for working-class wages, job security, and safety-net benefits, along with its restrictions on financial speculation and monopoly concentration—had become too firmly embedded in economic and legal doctrine. In 1971, corporate lawyer Lewis Powell, believing that consumer advocates such as Ralph Nader were undermining confidence in "the profit system," sent a confidential memo to the Chamber of Commerce urging an all-out offensive against what he called the New Deal and Great Society's "Attack on [the] American Free Enterprise System."[37] Powell was shortly thereafter appointed to the Supreme Court.

Powell's timing was ideal for recruiting to the "free enterprise" cause. In the early 1970s, economic growth slowed. At first, wages and profits stalled across the board. But that gave business owners and wealthy elites who had previously tolerated New Deal reforms a big incentive to join the "splinter group" Eisenhower had thought would remain marginalized—those who wanted to increase businesses' *share* of total revenue by gutting safety-net programs, eliminating labor laws, deregulating industry and finance, and lowering taxes on wealth. The Heritage Foundation, now best known as the architect of the Project 2025 campaign, was founded in 1973 to help implement the Powell agenda.

By the 1980s, as investigative journalist Jane Mayer has shown, Powell's offensive was being enthusiastically pursued by a coterie of super-wealthy families intent on repealing restrictions on stock buybacks and leveraged buyouts, shedding mandated healthcare and pension benefits, deregulating the financial sector, rolling back unionization, and reducing taxes on corporate profits and inherited wealth. As historian Nancy MacLean demonstrates, many of these "free market" proponents, heeding Eisenhower's warning that such actions would be punished at the ballot box, also began what turned into a decades-long campaign to remove the "constraints" democracy imposes on the pursuit of profit and accumulation of wealth.[38]

Powell had particularly recommended the recruitment of jurists to the "free enterprise" cause, calling the judiciary "the most important instrument for social, economic and political change." The Federalist Society, formed in 1982 and committed to "Rolling Back the New Deal" in the words of one of its conference titles, became one such recruiting agency. Its efforts to place sympathetic judges in high positions have paid off handsomely. The 2010 Supreme Court ruling that corporations' political campaign spending counts as free speech was one sign of its success. Today, six members of the current Supreme Court are or have been members of the Federalist Society: Roberts, Alito, Thomas, Kavanagh, Gorsuch, and Barrett.[39]

During the second half of the 1970s, as the pro-business coalition mobilized to tear down the New Deal and Great Society programs of the 1950s and 1960s, another coalition was gearing up to rebuild the marriage, sex, and gender system of that era. In 1977, conservative activist Phyllis Schlafly kicked off her ultimately successful campaign to defeat the ERA,[40] utilizing now-familiar arguments about the danger of unisex bathrooms. That same year, the popular singer Anita Bryant mounted a national antigay crusade under the now-equally-familiar slogan "Save Our Children."

Since the late 1970s, groups claiming to defend "free markets" have increasingly made common cause with groups claiming to defend "traditional" gender roles, sexual mores, marital norms, and "Christian family values." Wealthy individuals and politicians who want to deregulate Wall Street and repeal restrictions on corporate and billionaire entitlements forged alliances with groups wanting to re-regulate women's bodies and reimpose restrictions on people's sexual and marital choices. Many Christian conservatives returned the favor, as when Moral Majority founder Jerry Falwell Sr. insisted that God himself endorses the "free market" agenda of "property, ownership, competition, work, and acquisition."[41]

Some may find it hard to reconcile such a supposed endorsement with the biblical pronouncement that "love of money is the root of all evil" and the New Testament's exhortations to feed the poor and shelter the homeless. Nevertheless, people who detest restrictions on "free enterprise" and people who detest the cultural libertarianism that free enterprise encourages have increasingly made common cause. Today's pro-wealth cause is highly dependent upon voters who believe they are voting for "family values."[42]

THE TRIUMPH OF THE PRO-WEALTH AGENDA

In public, both groups place more emphasis on restoring the sexual, gender, and marriage norms of the 1950s than on rolling back the New Deal's protection of workers and consumers. But in practice, if not preaching, pro-business advocates have until recently been more successful than pro-marriage advocates in implementing their agenda. Recall the Rand Corporation economists' estimate that if the equitable distribution of income growth in the period from 1945 to 1974 had continued, by 2018 the income of people in the bottom 90 percent of the population would have been 67 percent higher than it actually ended up. What happened in reality?

Over the forty-three years between 1975 and 2018, those economists calculate, the richest 10 percent of Americans managed to rake in a mind-boggling $47 trillion dollars *more* than they would have if the trends of the previous era had continued. Meanwhile, the bottom 90 percent got $47 trillion *less*—an average of *$2.5 trillion less each year.* As *Time* magazine summarized these findings, that would have been "enough to pay every single working American in the bottom nine deciles an additional $1,144 a month. Every month. Every single year!"[43]

The result? A 2025 report by the Federal Reserve found that as of December 31, 2024, the wealthiest 10 percent of households held 67.2 percent of total household wealth, while the bottom 50 percent held just 2.5 percent.[44]

All this has made it much harder than it once was for young male wage earners to live up to the expectations of male breadwinning that undergirded the marriage trends of the 1950s and 1960s.

According to a 2017 Census Bureau study that accounted for inflation by measuring in constant 2015 dollars, back in 1975 only 25 percent of men aged twenty-five to thirty-four had incomes lower than $30,000 per year. By 2016, also measuring in 2015 dollars, 41 percent of young men in the same age group were making less than $30,000.[45]

Since the late 1960s, the typical twenty-five- to twenty-nine-year-old male worker has been paid a lower starting wage than his counterpart who joined the workforce earlier in the postwar era. As a result, he has also earned less *over a lifetime* than a similar man the same age who entered the workforce in the 1960s. Most of the decline in men's lifetime earnings since the late 1960s is a result of lower incomes while working rather than fewer years spent in the labor force.[46]

No wonder many Americans feel robbed of the "better future" they'd come to believe was an American entitlement. And adding insult to injury, the growth in inequality has reorganized daily life in ways that continually highlight the special privileges accorded to the wealthy and denied to the rest of us in a nominally egalitarian society.[47]

People in the top 10 percent of the income distribution now account for half of consumer spending. As a result they get 90 percent of most companies' attention. In 2005, the financial institution Citigroup issued an "Industry Note" memo on investment strategy, identifying America as a "Plutonomy," where "the rich absorb a disproportionate chunk of the economy." The memo went on to cheerfully advise investors on stocks that would flourish in a plutonomy.[48] But for people excluded from the plutonomy's new perks, such as concierge medical practices, separate elite entrances into public venues, designated "valued customer" telephone numbers, and line-skipping privileges on Disneyland rides, being forced to abide by inconveniences once shared by all increasingly feels like a badge of disrespect. One study found that when airline passengers who purchased coach tickets have to walk through the first-class cabin to get to their seats—after having waited for first-class passengers and frequent fliers to board ahead of them, then often discovering that the overhead luggage bins are already full—this visceral demonstration of class inequality is associated with twice as many air rage incidents as when everyone boards through the middle of the plane.[49]

All these changes help explain why many Americans have become susceptible to "past-sickness," pining for a time when opportunity and respect seemed in easier reach. The sense of injury many working-class and lower-middle-class Americans feel is not "all in their head." However, many have misdiagnosed the source of that pain, concluding that their prospects have receded because they've lost their traditional racial and gender privileges. They think White men's economic prospects and sense of dignity might start being "great" again if they didn't have to compete with Blacks or other minorities and if women went back to being homemakers.

But most of the progress White workers made during the postwar decades wasn't due to any *increase* in the long-standing injustices perpetrated against working people of color, even though those injustices continued to be widespread. Rather, it was due to a *decrease* in the long-standing injustices that employers, banks, and the super-rich had traditionally been allowed to perpetrate on workers and consumers. And ironically, the relative privileges White men received from racism and sexism back then actually made them more vulnerable to later attacks on their wages, working conditions, and social benefits.

THE DOUBLE-EDGED SWORD OF WHITE MALE "PRIVILEGE"

White people who are disadvantaged compared to people above them in the economic and educational hierarchy (who are still mostly other Whites) get valuable benefits when their color gives them a competitive advantage over people with roughly similar education or skills. But in the long run, the existence of a two-tiered wage and benefit system based on *privilege* for one group of workers instead of *rights* for all is a trap.

In the early twentieth century, for example, the fact that Black men were excluded from certain occupations meant employers could recruit Southern Black workers as strikebreakers when White workers went on strike, only to fire them when the strike was broken, hurting both groups. In the 1970s and 1980s, manufacturing jobs literally "went South" as employers moved to states where union drives had historically failed because White workers resisted working with Black ones. And throughout the country, racial jealousies have often undercut the ability of working Americans to defend the social safety net on which most of us need to rely at some point in our lives. As legal scholar Ian Haney López argues, fanning racial tensions has long been one of the most potent weapons that elites and demagogues have waged against economically egalitarian social policies.[50]

Sexism often works the same way. Today's army of temporary and contract workers, with no job security, health insurance, overtime protection, pensions, or guaranteed hours, is the direct descendant of the 1950s and 1960s temp industry that male union leaders failed to contest because it supposedly let their daughters and wives earn "pin money" as Kelly Girls without competing against full-time male workers. Instead, it offered a blueprint for how to get rid of full-time workers and mandated benefits.

In 1971, Kelly Services ran an ad describing the type of temporary worker they offered, calling her the "Never-Never Girl." Her description should sound eerily familiar to today's "independent contractors" and gig workers. "Never takes a vacation or holiday . . . Never costs you a dime for slack time. (When the workload drops, you drop her.) Never has a cold, slipped disc or loose tooth. (Not on your time anyway!) Never costs you for unemployment taxes and Social Security payments. (None of the paperwork, either!) Never costs you for fringe benefits."[51]

Over the past 50 years, Americans have experienced the piecemeal repeal of two contracts that most people in the 1950s thought were pretty much iron-clad: the postwar sex, gender, and marriage pact and the postwar labor, capital, and government pact. We have to negotiate new contracts, and that will be a challenging process. But first we have to discard the idea that if we could restore the gender roles and marriage patterns of that era, that would pretty much take care of things.

I don't want to downplay the challenges posed by our emerging new gender, sexual, and marital norms. While they've reduced many old injustices, they've also created some new risks and dilemmas. According to the National Crime Victimization Survey, which captures more incidents than police reports, violent rape has declined fairly steadily since the 1980s. Rape and sexual assault rates fell by 81 percent between 1993 and 2005, then spiked in 2018, but in 2022 were still 56 percent lower than in 1993. Nevertheless, underreporting remains a serious problem, and contemporary dating and sexual practices have created new ambiguities about what constitutes sexual consent, especially among people still influenced by traditional double standards. Additionally, although the dangers of the hooking-up scene have been exaggerated, as I show in chapter 8, it does provide sexual predators with potential targets.[52]

The widespread acceptance of sexual expressiveness and imagery has been liberating in many ways. But the ubiquitous sexual objectification of girls and women in popular culture has negative effects on their self-image and aspirations. The male-oriented pornography so easily available on the internet miseducates boys and young men about what "turns on" girls and women while offering a trove of demeaning images that can encourage sexual harassment among even very young teens.[53] And I shudder to imagine the directions in which new AI-generated pornography may go!

We must acknowledge and try to mitigate the downsides of changing social mores and behavior patterns. But we need to be realistic about what we can or should seek to reverse. Consider recent calls to roll back unilateral divorce, a practice that allows one party to get a divorce even if the other objects. There's no question that divorce can be very painful for the partner who wants the marriage to continue. But because states passed these laws at different times, economists Betsey Stevenson and Justin Wolfers had what was effectively a controlled experiment to examine the consequences. In states that adopted unilateral divorce between 1976 and 1985, divorce rates rose sharply over the next decade, reflecting pent-up demand. Then the rates tapered off and even fell. Meanwhile, however, the suicide rate of wives declined by about 20 percent, while domestic violence rates dropped by somewhere between a quarter and a half.[54]

Perhaps the most widely circulated argument about the need to reverse recent changes in marriage and relationship patterns is the claim that our new acceptance of divorce and unwed motherhood is the reason America has such exceptionally high murder rates, far higher than those in Europe and other developed countries such as Canada and Japan. So I'll end this chapter with just one striking example of how wrong-headed it is to think that Making America Married Again—or "MAMA" as I like to call it—would solve the social problems of our era.

MYTHS ABOUT MURDER AND MARRIAGE

When violent crime and murder spiked in the 1980s and early 1990s, commentators leapt to attribute this to the increase in single parenthood since the 1950s and 1960s. In 1995, criminologist John DiLulio ignited a bipartisan push for mass incarceration when he warned that the proliferation of "fatherless" and "godless" families had produced a generation of "depraved" young "super predators," with the next generation on track to be even more violent.[55] Yet the prediction that the decline in married-couple families would produce an ever-escalating murder rate turned out to be completely wrong. In light of recurrent claims about "skyrocketing" crime rates in recent years, it's worth tracking what actually happened during the decades since the 1950s.

In 1960, only 8 percent of children didn't have a father in their home, and in 1970 only 11 percent. By 1980, that number had jumped to 18 percent and by 1985 to 21 percent.[56] Bear in mind that historically, most homicides are committed by males aged eighteen to twenty-nine. So if supposedly "fatherless" families were the main cause of rising homicide rates, we'd expect murder rates to have skyrocketed between the mid-1990s and 2014, when children born between 1980 and 1985 were in the violence-prone age range of eighteen to twenty-nine.

But that's not the way things played out. In 1960, when eighteen- to twenty-nine-year-olds would have been born between 1931 and

1942, there were 5.1 homicides per 1,000 people each year. Homicides rose in the late 1960s and the 1970s, hitting an all-time high of 10.4 per 1,000 people in 1980, when men aged eighteen to twenty-nine would have been born between 1951 and 1962. It then hovered between 8 and 9 per 1,000 during the 1980s before rising to 9.8 in 1991 and remaining above 9 until 1993.[57]

After that, however, the homicide rate began a long-term fall. Between 1996 and 2014, *even as the record number of "fatherless" males born between 1980 and 1985 reached their most violence-prone ages,* the homicide rate steadily declined, bottoming out at 4.4 in 2014, *the lowest rate since reliable national records began being kept in 1960—in fact, marginally lower than in 1960!*

In 2020, during the pandemic, the murder rate shot up by 27 percent, the largest single-year rise since 1960. Yet even after that dramatic increase, the homicide rate remained lower than its historic highs in 1980 and the early 1990s. And in 2023, the murder rate *fell* at the steepest rate on record, bringing 2023 and 2024 homicide rates back to much lower levels than the 1990s, and in some cities, to the lowest rate since the 1960s.[58]

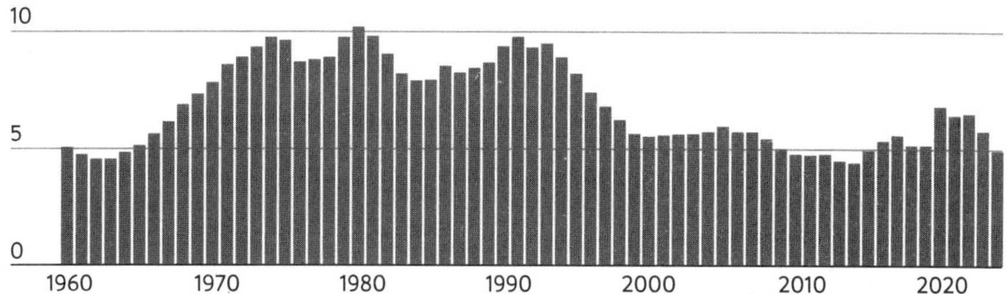

As this book went to press, murder rates for 2025 were looking to end up similarly low in comparison to the 1990s. Yet a July 30, 2025, poll by YouGov found that a majority of Americans believed murder rates had *increased* since 1990, with more than a third saying it had "increased a lot." Such is the power—and the danger—of nostalgia, especially when amplified by ideologues.[59]

Families in America, especially parents with children, face serious challenges today. Not all of them meet those challenges successfully. But blaming contemporary problems on people's abandonment of "traditional" family values is not helpful.

Shifting values since the 1970s explain why many Americans now feel comfortable delaying marriage, engaging in unmarried cohabitation, intentionally remaining single, getting a divorce, or questioning their gender or sexual identity. But they don't explain the fact that the social groups who tend to be most accepting of new values about women's rights, same-sex relationships, and trans rights—and least disapproving of divorce and unwed motherhood—are actually the sectors of the population most likely to marry and least likely to divorce.

The most serious problems we face today, in or out of marriage, result from the interaction between our expanded options for conducting a successful life outside marriage, our reduced prospects for fairly shared prosperity, and the persistence of many all-too-traditional gender and sexual double standards.

In the next two chapters I show how the simultaneous polarization of economic prospects and relationship patterns has led to widespread misunderstandings of the causes and consequences of changes in marriage. Clinging to "traditional" family values and gender habits under these new conditions can actually sabotage people's marital prospects and outcomes.

Chapter 7.

HAS MARRIAGE BECOME A LUXURY GOOD?

Despite all the talk about marriage becoming obsolete, most Americans still get married. But what convinces them to "tie the knot" and how they decide *when* to do that has changed dramatically.

Over the years I've interviewed many men and women who married in the 1940s, 1950s, and 1960s. When I asked how long they knew each other before marrying, I was always struck by how rapidly their courtships had proceeded. Aside from couples who were high school sweethearts, they typically reported seeing each other just seven or eight months before setting a wedding date. This is close to sociologist Frank Furstenberg Jr.'s estimate that the average length of time a 1950s couple dated before marriage was only six months.

By way of contrast, a 2018 survey of more than two thousand couples aged twenty-five to thirty-four found they'd known each other an average of six and a half *years* before marrying. Another study of couples who'd cohabited before marriage found that on average, they'd *lived* together for more than two and a half years before getting wed.[1]

When I asked people from that earlier era why they felt comfortable marrying so quickly, they often replied "that's just what you did." Some added the phrase "when you fell in love." A few women said "when you started having sex." And some said "we had to," meaning the woman had gotten pregnant.

When pressed to elaborate, most people provided variations on the idea that getting married was what you did "when you were ready to grow up." Men said "it was time to settle down" or "to get a serious job." Women said they wanted "to have a home of my own" or "to start a family" or "to stop depending on my parents."

No one described holding off marriage until they'd saved a significant sum of money. Indeed, among couples who met in college, several women reported dropping out of school to marry, then taking a job to support their new household until her husband finished college and could replace her in the workplace. It was jocularly called getting your PhT, for "putting hubby through."

FIRST COMES LOVE, THEN COMES COHABITATION

Nowadays the reasons people give for deciding if and when to marry are strikingly different. Love is essential, but not usually enough. For most couples today, *cohabitation* is what you do when you fall in love. A full three-quarters of couples who married between 2015 and 2019 had lived together first. But not all cohabiting couples who love each other get married. Something more than love is needed for most to take that next step.[2]

In contrast to the postwar era, people today consistently say they plan to wait to marry until they and their partner have achieved financial independence, demonstrated their personal responsibility, gained enough education or job experience to have good prospects for a secure future, and accumulated a nest egg. Being free of debt is also important. As late as 1979, outstanding student loans did not cause people to delay marriage. Since the late 1990s, that's changed.[3]

Marriage was once one of the *first* steps people took on the road to independent adulthood. Today for most people it's what they do after they've traveled quite some distance along that road. People once viewed marriage as the "cornerstone" of a successful adult life, says sociologist Andrew Cherlin. Increasingly, they now see it as the "capstone"—the last piece that completes the structure of their lives.[4]

As one woman in that 2018 poll explained her thinking, "I'd like to know who I am and what I'm able to offer financially and how stable I am, before I'm committed legally to someone. My mom says I'm removing all the romance from the equation, but I know there's more to marriage than just love."

Much of that "more" involves secure earnings prospects. In a 2019 survey of cohabiting couples who said they'd like to get married someday, a majority reported that one reason they weren't yet married was because they or their partner were not financially ready for marriage. Forty-four percent said they weren't yet far along enough in their job or career.[5]

People from middle-income backgrounds express the desire to establish themselves in a profession and be able to buy or rent a better home before they take the plunge. Lower-income Americans list more modest prerequisites, but they, too, have a "marriage bar" they feel they should meet. They want to be sure they can pay their bills each month without needing help from family, friends, or government programs and to have saved enough to throw a wedding to which they can invite friends and family.[6]

People's new ideas about where they must *be* in their lives in order to marry have interacted with the changing job and wage structure described in chapter 6 to produce a growing economic and educational divergence in marital patterns. Up through the 1970s, people at all income and educational levels married at similar ages and rates. The only exception was highly educated women. Until the 1960s, women with a college or postgraduate degree—then a much smaller group than now—were more likely to postpone or even forgo marriage than less-educated women.

Today, the educational gradient in women's likelihood of marriage goes in the opposite direction. By age forty to forty-four, only 16 percent of women with a bachelor's degree and 14 percent of women with a master's degree have never married, compared to a full quarter of women with a high school education or less.[7]

Less-educated women in committed cohabiting relationships have also become less likely to transition to marriage than their more highly educated counterparts. Between 1995 and 2005–2010, the proportion of women with a high school education or less who married their cohabiting partner within three years fell from 40 to 20 percent, while the proportion of college-educated cohabiting women who married within three years remained unchanged at 46 percent. Almost half of both groups (45 percent) had reported *intending* to marry when they first began living together.[8]

In the 1950s and 1960s, men aged twenty-five and older at all educational levels were equally likely to have married. Today, however, men with lower levels of education, like their female counterparts, are significantly less likely to have married than more-educated men.[9]

Education is usually a rough stand-in for income, so it's no surprise that marriage rates by income show a similar but even more dramatic divergence. As of 2021, among all men aged forty to forty-four earning $25,000 to $40,000 per year, 32 percent had never been married. Among men the same age earning $75,000 to $100,000, only 16 percent had never married. And although many high-earning women delay marriage while they establish their careers, by age forty to fifty-four, women who earn more than $75,000 a year are significantly more likely to have married than lower-earning women.[10]

Looking at earnings alone doesn't provide a full picture of how much economic resources influence marriage decisions. The extent to which a person's job offers predictable schedules and healthcare also counts. People working split shifts or nonstandard hours are less likely to marry than otherwise comparable workers. In fact, a substantial portion of the educational gap in entry into first marriage seems to be connected to the higher quality of the jobs available to more educated individuals. This helps explain why union membership raises the chance that a man will marry, regardless of his education, since union contracts typically offer health insurance and predictable schedules to all members.[11]

Low-income marriages have long been more likely to experience disruption than high-income ones. But in the 1950s and 1960s, highly educated women were more likely to get a legal divorce than less-educated women. As divorce became more accessible in the early 1970s, however, the divorce gap by education reversed and has steadily grown.[12]

Among women who married in the late 1970s, the percentage whose marriages dissolved within ten years was six points lower for women with a college degree than for women with a high school diploma. Among women who married in the early 1990s, that gap had grown to more than 20 percentage points. As of 2015, a college-educated woman had an almost 80 percent chance of reaching her twentieth wedding anniversary while a woman with a high school education or less had only a 40 percent chance.[13]

EXPLAINING THE CLASS GAP IN MARRIAGE

The growing income and educational divide in marriage patterns has led some commentators to argue that marriage has become a "luxury good," a status symbol, or even a "trophy"—the reward couples give themselves for successfully navigating a competitive educational and economic environment and meeting the increasingly high standards most Americans now hold for relationships.

Other observers counter that it's a mistake for people to view marriage as the culmination of their interpersonal journey because marriage is actually a springboard to economic success and personal well-being. They claim there'd be less poverty, more gainful employment, and more happy, healthy people in America if everyone understood that getting married is the *gateway* to economic and emotional security rather than the prize you collect at the end of your journey.

Pro-marriage advocacy groups such as the National Marriage Project point out that in the postwar era, poor and lower-middle-class Americans were "markedly more likely to get and stay married [than today], even if they did not have much money or a consistently good relationship. They made do."[14] And making do, they argue, is what allowed working-class people to make good.

Today, marriage advocates claim, "new cultural values" promulgated by the affluent middle class have set such "a high financial and emotional bar for marriage" that many poor and lower-middle-class couples wrongly believe they don't have the "emotional and economic resources" needed to make marriage work. Such couples, they suggest, are missing their best chance to *acquire* those resources.

"Marriage is a wealth-building institution," argues the author of a book titled *The Ring Makes All the Difference,* because when people marry, they earn more, save more, and become more personally responsible. In a 2015 *Washington Post* article titled "Don't Be a Bachelor," Bradford Wilcox, director of the National Marriage Project, scolded men who think they should delay marriage until they're making more money—along with "women who spurn low-wage men"—for failing to see that "marriage has a transformative effect on . . . emotional health and financial well-being." It spurs men to "work harder" and stick with their jobs longer. As a writer in *The Federalist* approvingly summed up the thesis of a 2024 book by Wilcox, "Want to Be Rich and Happy? Get Married."[15]

Is getting married a stepping stone in what some people call "the success sequence"? Or is marriage something people do after they've already checked off most boxes—good education, steady job, financial security, personal responsibility? Is marriage the starting point for a successful life or the shingle you hang out when you've arrived?

My view of marriage lies somewhere in between. People who claim marriage *creates* economic success and personal happiness typically confuse the economic, social, and psychological factors that lead people into beneficial, lasting marriages with the effect that simply *getting married* has on people.

On average, married people are happier, healthier, more economically secure, and less prone to crime than the unmarried. But on average, individuals who are happier, healthier, more economically secure, and less crime-prone are more likely to marry in the first place. Responsible, well-adjusted, non-depressed individuals with good employment histories or earnings prospects are simply more attractive as potential partners.

It's delusional to think that getting married will "transform" an individual's economic prospects or personal responsibility. In actuality, researchers have demonstrated that the increases in work effort and earnings and improvements in behavior often attributed to a person *getting* married typically begin well *before* marriage. They are precursors to—and usually prerequisites for—being accepted as a marriage partner. Individuals who won't or can't make these changes are less likely to marry—or to sustain stable relationships in or out of marriage.[16]

Sociologist Philip Cohen points out that there's a "marriage queue," and people don't end up at the back of the line by accident. The majority of women and men who are not marrying today, Cohen notes, live in low-income communities that offer a low likelihood of finding—or becoming—a partner who can offer economic security and consistent personal support.[17]

Black women in such communities face especially formidable odds of finding a partner who can consistently help with providing, due in part to job discrimination and in part to racial disparities in the mass incarceration campaign that accelerated in the 1980s and 1990s.* Looking at fifty large metropolitan areas in the United States, Cohen calculates that there are only sixty employed unmarried Black men for every one hundred unmarried Black women. Sociologist Christina Cross points out that on average,

* Economists John Schmitt and Kris Warner have calculated that incarceration and the job-search penalties of having a felony conviction explain almost 75 percent of the 1979 to 2008 decline in the employment rate for men without a high school diploma. On average, a criminal record reduces the likelihood of a job offer by 50 percent—and by more than that for Black applicants.

when a Black woman does marry, she gains 60 percent less in assets from her partner than when the average White woman marries.[18]

When people from low-income communities forgo or delay marriage, they seem to be making, consciously or not, fairly clear-eyed assessments of their own or a potential partner's chance for a successful marriage compared to others in their social network. Economist Tara Watson and sociologist Sara McLanahan found that between 1980 and 2000, as job security deteriorated and real wages of less-educated men declined, there was a sharp drop in the marriage rates of twenty-five- to thirty-four-year-old men, Black and White, in the bottom quarter of the income distribution. What best predicted a man's likelihood of marriage in those two decades was not his own absolute income but his income relative to the median wage of men in his local reference group. The more a man fell below that median, the less likely he was to marry.[19]

The declining wage and job stability of less-educated young men, combined with the still low but increasing earnings opportunities that have opened up for women in low-income communities since the 1970s, have changed the calculus for a woman considering whether to marry someone she is seeing, even if she becomes pregnant. She must weigh the advantages of pooling resources against the danger of being legally bound to someone who might be unable to consistently contribute to or might even misuse the couple's resources.[20]

In other cases, low-income men select themselves out of the marriage market. Some don't want to face expectations or demands they can't meet. Others, unable to achieve mainstream definitions of masculine success, compensate by adopting an outlaw or hypermasculine identity that makes stable relationships unlikely.[21]

Still, while I don't think marriage offers a dependable path to long-term security, I don't believe it's nothing more than a "trophy" people hang on the wall once they've already reached their economic or educational goals. Marriage can be a high-yield investment, producing significant financial and interpersonal benefits for a couple over the years. But it's an investment that requires a substantial buy-in and serious long-term commitment of resources. And it carries more risks than it did when neither partner had many options to pull out of the deal.

CALCULATING THE RISKS AND REWARDS OF MARRIAGE:
They Vary by Class and Race

I've come to think of modern marriage as analogous to a high-stakes real estate deal, with feelings as well as finances, well-being along with wealth, on the line. Most people want to be sure they and their partner can each contribute their fair share of the material and emotional down payment and ongoing maintenance fees that a successful marriage now requires. They know that entering a marriage without those personal and material assets greatly increases the risk of default.

A good marriage can benefit couples at any income level. It permits them to pool incomes, share resources, divide household tasks and childcare, and provide each other emotional and practical support. In fact, researchers Daniel Carlson and Ben Kail recently discovered one way in which marriage is actually associated with *greater* well-being for low-income couples than for their more affluent counterparts. Among impoverished people in distressed communities—but only among such people—married individuals, on average, report significantly higher levels of psychological well-being and lower levels of depression than their never-married counterparts.[22]

Carlson and Kail suggest that the reason low-income married Americans have this advantage over their never-married counterparts is because individuals in impoverished communities face many more external stressors than individuals in affluent communities, with far fewer sources of support. Money is tight and food or housing insecurity never far away. Crime is a constant concern. Dependable networks of friends and family are hard to come by. Trust in others, including police and other public agencies, is low. And unlike more affluent people, low-income individuals can seldom alleviate stress by going on vacation, offloading unpleasant household tasks, or seeing a therapist. Under such conditions, a reliable, supportive spouse is a godsend. Unfortunately, however, the same things that make a well-functioning marriage so helpful to people in such circumstances also make a well-functioning marriage hard to find and sustain.

Some individuals in low-income communities are not good candidates for marriage in the first place, having turned to stress reducers that have destructive consequences, such as drugs or alcohol,* sought support networks in gangs, or become involved in criminal activities. But even for couples with good habits and strong relationship skills, the chronic stress of economic scarcity and unpredictability, punctuated by the higher risk of health crises and other emergencies in low-income populations, makes it difficult to engage in the consistent mutual support that all Americans, whatever their class, race, or ethnicity, increasingly expect from a marriage.

---

* Experiments with primate groups where low-ranking individuals are bullied or excluded find that such stressed individuals will choose cocaine over food when given the chance. This is not something you can blame on their poor family values or lack of marriage. Moises Velasquez-Manoff, "Status and Stress," *New York Times*, July 27, 2013, https://archive.nytimes.com/opinionator.blogs.nytimes.com/2013/07/27/status-and-stress/.

On average, low-income individuals value marriage at least as much as people with higher incomes. But financial unpredictability, food or housing insecurity, and indebtedness worries, along with the discriminatory treatment that poor people often experience, undermine people's ability to conduct their lives and relationships the way they might wish. Fewer than 40 percent of food and retail workers in America can count on at least two weeks advance notice of their work schedules. More than 70 percent report experiencing at least one last-minute shift change within the last month. These changes make everyday life, as well as monthly income, highly unpredictable.[23]

In laboratory experiments, researchers have shown that couples randomly exposed to stressful conditions interact with each other and engage in problem-solving much less successfully than when they are not under stress. Couples who are normally affectionate, collaborative, and forgiving with each other become hostile when confronted with financial strain and other stressors related to poverty. They react negatively to minor annoyances and are less likely to engage in behaviors that bolster a relationship, such as expressing appreciation for helpful behavior or responding positively to a partner's attempts to connect.[24]

One study of Black, White, and Hispanic newlyweds in low-income neighborhoods found that financial challenges were a stronger predictor of negative behavior and communication patterns than their overall satisfaction with the relationship or stressful childhood experiences such as parental divorce. And researchers who followed a group of families over four years discovered that in periods where the couple or an individual was experiencing high stress levels, they were much more likely to engage in the kind of "malevolent attribution" I discussed in the introduction, interpreting any negative or irritating behavior by their partner as intentional and selfishly motivated.[25]

Coping with insecurity and scarcity reduces people's emotional and intellectual bandwidth. For example, low-income individuals who do as well as people with higher incomes when assigned emotionally neutral tasks exhibit sharp reductions in reasoning power and perceptual abilities when assigned tasks of equal difficulty that trigger reminders of their own income shortfalls.[26]

Chronic stress also increases the likelihood that one or both partners will engage in behaviors that take a relationship to the breaking point. Among higher-income couples, psychologist Benjamin Karney reports, the most frequent reasons cited for divorce are incompatibility, lack of love, poor communication, and/or personality clashes. By contrast, lower-income and less-educated couples "are significantly more likely to cite physical abuse, substance abuse, and failure to contribute to the household."[27]

Before anyone jumps to the conclusion that upper-income people are naturally less abusive than lower-income and less-educated ones, consider a study of how the Great Recession of 2007 to 2009 impacted intimate relationships. The authors found that the worsening labor market conditions created a sharp rise in the prevalence of domestic violence among educated women, to the point that it reached levels typically experienced by their more disadvantaged counterparts.[28]

Differences in income and education, however, explain only part of the variations in relationship patterns in America. In all racial and ethnic groups, individuals with more education and income are more likely to marry and less likely to divorce. But researchers still find significant racial-ethnic differences in marriage and divorce rates even after they think they've controlled for socioeconomic and educational status, as seen in this chart showing differences in the marriage rates of White, Black, Hispanic, and Asian men by education.[29]

Percent of never-married thirty-five- to thirty-nine-year-old men by education			
	HS degree or less	Bachelor's degree	Master's degree or more
Whites	38	23	18
Blacks	57	36	29
Hispanics	37	29	22
Asians	34	24	14

MARRIAGE IN BLACK AND WHITE

Most research on racial-ethnic differences in marriage patterns has compared Whites with African Americans. On average, Black Americans have the lowest marriage rates of all racial-ethnic groups and the second-highest divorce rates, surpassed only by Native Americans.[30] Many observers argue that the higher rates of non-marriage among Blacks at all income and educational levels stem from cultural differences in the value placed on marriage.

There are certainly important cultural differences between American Blacks and Whites, including a longer tradition among African Americans of women's independence and employment outside the home, as well as greater emphasis on extended family obligations over marital self-sufficiency. But ample research confirms that the majority of Black Americans value and desire marriage.[31]

In my view, many differences often attributed to distinctive racial traditions are actually a result of America's distinctive *racist* traditions. These have created an accumulation of economic, social, environmental, and personal stressors for African Americans that simply have no counterparts among Whites for which researchers can "control."

For example, two-thirds of Black children born between 1985 and 2000 were raised in neighborhoods where the poverty rate was 20 percent or more. This was true of just 6 percent of White children. Comparing Blacks and Whites with the same educational credentials ignores the fact that Blacks are less likely than Whites to have attended well-funded high schools and high-prestige colleges. Even among Blacks and Whites with the same earnings, Blacks typically have fewer assets and lower inheritance prospects, making for a much less secure personal safety net.[32]

Equally important, Black Americans in all educational and economic categories are routinely exposed to racially discriminatory messages and experiences whose severity has no counterpart among White Americans, even impoverished Whites, although such individuals also routinely encounter disrespectful treatment from authority figures and abusive behavior by police.

Studies consistently confirm that experiencing discrimination and prejudice harms people's mental and physical health. It is just as likely as economic stress to make people negative and antagonistic in their interpersonal relationships.[33]

The research that may come closest to controlling for the differences in Black and White marital patterns lies in two studies of the military—the one and only area of American life where Blacks and Whites attend the same schools and get the same medical care, wages, housing, and recreational activities. In that population, sociologist Jennifer Lundquist found, Black enlisted soldiers had the same rates of marriage as their White counterparts—and *lower* rates of divorce.[34]

A follow-up study by Jay Teachman and Lucky Tedrow suggests that the second finding wasn't because the Army was recruiting a less-divorce-prone type of person, but because it had created a less-divorce-prone environment. And that must have involved something more than equality in material conditions of life, vital though that precondition was, because the Army was the *only* branch of the military that substantially reduced the likelihood of divorce for Black men.

The extra ingredient, the authors concluded—and one that is especially relevant in today's debates about the value of diversity and inclusion efforts—was that in addition to equal pay and equal housing, the army had twice the proportion of Blacks in the officer level and in the top three ranks of enlistees as any other branch of the services. This allowed Black enlistees to see examples of upward mobility that were "not limited to tokenism," producing the kind of confidence in future progress that is predictive of positive interpersonal interactions in all racial-ethnic groups.[35]

Divorce rates among Native Americans are even higher than among Black Americans. In part that's because they share similar risk factors. Native Americans have the highest poverty rates and lowest educational completion rates among America's racial and ethnic groups. Unemployment on reservations is five times the national average.[36]

But in addition, American Indian communities are still dealing with the historical trauma created first by settler and military massacres and expulsion from their lands and then by the forcible removal of thousands of their children to boarding schools where they were immediately stripped of their clothes and hair styles and forbidden to practice the language, religion, and cultural traditions of their kin. The removal of so many children from access to elders of their own culture over so many generations, right into the 1970s, along with the widespread physical and sexual abuse that went on in those schools, left lasting psychological scars. So did adoption and foster-care policies that took an estimated 25 to 35 percent of Native children from their families and placed most of them outside their tribal communities.[37]

THE DEMISE OF THE MIDDLE-CLASS MALE BREADWINNER

Economically and socially marginalized groups and individuals are not the only people facing relationship stresses caused by the erosion of men's real wages. For many middle-class families, almost all their economic progress since the 1970s has been due to the growing labor force participation of wives. A 2020 study of work and income trends in the middle 60 percent of households found that women's increased contribution to family income accounted for 91 percent of families' total income gains between 1979 and 2018.[38]

Women's expanded contribution to household finances is partly due to an increase in women's pay rates, thanks to feminist campaigns against discriminatory pay. But part is due to a sharp expansion of women's work hours. When married women worked outside the home in the 1960s and 1970s, they often worked part-time. Today more than two-thirds of dual-earner couples in the middle 60 percent of the income distribution have a combined workweek of 80 hours or more.

Meanwhile, the earnings gap between the highest- and lowest-paid individuals has widened, even among college graduates, and the wealth gap between the rich and the middle has soared. In

1963, the richest families had thirty-six times as much wealth as families in the middle of the wealth distribution. By 2022, they had seventy-one times as much.[39]

International studies show that wherever such inequality has mounted, parents have become increasingly anxious about their children's future, spurring them to engage in intensive, child-focused parenting aimed at fostering high achievement and competitive advantage. Sociologists Melissa Milkie and Catharine Warner argue that America's inadequate government and workplace supports explain why mothers in the United States feel especially pressured to focus on cultivating their children's skills and personal resumés in order to "safeguard" their place in the social hierarchy.[40]

All these work and family trends combine to create a serious time and energy crunch for couples at almost every income and educational level. And scarcity of time and energy is as corrosive to relationship quality as scarcity of money.

Still, "pro-marriage" advocates are right about one thing. Americans' standards for what constitutes an acceptable marriage are much higher than they used to be. As someone who has spent decades studying the misery that can ensue when standards for marital relationships are low, I'd say that's mostly a good thing. But people's higher expectations, combined with the new possibilities for leading a successful and satisfying life outside marriage, have increased the work it takes to keep both partners committed to staying the course. To be successful today, relationships require more time and effort, better negotiating skills, more give-and-take, and more willingness to step outside traditional gendered comfort zones than in the past.

Meanwhile, even as we expect more from our personal support systems than we used to, we get less from our societal ones. Full-time

American workers used to work about one hundred *fewer* hours a year than workers in Western Europe. Now they work considerably longer. On average, Americans work three hundred more hours a year than our French counterparts and four hundred more than Dutch workers. Yet we have less access to paid vacations, subsidized healthcare, paid sick days, paid parental leave, and affordable childcare.[41]

On top of that, new ideals about gender and sexual equality have spread unevenly among the population, generating fierce opposition in some quarters and angry frustration at their slow spread in others. Even people who embrace the new ideals find it hard to discard some of the historically conditioned assumptions and behavior patterns that undercut our ability to build the relationships we want. In the next chapter I discuss some of the things we're learning about the changing "rules" of marriage formation and marital satisfaction—and how to play by them.

Chapter 8.

THE NEW "RULES OF ENGAGEMENT"

What Makes a Modern Marriage Work?

Most of the relationship "instruction manuals" we've inherited from the past have been rendered obsolete by what sociologists call the "deinstitutionalization" of marriage. By that they mean the gradual erosion and in many cases outright collapse of the social norms, laws, public policies, and economic arrangements that historically pushed people into marriage, penalized individuals who didn't or couldn't marry, provided special rights for individuals who did marry, determined the role each partner must play in marriage, and mandated who could or couldn't leave a marriage.[1]

For thousands of years, being married—or being unable to marry—was what largely determined people's work duties, personal obligations, and legal rights. Since the 1970s, however, the once firm line between the rights and responsibilities of married and unmarried individuals has blurred. Domestic partner laws and other new social policies now let cohabiting couples claim many protections and privileges formerly reserved for married people. Conversely, while being unmarried carries fewer social penalties than in the past, it no longer exempts people from responsibilities they've incurred to children or former long-term partners. An unmarried romantic partner can sue for a share of joint assets or even for what used to be called "spousal" support. A child born out of wedlock is entitled to inherit from the father and even from distant kin of both parents.

More people have the right to marry than in the past, but marriage is now much easier to exit. And although the economic costs of breaking up can be heavy, divorce no longer jeopardizes people's social status, job prospects, or political ambitions the way it used to.

Historian Nancy Cott points out that the "deinstitutionalization" of marriage has changed intimate relationships in ways similar to how the "disestablishment" of the Church of England changed religion.[2] England, along with several American colonies, had a legally "established" religion, supported by government funds. Members of the church got special preference in government contracts, military commissions, university admissions, and applications for business licenses. In exchange, they were required to attend services and accept church doctrines, creeds, hierarchies, and rituals of worship. Nonmembers of an established church could sometimes even be expelled from the community.

When a church was "disestablished," it didn't disappear. But people's decisions about what if any church to join became, as American legislators often put it after the Declaration of Independence, "a matter of private judgment." And once a religious establishment could no longer count on people joining or staying because it was the only way to get legal, economic, and political benefits unattainable elsewhere, it had to consistently provide people with the spiritual fulfillment and emotional support they craved. A disestablished religion would never again enroll or retain such a high proportion of the population as when it was "the only game in town."

Today, the same holds true for marriage in countries where legal and social changes have made getting or staying married "a matter of private judgment" rather than social or economic compulsion. Sociologist Philip Cohen recently looked at dozens of countries and calculated how much the percentage of women aged forty to forty-four who were married had slipped over the past half century. In 1970, 82 percent of American women in that age group were married. By 2021, that had fallen to 62 percent. In Canada the percentage fell from 84 percent in 1976 to 58 percent in 2016, in Britain, from 88 percent in the early 1970s to 61 percent in 2011. During the same time period, Belgium went from 88 percent of that age group married to 61 percent, Spain from 84 to 69 percent, and Portugal from 83 to 69 percent.[3]

Cohen *did* find some countries where the percentage of forty- to forty-four-year-old married women had held steady or even increased. These included Yemen, Syria, South Sudan, and Saudi Arabia. That list tells us quite a lot about what kind of social system it would take to rebuild a "culture of marriage" elsewhere.

The fact that people no longer see marriage as mandatory doesn't mean marriage rates are doomed to keep shrinking until marriage disappears, or that we can't improve the odds of people marrying successfully. But society faces a new reality. Now that there are ways to achieve economic security, political advancement, social respect, legal protections, and a loving partnership without getting married, people are less inclined to enter the institution solely for practical advantages that may not be better than what they can get outside marriage. They want different things from marriage than they used to, and they engage in more protracted comparison shopping.

THE CHANGING "RULES OF ENGAGEMENT"

The changing gender, sexual, and marital patterns described in this book, combined with new economic and work challenges, have transformed the "rules" that once predicted who would marry, when they would marry, what would create marital satisfaction or conflict, and whether people would divorce.

Consider how people decide when to marry. From 1950 to the 1970s, early marriage was the societal norm. Not until 1980 did the median age of marriage for women hit twenty-two. For men it was only twenty-three until the second half of the 1970s. Between 2008 and 2023, however, men's median age at first marriage increased by more than two and a half years, to 30.6. For women it increased by exactly two and a half years, to just shy of twenty-nine for females.[4] And not only do half of all men and women marry for the first time at an older age than the median, but the range of ages above that median is more spread out than ever before.

In the postwar era, marrying young wasn't just more economically feasible. It was a smart move, the best way to "make sure all the good ones wouldn't be taken," as one woman told me her mother advised her. The prominent parent-education author Sidonie Matsner Gruenberg warned in 1953 that "a girl who hasn't a man in sight by the time she is twenty is not altogether wrong in fearing that she may never get married."[5]

Gruenberg was exaggerating only a bit. In that era a woman who wasn't married by twenty-five or twenty-six was considerably less likely to *ever* marry than her younger counterparts. And if she *did* "land" a husband at the "advanced" age of her late twenties or early thirties, she might not keep him. According to three noted sociologists who analyzed marriage and divorce data from the 1960s, marrying after her mid-twenties raised a woman's risk of divorce.[6]

Today, by contrast, the sociologist Cohen calculates, each year a woman waits to marry, up to age thirty-four, steadily lowers her divorce risk. The risk doesn't rise again for women who marry later, and it actually falls even more for women who marry between age forty-four and age fifty-nine.[7]

Delaying marriage does pose some real challenges, however. For individuals who've completed their schooling, established themselves in occupations, and attained the financial security most Americans now consider a precondition for marrying, the problem is often how to reconcile the different schedules, demands, and even locations of each partner's already-established jobs, residences, and friendship networks.[8]

And for individuals still acquiring educational credentials and/or job experience and not yet ready to commit to marriage, the issue is how to handle their sexual urges, encounters, and relationships in the meantime.

THE CHANGING RULES, RISKS, AND REWARDS OF PREMARITAL SEX

Contrary to widespread belief, today's teens have their first sexual experience later, on average, than a few decades ago. Since 1993, the percentage of high schoolers who have had sexual intercourse has fallen for all grade levels.[9] But the rising age of marriage means that even people who postpone sexual initiation until after high school are much less likely to wait until their wedding night than their counterparts in the 1950s.

Also contrary to rumor, dating is not dead. Some young people have even started using temporary cohabitation as an intensive form of dating.[10] But for many, having uncommitted casual sex is the way they handle at least part of the extended period of time when they are physically and emotionally ready for sex but not for a relationship that might interfere with educational plans or long-term aspirations.

Casual sex doesn't have to be callous or careless. But after centuries of indoctrination in the sexual double standards of both aristocratic patriarchy and market-based democracy, Americans lack a widely-agreed-upon script for how to have uncommitted sex in a guilt-free, safe, and nonexploitative way. So it's no wonder casual sex evokes ambivalence and sometimes leads to crossed signals.

Consider the hookups that are now a normal part of life on residential college campuses. These are erotic encounters that may involve anything from heavy kissing to sexual intercourse. Although explicitly defined as casual, with no expectation of any ongoing contact, hookups do sometimes lead to serious relationships. Indeed, one (nonrandom) sample of 1,000 unmarried individuals aged eighteen to thirty-four found that of the 418 individuals who married within the next five years, almost a third reported that their relationship began as some kind of hookup.[11]

Still, most hookups don't turn into long-term relationships. The most extensive study of hookups comes from a survey of twenty-four thousand students from two colleges and universities taken between 2005 and 2011.[12] A follow-up study analyzed surveys taken from almost four thousand students from thirty-four colleges between 2019 and 2024.

In the larger survey, fewer than half the respondents who reported having hooked up said their most recent hookup had involved sexual intercourse. More than a third said it was confined to "making out," with no genital touching. The rest reported either genital stimulation or oral sex. Most hookups were with someone the respondent knew—often someone they had hooked up with before. Only 13 percent of respondents reported not knowing their partner at all before hooking up.

While hookups aren't typically the terrible experience sometimes portrayed in the popular press, neither are they the epitome of free-spirited sexual liberation. Fewer than 15 percent of the women and 13 percent of the men in the survey said they regretted their most recent hookup. But only 48 percent of men and 45 percent of women reported being "glad" about it. The rest were sort of "meh"—neither glad nor regretful.

Overall, heterosexual women have more to lose from hooking up than their male partners, since they may face "slut-shaming" gossip or find that a man they hooked up with disrespects them (but not himself) for doing so. And there is always the danger of being coerced into unwanted sex, a risk that gay men also face. Nevertheless, many women report that despite its drawbacks, hooking up is preferable to prematurely entering a long-term relationship.[13]

Some of the worst aspects of the hookup scene, from disrespect to sexual coercion, result not from too liberal sexual ethics but from too great adherence to older sexual norms and double standards. For example, about half of men and women who hook up report having engaged in binge drinking (four or more drinks for women; five or more for men) before doing so, largely to overcome their inhibitions about engaging in casual sex. Such heavy drinking and/or drug use is involved in the majority of campus rape cases. Even aside from those worst-case scenarios, each additional drink a student recounted having before or during a hookup was associated with a lower level of reported sexual enjoyment.[14]

Still, hookups aren't the whole story for college students. Many students also date during their college years. And in between the "just sex" of a hookup and the public visibility of dating or living together, students often engage in a more private exploration of personal and romantic compatibility that usually starts with texting and video chatting but is referred to as "talking." As one of my students described her developing relationship with a young man in our class, "we hooked up a few times, but then we started talking."

"Talking" is almost always a first step toward dating. But in keeping with the uncertainty surrounding relationships initiated before individuals feel ready to make any serious commitments, individuals also use the phrase "*just* talking" to minimize their own or others' expectations that a serious relationship is in the cards.[15]

After people leave school or move away from the community in which they grew up, meeting trustworthy sexual and romantic partners becomes ever more complicated. The decline of "third spaces"[16]—places other than home or work where people can hang out, meet, and socialize—helps explain why dates made online are now the main way most couples meet once they are out of school.[17]

A 2022 Pew Research poll found that more than half of single Americans under thirty and almost 40 percent of thirty- to forty-nine-year-olds had used a dating site or app in the past year. Here, too, reviews are mixed. Fifty-three percent of respondents found it positive overall. But 35 percent said it was "somewhat negative" and 11 percent "very negative."[18] Some of the disappointment, I suspect, stems from the fact that dating sites heighten the importance of looks—and also of credentials—in people's decisions about whether to contact each other. Neither of those is a good indicator of compatibility. New AI matchmaking apps may help, assuming they don't "hallucinate" too often, since they can ask for and provide much more detailed information about people's interests.[19]

Overall, most of the problems people face in navigating their protracted period of premarital—and in some cases permanently nonmarital—sexual and romantic exploration arise not because our sexual mores have changed too much, but because they haven't changed enough. We don't yet have a widely accepted model for how to handle uncommitted sex in an egalitarian, mutually considerate, and self-respecting way. Old expectations about men taking the initiative clash with new resentments about male pushiness. And gendered double standards about sex are still widespread enough to inspire guilt, shame, and hurtful or downright exploitative behavior.

Still, whatever the dilemmas and downsides associated with the prolonged period of sexual experimentation most people now go through in their twenties and into their thirties, there's one worry they can dismiss: Accumulating a lengthy sexual résumé does not hurt a person's chance of getting married. Men and women who have multiple sex partners as young adults are no less likely to marry than those who are more abstinent, although they tend to marry later.[20]

Some research has suggested that having multiple premarital sexual partners is associated with lower levels of happiness in marriage, but I'm skeptical there's any cause-and-effect relationship. I'd bet that it's not how many people you've slept with, but how you've treated the people you slept with—or allowed them to treat you—that will predict the quality of your marriage.

AFTER THE WEDDING: The Changing Rules of Marital Satisfaction and Stability

At some point in the 1960s or early 1970s, delaying marriage or pursuing higher education stopped raising the likelihood that a woman would never marry or would experience divorce. But marrying a man less educated than herself raised a woman's risk of divorce significantly. Among couples who married between 1950 and 1979, the chance of divorce was 34 percent higher when the wife had more education than her husband, even if the woman's greater education did not result in her outearning her spouse.

This is another "rule" that has been overturned. Among couples who married in the 1990s and later, wives' educational advantage no longer raises the risk of divorce.[21]

What about when a woman has higher earnings than her husband, or a high-powered career? As late as 2006, an editor at *Forbes* could cite dozens of research studies supporting a column warning male readers that if they wanted a wife who would respect them, be faithful, and wouldn't leave them, "don't marry a woman with a career."[22]

Yet by 2006 the studies the journalist cited were already a decade out of date. Yes, among marriages formed in the 1960s and 1970s, those where the woman earned more money than her husband were more likely to end in divorce than those where the man outearned his wife. But sociologists Christine Schwartz and Pilar Gonalons-Pons have found that among couples who married in the 1990s and later, a wife's higher earnings no longer raise the risk of divorce.[23] Some older norms do persist. While a wife's full-time employment is not associated with a couple's added risk of divorce, a husband's *less-than-full-time* employment is.[24] Still, men and women have become increasingly comfortable with gender equality in work and other arenas of public life. Couples who blur or even reverse conventional roles in activities *outside the home* are no longer at added risk for divorce.

But what about *inside the home?* For most of the twentieth century, the distinction between what men and women did in and around the home was even more rigid than what they did outside it. Husbands did "manly" activities such as yard work, garbage removal, household repairs, and chores involving machinery. They did not change diapers,* do laundry, wash dishes, mop floors, or handle everyday cooking. That was women's work.

In the 1950s, the association of "core" household chores with femininity was so strong that the sight of a husband doing dishes or laundry was taken as a sure sign of a troubled marriage. One memorable scene in the iconic 1955 film *Rebel Without a Cause,* starring heartthrob James Dean as a rebellious teen, signaled the family pathology that supposedly explained the boy's problems: His father, wearing an apron, takes a tray of food upstairs to his wife, drops it, then anxiously falls to his knees to clean it up "before she sees it."

Today, by contrast, one of the sure signs of a troubled marriage is when a woman *fails* to see her husband don an apron or clean up a mess. Sharing routine household chores has become an ever more important component of marital satisfaction and stability. Interestingly, the chore that seems to provoke the greatest discontent when not shared is dishwashing. A 2006 household survey found that among couples where the wife did most of the dishwashing, 41

* When I interviewed more than one hundred women who raised families in the 1950s and 1960s for my book *A Strange Stirring,* only a handful could remember their husband *ever* changing a diaper.

percent of the women said their relationship was in trouble, compared to only 20 percent of women in marriages where dishwashing was shared equally.[25] Obviously, what couples see as a fair division of labor depends on many factors: how many hours one or both work outside the home; what their views are about "traditional" gender roles; and even their definition of what household activities count as work versus leisure and which ones are required or discretionary. Despite differences in such beliefs, the overall tendency is clear. Couples with egalitarian arrangements of household labor and childcare report increases in their levels of love over time. Couples with "traditional" divisions of labor report declines, no matter how high the quality of their romantic relationship at the start of their relationship.[26]

The increasing preference for egalitarianism is especially clear in a new long-term study of marriage trends in the US and West Germany. While divorce rates are affected by many different factors, the researchers found that marriages in which couples spend similar time in paid and unpaid work have become more stable over time in both countries, while marriages marked by dissimilarity in both paid and unpaid work time have become less stable. They suggest that since the 2000s, the lowest divorce risk is in marriages where husbands and wives put in similar hours of paid and unpaid work.[27]

Conducting in-depth interviews with a diverse group of midlife Americans for a forthcoming book, sociologist Kathleen Gerson identified four main ways that people meet the challenge of dividing work and caregiving responsibilities—male breadwinning with female homemaking, dual-earning with one person doing more earning and one doing more household work, egalitarian dividing of earning and caring, and sidestepping the issue by remaining single and childless. Individuals in couples who equally shared work and caregiving reported the highest levels of satisfaction. And a substantial proportion of people in other arrangements said they would have preferred an egalitarian division of work and care, suggesting that their current pattern, even if they were happy with it, was a second-best alternative.[28]

Yet in the 2006 household survey whose findings on dishwashing I cited earlier, fewer than a third of the heterosexual couples reported sharing most chores equitably. And even among those who did say they divided the tasks equally, a significant number nevertheless said they were dissatisfied with their relationship.

Some might think this means that achieving egalitarianism in housework actually doesn't make much difference to marital satisfaction. But University of Utah sociologist Daniel Carlson wondered if there were discrepancies in the way different couples defined and implemented equality. And in investigating this, he discovered that couples who operated on a "separate but equal"—as opposed to a mutually shared—domestic routine were the most discontented.

DIVIDING VS. SHARING:
It Makes a Difference

Carlson asked the couples who claimed to equally share the top five routine household chores (cooking, dishwashing, cleaning, laundry, and shopping) exactly *how* they organized that—whether they divvied the chores up, each partner taking all of some tasks and none of the others, or whether they shared some or all of the chores, either by doing them together or taking turns doing them. The choice of one method over another turned out to have a big impact on people's marital satisfaction.[29]

Among couples who did a roughly equal amount of housework, the ones most satisfied with their relationships were those who alternated or jointly performed all five routine tasks they were asked to report on. Ninety-two percent of those men and 100 percent of those women said they considered their housework arrangement fair to both partners. Among men and women who equally shared three or four chores, a large majority also thought their arrangement was fair. But among couples who reported they split the household chores fifty-fifty but didn't share any of the same tasks, only half the men and women thought their arrangement was fair.

Some research has suggested that housework equality is a zero-sum game—that men's marital satisfaction decreases as their share of housework increases.[30] But Carlson found that men who equally shared three or more routine chores with their partner were *just* as satisfied with their marital relationship and housework arrangement as men who did *no* housework at all! This was true even in the small number of households where the man did *more* total housework than his wife.

Women's satisfaction also differed sharply depending on whether they shared or divided the chores. Those who divided the total number of tasks equitably with their partner but didn't jointly perform or alternate any task were almost as dissatisfied as women who did *all* the routine housework.*

It's relatively easy to understand why women who do half the housework but whose husbands don't share any of the same tasks aren't happy. The majority of chores that came to be seen as a wife's responsibility after the demise of the household economy were very different from her traditional tasks of spinning cloth, curing bacon, preserving fruits and vegetables, brewing beer, and

* In fact, the difference between the level of dissatisfaction in the two groups was so small that it didn't reach statistical significance.

making cheese. Those tasks required skill, commanded respect, and often contributed significant amounts of cash to the family. But when men started earning wages away from home to *purchase* such goods, wives were left with the monotonous, onerous, and low-status tasks previously delegated to children or servants. After two hundred years of practice, they are assumed to be—and often are—better at these chores than their husbands.

Yet these tasks offer little flexibility about how and when they are done, confer a minimal sense of accomplishment, and garner none of the admiration that often greeted the products of an old-time housewife's work. Cooking dinner is the only routine chore that is sometimes praised. Dishwashing, laundering, sweeping, tidying up, scrubbing the toilet, and shopping go unremarked unless they don't get done. No wonder women are unhappy when they do them day after day.

But why are men who share or alternate chores just as happy with their relationships as men who do *no* chores? Part of the answer may be that it's unpleasant to have an unhappy wife. My mother's favorite T-shirt put it this way: "If Mama ain't happy, ain't NOBODY happy." Perhaps more important, sharing chores requires good communication. It creates empathy and appreciation for both partners' work, alleviating any suspicion that the other "has it easier."

Furthermore, once a man experiences how much previously invisible planning, effort, and "touch-up" work go into the "unskilled" tasks usually assigned to women, he is more likely to recognize the prior division of labor as unfair. And considerable research suggests that unfair relationships take a subtle toll even on people who benefit from them.[31]

So how do we *get* to a fair division? Comparisons of same-sex and different-sex couples provide important clues. Overall, women in heterosexual couples tend to be the most dissatisfied with the division of household chores. Men in same-sex couples are the most satisfied. Women in lesbian couples fall somewhere in between.

Among all couple types, a major predictor of satisfaction is whether they had an explicit conversation with their partner about how to organize the household labor and whether they were happy with how that discussion went. Same-sex couples are more likely than different-sex couples to have such conversations and to report feeling satisfied with the outcome.[32]

A successful discussion often leads to the kind of sharing that the people in Carlson's study found most satisfying. But a good conversation can also result in specialization that is mutually satisfactory, if it stimulates a couple to divide tasks on the basis of each partner's particular likes and dislikes rather than on the basis of gender stereotypes. Again, same-sex couples have an advantage here. Since they can't assume one partner is better at conventionally "male" tasks and the other at "female" ones, they tend to divide tasks more creatively and flexibly than different-sex couples.

Still, even after "talking it out," actually *working it out* remains a challenge. On top of the tremendous logistical challenges that arise when couples try to equally share or alternate paid work, housework, *and* childcare, both men and women have to contend with a welter of unconscious earworms, blind spots, emotional triggers, and hard-to-break behavior patterns that sabotage equality. This is where historical and sociological perspective can come in handy.

GENDERED "CALLS TO DUTY"

Most women, for example, have been socialized to hear a call for quick action when they see a messy room or dirty kitchen—a call that doesn't register on many men.[33] So when a man procrastinates about cleaning something he was supposed to take care of, the noise in his wife's head will usually drive her to do it—often with a resentment that is only exacerbated if he tells her, "I was *going* to do it."

I sometimes wonder whether the urgency many women feel about having an orderly house is a holdover from the new class aspirations that turned female domesticity into a status symbol during the late eighteenth and early nineteenth centuries. Keeping things "neat and tidy" hadn't been a priority—and seldom even a possibility—for wives in the era of the co-provider family economy. Their diaries testify to living spaces filled with spinning wheels and sewing supplies and kitchens cluttered with gutted chickens, bloody pig haunches, beer being brewed, bacon being cured, vegetables being pickled, and preserves crowded onto every flat surface.

By the nineteenth century, however, a "neat and tidy" house had become the way a family could demonstrate it had the luxury of using its dwelling as a place to relax—and show off to others—rather than as a workplace. A woman who didn't keep a neat and tidy house was not only an embarrassment to her own sex but also to her family's class aspirations.

Even now, women experience social stigma when their dwellings don't meet the high standards of order and cleanliness expected of females but not of males. In one experiment, researchers showed people pictures of a messy room and a relatively clean room, telling some that the room was occupied by a man and others that it was occupied by a woman. When observers were shown a room that wasn't particularly messy, their standards for classifying it as "clean" were higher when they thought it belonged to a woman rather than a man, and they suggested that the woman would be judged negatively by others for any mess.[34]

The observers didn't view a messy room as less messy when they thought a man rather than a woman was the occupant. In fact, that often inspired them to voice negative stereotypes about male messiness. But they didn't seem to think the man would face negative social judgments about living with the mess. "That's just the way men are." As we saw in the stereotypes about altruistic femininity and toxic masculinity discussed in chapter 3, seemingly positive stereotypes about women often get them extra work instead of extra rewards, while seemingly negative stereotypes about men can actually bolster male privilege.

It's worth noting, however, that men have their own "calls to action," many of which most women don't notice or just assume their male partners will answer. Leaves poking over the edge of the roof are a summons to clean the gutters. A dripping faucet calls for changing the washer. An imminent cold spell says it's "time to wrap the pipes and check the antifreeze." A nasty smell means "check the crawl space for dead animals."

One source of tension in contemporary households is that modern technology and city living have reduced the number of occasions when men need to do (or even learn *how* to do) the kinds of chores that used to make their wives think doing all the dishes wasn't such a bad deal.

Other gender habits from the past two hundred years also sabotage efforts to build egalitarian marriages. Men often exhibit what psychologists call "learned helplessness," expressing their willingness to do a chore that was once thought "women's work" but then asking for so much direction and doing such an inadequate job that the woman decides it's easier to do it herself.

Conversely, though, many women exhibit a "learned help*ful*ness" that also undercuts egalitarianism. Having taken on the role of domestic "experts" when husbands became "breadwinners," we doubt men's ability to do it right—and by "right," we mean the way we do it. Sometimes a woman gives so much direction—or correction—to a man's performance of a task that it prevents him from developing any feeling of "ownership" over it. Researchers call this behavior "gatekeeping."

Despite having warned other women against gatekeeping for years in public lectures, I have often found myself rearranging the dishwasher to my personal satisfaction after my husband fills it. My husband does more than his fair share of most routine chores. But after catching me at this a couple of times, he started leaving dishes on the counter. Why should he put them in the dishwasher, he asked, if I'm just going to rearrange them?

That's a pretty reasonable question. So it's not surprising that when Eve Rodsky interviewed men for her book *Fair Play,* she found that the ones most satisfied with their domestic arrangements and most invested in keeping them equal were those who felt their wives trusted them to carry out tasks without interference, advice, or after-the-fact adjustments.[35]

We're still a good way away from equality in domestic labor, but there's been significant progress in recent years, given how lopsided the work was throughout most of the twentieth century. A 2025 study found that the gap in the time men and women spend doing the routine chores often thought of as "female" jobs shrank by 40 percent in the period between 2003–2005 and 2022–2023.[36]

In fact, growing numbers of childless heterosexual couples have been achieving an essentially egalitarian division of household chores. The biggest domestic inequalities are now associated with the transition to parenthood.[37]

PARENTHOOD SHOCK

Once a child arrives, few parents can free up enough time from paid work to equally share the added labor needed to manage a household with a child in it while still working enough to meet household expenses. And few Americans have access to support systems that make it possible for couples to alternate work and family responsibilities.[38]

Among heterosexual couples who can afford to have one partner quit or cut back at work in the early months or years of parenthood, many factors tilt the scales toward that partner being the woman. If she's the biological mother, she needs time to recover physically. If she plans to nurse, she needs more flexibility than most workplaces offer.

The US is one of the few industrialized nations that fails to guarantee paid maternity leave to all its citizens, but paid or unpaid, women tend to have more access to parental leave than men, and they face less stigma for taking it. Meanwhile, in addition to the man being more likely to be the higher earner in the family, making his taking unpaid leave a bigger sacrifice for the family, men often get a "fatherhood bonus" for *not* taking leave. This might better be called a "non-parenting bonus," since it rests on the expectation that a man will increase his work efforts and hours once he has "a family to support." He often forfeits that bonus if he doesn't.

Long-standing cultural norms and psychological earworms reinforce these patterns. Mothers tend to feel guiltier than fathers about being away from children and more ambivalent about losing the domestic and childrearing authority that comes with being the primary parent. So even when a woman would prefer to combine work and parenting equally, she is often more willing—or feels more social pressure—to sacrifice work rewards than to lose out on parenting time. And although it's beginning to change, stay-at-home dads still face—or at least feel—social stigma for not being breadwinners.

The hard choices posed by the competing demands of paid work and parenting are not unique to heterosexual couples, as Haley Swenson of the Better Life Lab explains in her afterword to this book.[39] And the solution of having one partner specialize in home duties and one in paid work is not necessarily unfair, despite the ambivalence and conflict it can create.

Nevertheless, while it often makes sense to have the wife in a heterosexual marriage be the primary parent in the early years, that decision frequently interacts with long-standing gender patterns to turn temporary asymmetry in the division of labor into self-perpetuating inequality. Many women find it difficult to get back on a promotional track when they reenter the workforce, having fallen off a career ladder that was already harder to scale than for men. And not infrequently they face discrimination based on the assumption that their maternal commitments will interfere with their paid work.[40]

While focusing on home and childcare tends to cost a wife experience, visibility, and opportunities for advancement in the world of paid work, her partner, especially in a heterosexual marriage, faces the opposite problem. Focusing on paid work in the aftermath of a child's birth deprives a man of experience, visibility, and advancement in the world of childrearing. Once a woman has a significant head start in the skills, norms, and social networks of parenting, it's easy for her husband (along with teachers, friends, and medical personnel) to start treating her as the "project manager" of family life, and to keep doing so even after she has gone back to paid work. The future Supreme Court Justice Ruth Bader Ginsberg once felt it necessary to write to her son's school counselor: "This child has two parents. Please alternate calls."[41]

Conversely, a woman who has been a full-time at-home mother can get in the habit of considering herself such an expert that gatekeeping becomes gate*closing*.[42] I thought I'd learned my lesson after my husband stopped loading the dishwasher. Yet the first time our infant grandchild started wailing while my husband was holding him, I swooped in to take over—and was treated to a refresher course on how disrespected that made him feel.

For many different reasons, then, what starts out as a reasonable accommodation to the partners' differing situations and needs can exacerbate an unevenness in domestic expertise and daily habits that engenders (and in most cases I mean the verb literally) growing resentment over the long run. Getting to equity—or back to equity—takes planning, flexibility, compromise, and often, for heterosexual couples, "affirmative action" on the part of the man, adjusting his own professional or personal priorities in order to step up to the plate at home and facilitate his wife's entry or reentry into the world of paid work.[43]

In her afterword to this book, Swenson describes some of the diverse resources available to couples who seek to maximize fairness in their division of labor. But one critical requirement is that whichever parent works more outside the home must learn to recognize and respond to the new demands of running a household with children.

This is why getting paternity leave—and getting men in heterosexual couples to use it—is so important. The experience of actually doing hands-on care (especially when mom isn't around) helps men recognize just how much needs doing, along with how urgently it needs doing at any given time, and how much advance planning and ongoing monitoring it takes.[44]

Studies show that when men take paternity leave, they not only do more childcare and routine housework during their leave but continue to do so after they return to their paid jobs. In the long run, says sociologist Richard Petts, "such men remain more engaged in their children's lives, their partners report greater relationship satisfaction, and the parents are less likely to divorce."[45]

Indeed, after studying a sample of approximately fourteen thousand children born in the US in 2001, Petts and his colleagues found that over the first six years of parenthood, 32 percent of heterosexual couples in which the father had taken no paternity leave ended up divorcing. Among couples where the father had taken four weeks of paternity leave, only 12 percent of these marriages dissolved.[46]

Fascinating new research suggests that actively caring for infants causes changes in men's brain activity and hormone levels that are very similar to what occurs in women who actually give birth. When they care for infants, both men and women experience a decrease in testosterone, the hormone associated with mobilizing aggressive and competitive behavior, and an increase in oxytocin, the hormone associated with feelings of love and connection with others. Their brains even seem to "streamline" themselves in ways that focus greater attention and attachment to babies. And the more time men spend caring for babies, the more extensive these changes are, expanding their caring horizons.[47]

There are many reasons to demand more extensive social supports for childrearing, not only during the first months but throughout the early years. A recent study gives one indication of how much difference such support can make for mothers—and by extension for their children—whether they work outside the home or not. The researchers compared postpartum depression trajectories in the US, the UK, and Australia. Initially, American mothers with postpartum depression had, on average, less severe symptoms than their counterparts in the UK and Australia. But their symptoms took considerably longer to recede over the years. In fact, by the time their children turned six, those American mothers had higher depressive symptoms than their UK and Australian counterparts, whose symptoms had abated more rapidly. At least in part, the authors suggest, the more rapid recovery from postpartum depression in the UK and Australia probably reflects these countries' stronger support systems for parenting infants and young children.[48]

BUT WHAT ABOUT OUR SEX LIVES?

Let's face it. Establishing and maintaining an egalitarian marriage is hard work. It takes time and energy to challenge embedded work practices and inadequate social policies while also trying to revise long-established assumptions and habits inherited from the past. So even when the journey toward an egalitarian marriage doesn't involve conflict, it's not always erotic.

In fact, some commentators argue that achieving equality can undermine a couple's sexual desire and pleasure. Yes, they admit, egalitarian couples feel closer to each other than couples in more traditional gender arrangements. They are more likely to be satisfied with the division of labor in their households. But being "content" with your relationship, such commentators say, is a poor substitute for being excited by it. One early study of egalitarian couple relationships concluded that they foster a "sibling-like" affection that stifles sexual passion.[49]

In 2014, *The New York Times Magazine* ran a cover story whose title asked the question "Does a More Equal Marriage Mean Less Sex?" The answer, according to its author, psychologist Lori Gottlieb, was yes. "In an attempt to be gender-neutral," Gottlieb argued, "we may have become gender-neutered."[50]

Gottlieb quoted therapist Esther Perel as saying, "Egalitarian marriage takes the values of a good social system—consensus-building and consent—and assumes you can bring these rules into the bedroom. But the values that make for good social relationships are not necessarily the same ones that drive lust." In fact, Perel told Gottlieb, "most of us get turned on at night by the very things that we'll demonstrate against during the day."

A few years later, sociologist Mark Regnerus made an even more dramatic pronouncement: "Equality between the sexes," he declared, "is leading to the demise of sex. . . . We cannot have both eros and strict equality between the sexes. Saving one requires sacrificing the other."[51]

Both Gottlieb and Regnerus based their claims on a 2013 article showing that couples in which men did a larger share of conventionally "feminine" tasks such as cleaning, laundry, and dishes had less frequent sex than couples with a more "traditional" division of labor, and the women reported lower sexual satisfaction. For heterosexual couples, the authors concluded, stereotypically masculine and feminine behaviors serve as sexual "turn-ons," while violations of "traditional" gender norms dampen sexual desire.[52]

That was certainly the view of most nineteenth-century marriage commentators. It remains a major theme of many romance novels even today. But as sociologist Virginia Rutter argues, it reflects an erotic imagination that is "stuck in the past."[53] Literally!

The 2013 study suggesting that gender egalitarian housework was a sexual turn-off was based on data collected from a sample of marriages formed in the 1970s and 1980s, almost half a century ago.

By contrast, when researchers examined marriages formed during the 1990s and first few years of this century, they found that on average, partners with egalitarian housework arrangements reported enjoying sex just as much, and actually having sex more frequently, than couples where the woman did most of the so-called "feminine" chores. The highest levels of sexual enjoyment were reported by men and women who shared childcare equally. Conversely, a 2022 study of more than one thousand women with children found that doing a high proportion of household labor was associated with "significantly lower sexual desire" for their male partner.[54] So much for equality sounding the death-knell of heterosexual eroticism.

Of course, no couple, gay or straight, is immune from the waning of sexual desire that can stem from what psychologists call "hedonic adaptation"—our tendency to start taking for granted, or even losing interest in, activities and experiences that initially excited us.

Advocates of "tension" and "mystery" in relationships are right about one thing: Arousal associated with uncertainty and anxiety *can* trigger sexual desire. In a 1974 study, social psychologists stationed an attractive woman at the end of a bridge and had her ask men who had just crossed it to take a survey. Afterward, she gave them her phone number, ostensibly in case they had anything to add.

Then the woman positioned herself at the end of a different bridge—only this time, it was a suspension or swinging bridge on which people had to struggle to keep their balance—and followed the same script. Men who had walked over the swinging bridge were considerably more likely to call the woman and ask her out than men who had crossed the stable bridge. They had interpreted their anxiety arousal as sexual attraction.[55] The romance novels I described in chapter 4 got that much right.

But while uncertainty and anxiety can boost excitement in the short run, they are poor recipes for a lasting relationship. Most of the time we need our long-term partner to be comforting, calming, and accommodating.

Fortunately, researchers have discovered that it's relatively easy to trick our libido into feeling the arousal associated with challenging or anxiety-producing interactions without the destructive long-term side effects. It turns out that the bridge experiment provides an almost literal clue as to how: *Being thrown off balance*—intellectually, emotionally, or physically—can ignite the arousal our brains associate with sexual desire without sacrificing the security and trust of an egalitarian relationship.

Scores of research experiments show that exciting, challenging experiences activate stronger feelings of romantic passion than comfortable ones. They don't have to involve rock climbing or whitewater rafting, although those can work. In one experiment, something as simple as completing a difficult obstacle course caused couples to report greater feelings of passionate love than couples given a less challenging exercise.[56]

Emotional risk-taking can also reignite feelings of passion. One study assigned four groups of married couples to go on different types of dates. In two of the groups, each couple went out as a twosome, but half those couples were instructed to chat about comfortable, everyday things and the other half to discuss emotionally laden topics and issues requiring high levels of self-disclosure. Couples in groups three and four were assigned to go on a double date with a couple they didn't know, with half assigned to do the small-talk exercise and the other half to tackle the more emotional and self-revealing topics.

The self-disclosure task boosted feelings of relationship satisfaction more than the small-talk task for everyone. But the people who engaged in this with another couple reported especially enhanced feelings of intimacy and attraction toward each other. Such studies suggest that a "double date" night might work better than an intimate outing for two in revving up desire.

One in-depth examination of five hundred middle-class, dual-career families found that the highest-quality time couples reported was the child-free time they spent together with other people. Women who spent more time with friends *in addition* to their husband were more satisfied with their marriages than women who spent more couple-time with their husbands.[57]

Yet the nuclear family model we inherited from the 1950s emphasized family "togetherness" to the point that psychologists cautioned people against "neglecting" their spouse by spending too much time with friends or extended family. Wives were advised against allowing aging parents to live with them, since that might dilute their attentiveness to their husband.[58]

We've come a long way from that Ozzie and Harriet ideal, but marriage still tends to shrink people's social networks rather than expand them the way it did in the prehistoric era and continues to do in many small-scale communities. Using national survey data from the early 1990s through 2012, for example, sociologists Natalia Sarkisian and Naomi Gerstel found that married individuals were significantly less likely than their single counterparts to frequently visit, socialize, and provide emotional or practical assistance to family members, neighbors, friends, and coworkers. They also spent less time in casual social interactions with strangers.[59]

Married people who fall into these patterns are missing out on important sources of support. UCLA social psychologist Benjamin Karney points out that maintaining supportive friendships results in more satisfying marriages. People who socialize frequently with good friends report fewer symptoms of depression. And so do their *partners*, even when they haven't been in on the socializing.[60]

I would never underplay the extra rewards that come with a good marriage. But these research findings bring us back to a point I made at the beginning of this book: Most of the things that make for a healthy and fulfilling single life also make for a healthy and fulfilling marriage, and vice versa. They involve being—and staying—connected to others, as well as pursuing socially engaged interests and goals.

Even just engaging in sociable interactions with people you meet in the course of a day has a marked effect on people's well-being. Casual friendly exchanges with baristas at the local coffee stand, clerks at the local store, members of the same gym, fellow dog owners at the park, and even random strangers in a line or a waiting room can brighten our day—and sometimes our entire week—while giving us the satisfaction of knowing we've brightened someone else's. Such interactions with "Consequential Strangers," as one book title terms them, remind us that we're part of a bigger community—an important reminder in a society where we are often more closely "connected" with machines than with real, live people.[61]

There's no reason marriage can't support such connections. When my husband and I married, our wedding vows included a promise to our respective friends and families that they were not losing us to coupledom. Instead, we said, we hoped they would gain a new set of friends and social connections through the social networks we were each bringing to our marriage.

When our son and daughter-in-law married many years later,

they didn't ask the bride's father to give her away. Instead, taking a page from our Paleolithic ancestors, the bride and groom each gave their own parents away to the other parents, presenting the four of us with matching Hawaiian leis to symbolize the expanded social ties their union was creating.

AFTERWORD

by Haley Swenson

I work at the Better Life Lab at a nonpartisan think tank, New America, in Washington, DC, where I run our Better Life Lab Experiments, or BLLx initiative. Our mission is to empower families by developing innovative strategies to help them understand the kinds of relationship tensions Stephanie Coontz has described in this book and to more fairly share the load of housework and care work at home.

Between demanding workplaces—what Nobel Prize–winning economist Claudia Goldin calls "greedy jobs"—and ever-more-complex home lives and family relationships, far too many families are overwhelmed, stressed, and pushed beyond capacity, with potentially long-lasting consequences. Drawing on the work of academics, behavioral scientists, psychologists, therapists, family and couples counselors, and other experts—especially families who are successfully sharing the load—we have developed nearly forty original experiments designed to help busy families get stuff done, while encouraging family members to think longer and harder about the gender assumptions and habits that undermine gender equality at home and nudge them toward more egalitarian divisions of labor.[1]

We emphasize gender equality because, for the historical reasons

Coontz discusses in this book, women often bear the brunt of the physical housework, care work, and the cognitive and emotional work families rely on every day. But the US's unique lack of family-sustaining public policies like affordable, accessible childcare, paid family leave and paid sick days, and support for family caregivers and disabled people contributes to family stress for all kinds of families, whatever the gender of their members. Consider my own experience.

My wife and I met while working together at the Better Life Lab. We bonded over our shared commitment to these goals and soon over so much more. When we moved from just being colleagues to being close friends and eventually to dating, it was the first long-term relationship either of us had ever had with another woman. With our shared commitment to feminist values, moving in with her a year and a half into the relationship felt like fresh air.

Unlike my experience living with men, where I took the lead on all housework, here was a partner who, like me, already had a system for managing her house. I didn't need to come up with and introduce fair systems for handling cleanup or meals. Without my asking, she did her share of the cognitive, emotional, and physical work it took to create a comfortable life for us. She already had her own rules and the discipline to follow them: mop the kitchen every weekend, no dishes left in the sink overnight, the person who cooks does not clean up, and the bed must be made before we leave for work.

Most days, her rules worked great. I enjoyed a constantly tidy space and crawling into a made bed at night. When I did the dishes or put away laundry, I didn't feel that tinge of bitterness that comes from the feeling you're doing more than your share or that it isn't even going to be noticed or appreciated.

But on some days, I just didn't have the energy or commitment to follow through with my partner's rules. Maybe I didn't want to make the bed. Maybe I *wanted* my laundry to sit for a couple of days until I was less busy at work. But my commitment to her pushed me to keep trying to get things done in the way she liked, even as I slowly grew resentful of my wife-mandated housework.

Yet as she continued to take initiative in housework, financial management, and household maintenance, I also began to feel that I was falling short of an equal partnership. As I told a reporter at *The New York Times* in 2021, this left me feeling "like the dude" in the relationship.[2] I began to understand firsthand just how my past male partners might have felt when they told me their standards for when and how to clean up were just different from mine. "Sure," I'd think back then, "it just so happens that all men have a personal preference for mess, and all women are naturally tidier." But it turns out that not all women are naturally tidier, or at least not equally so.

I was raised in a house where clutter was an accepted part of life, where dinner dishes could wait until morning if we were too busy to get to them and clean laundry could accumulate in a hamper until you needed it. A deep clean might not happen until we were expecting company, at which point we'd need all hands on deck to pull the house into a state worthy of company. Suddenly, I felt the way my past partners had: Our standards were simply different.

My wife and I didn't have the baggage of gender roles and vastly different socialization that heterosexual couples face, and yet we still weren't on the same page about just what was fair and reasonable. Turning her rules into *our rules* was far more complex than it sounded. Any two people, same-sex or different-sex, who suddenly merge their lives, especially under one roof, must communicate and negotiate about how they expect their households to run. They can't expect things to work smoothly just because they love each other. And that's exactly the issue that our Better Life Lab has been trying to help couples manage.

My colleague Brigid Schulte, a former reporter at *The Washington Post* and the director of the Better Life Lab, has told the story of how she reset expectations and began to redistribute domestic labor in her marriage in her 2014 book, *Overwhelmed: Work, Love, and Play When No One Has the Time.*[3] One day she reached her breaking point and was seriously considering divorce. She went for a long walk with her husband, Tom, and they discussed their values as a couple—fun, quality time, care, equality, personal time for growth and learning. Then she wrote a long list of all the work it was taking to run their household and care for their two children. They had a frank discussion about just how much of it she was doing—the actual physical labor in addition to the logistics, planning, and emotional labor. They discussed how that reality did not square with their values, and Tom committed to change.

Brigid and Tom began small experiments with how they accomplished chores, agreeing to rules and standards that would keep them accountable: Last one out of bed makes the bed. Washing the dishes includes handwashing the pots. And if her husband didn't do his part, Brigid didn't "rescue" him as she had before. She held him accountable for the commitments they'd made. Over time, these rules became habits, and their life reflected their shared values. Brigid was happy again, and their marriage became stronger.

At the Better Life Lab, we set out to discover what other couples could learn from examples such as this. The quickly evolving field of behavioral science offered insights into habit formation and long-term behavior change. We learned about the power of "nudges," or environmental prompts—like a note on their work computer or a reminder in their calendar—that urge individuals toward the behavior they want to establish—say, taking on a more assertive role in dinner planning.[4] Research also suggested that having measurable goals was critical to change, so it was important for couples to get specific about what they wanted to change, not just set lofty, amorphous goals like "a fairer division of labor."[5]

From the family psychologist B. Janet Hibbs, Brigid and I learned of the need to understand the "three-person story"—in which couples should be willing to hear out "my story," "your story," and then what an objective, caring third person might say to describe a situation, helping them approach each other with fairness in these conversations.[6] The Gottman Institute provides research-backed tips for handling relationship conflicts in ways that nurture and build intimacy between partners rather than dividing them.[7] Professional gender facilitator Kate Mangino's *Equal Partner* is another excellent resource for anyone seeking to change their current household dynamic.[8]

In our own home, my wife and I, along with my sister, who moved in with us during the COVID-19 pandemic, turned to principles such as these to solve the problem of cleaning our three cats' litter boxes. Nobody enjoyed this housework task, but procrastination in this area came at a cost, as the smells and mess of a neglected box quickly made themselves known. Before instituting our system, one of us might ask, frustrated, "Whose turn is it to clean the box?" We could never quite remember and always hoped to be spared. So we pinned a list of our names to the fridge. A paper clip indicated who was on litter box duty. When they'd cleaned the boxes, they simply moved the clip down the paper to the next name. Now, we always knew whose turn it was, and we had every incentive both to be sure to update the chart when we were finished, and to clean the boxes as soon as possible before more time had passed and the job had become even messier.

A single experiment like this cannot reshape your household's entire division of labor overnight, but it can automate and simplify some of your most conflictual chores. In interviews with other families facing household challenges, we found that many had also come up with rules, tips, and charts for getting the work done fairly. One family with dual-earner partners and three children shared with us their custom of a "laundry party" to ensure putting away clean laundry didn't continuously fall to Mom. When all family members were present at home, they'd pile the clean laundry in one area and set a timer, maybe fifteen minutes or half an hour. They'd fold and put away as much laundry as they could before the timer went off. With everyone involved, they could get through what was in the past a huge, time-consuming task looming over Mom.

Building on these interviews and our own experience, we decided to focus interventions on one problem at a time, allowing couples to reflect on and discuss each change, in order to grow their awareness of the overall dynamics in their relationships over time. The idea was to use these interventions both to provide better ways to tackle individuals' biggest annoyances—say, that only the male partner is finding time for leisure, or that the laundry is perpetually piling up—and to raise the whole family's awareness of the work it takes to run their households.

We called the project Better Life Lab Experiments, or BLLx for short, to reflect the early stages of this research. We quickly attracted around a thousand subscribers to the project, our "beta testers." We asked them to try our experiments and then let us know how they worked, or, just as important, why they didn't. Joining is easy and free. Come to our website at NewAmerica.org, sign up for our latest experiments, and check out all the past experiments we've run.

Better Life Lab Experiments often begin by asking family

members to think about the ideal way they'd like their participation in an activity or their household to feel and be. Then it asks them to make some targeted changes so they have a better shot at achieving that, and, finally, to think about how that felt and what it suggests about how they should move forward.

One experiment addresses the gender gap in leisure time, for instance, by asking partners to consider how much time they each get per week on their own to relax and ideally what that would look like. Then it asks them to take turns being the other person's "leisure time" sponsor, making it their job to ensure their partner has time to themselves each week, despite a busy work and family schedule. Finally, we ask them to step back and discuss whether this division of *leisure*, as opposed to just the division of *labor*, feels fair.

To date we've designed nearly forty original experiments, some in collaboration with other researchers, and some with couples innovating in their households. We are careful not to oversell what our interventions can accomplish. As I wrote in a 2024 essay: "The truth is we're all tinkering around the edges of a problem with deep, structural roots. None of our solutions—my interventions, the cards, the apps, or a divorce—can offer affordable childcare, equal parental leave for both partners, or flexible workplaces with living wages and benefits, all of which are the foundation for equality between couples."[9]

But as Coontz argues, knowing the difference between what we can and can't solve at the individual level can reduce the acrimony involved in negotiating. In fact, admitting the limitations to how much we can accomplish through our own efforts may be critical to achieving the fairer and happier relationships we want. That's because research suggests couples who believe only a perfectly symmetrical division of labor will suffice may be the most resentful when this doesn't happen.[10] What seems to matter more than perfectly splitting the chores at any one time is making sure each partner feels that the overall organization and long-term outcome of their labor and leisure is fair.

In the early stages of developing BLLx, Brigid and I met Eve Rodsky, an executive advisor to family-run philanthropies, who began researching these questions after they'd become a significant source of tension in her own marriage.[11] Rodsky designed "the Fair Play system," a deck of cards representing each mental and physical household or family task, to help concretize the work that is often invisible to the partner not already doing it. She drew on a management strategy called "CPE," for "Conception, Planning, and Execution."

When someone takes on a task in the Fair Play system—say, weeknight dinners—they own all parts of the task, from deciding what to cook, to grocery shopping, enlisting the help of kids or other members of the family, through to preparing and serving the meal. Too often, female partners do the mental and emotional labor leading up to a task and then ask their male partner to execute the task or one of its components under their direction. This leaves the man stepping in as a "helper," rather than a full partner—and often unable to complete the task in a way that satisfies the woman because he wasn't aware of the larger context.

Rodsky encourages couples to discuss and establish a "minimum standard of care" for any task someone is assigned for the family. How to meet those minimum standards is the prerogative of the person doing the task. But he or she can't claim exemption from a different task if they decide to do *more* than that minimum. Each person is responsible for all the cards they hold.

In the last few years, tech entrepreneurs and venture capitalists have begun to take note of the increasingly mainstream conversations about how overwhelmed families are and how to address the unequal gender division of unpaid labor. A new array of apps helps families share their calendars, assign family members particular tasks, and track their progress on shared projects. One I particularly like is Milo, which works almost entirely over SMS, so my wife and I can text the bot our shorthand reminders and never have to open an app.

Will women become the keepers and maintainers of the apps, while men step in just to execute a few final tasks, keeping the invisible work of mental and emotional labor firmly gendered? Or can the apps help people redistribute the invisible as well as the visible labor? At BLLx, we have recently begun to experiment with integrating AI chatbots and apps into household routines and cognitive labor. I have written elsewhere about the kinds of prompts parents can ask AI to help solve, and of its ability to take pressure off both partners.[12]

However, entrepreneurs alone cannot solve all these problems, and their products often don't serve people with limited means. To our knowledge, Brigid and I run the only think-tank initiative dedicated to developing resources that are free to the public and have been tested with the input and contributions of diverse families in terms of how they can help people achieve a fairer division of labor at home. We hope other nonprofits and public institutions will join us in such research and innovation.

Meanwhile, in my own family, the work of running a home with my wife has gotten bigger and more complicated. Today we share not only housework but also care for our toddler son. Our roles—who does more paid work and who does more childcare—shift with our family's changing needs. The most significant lesson we've learned both as a couple and as people who research these issues has been the importance of trust. Some days my wife might be handling something big for the household, while I have time to relax. Other days, the opposite may be true. But we have worked hard enough at fairness that we each assume the other person is giving as much as they can to creating a household and family life that reflects our core values.

I no longer worry I am "the dude" in our relationship. Instead, I celebrate how lucky we are to be two modern-day married people who care deeply about the life we are building and how it works for both of us and our child.

ACKNOWLEDGMENTS

I began this book in early 2020, after my literary agent, Susan Rabiner, encouraged me to expand on several op-eds I had written for *The New York Times*, CNN, NBC, and other outlets, in which I discussed how understanding the history of marriage can help people contextualize contemporary debates and improve their own relationships. The project took longer than either of us anticipated.

Two months after signing the book contract I learned that my first grandchild was on the way and my son and daughter-in-law would need me and my husband to go live with them to help out during the COVID pandemic. That slowed the book writing down considerably. In addition, I didn't factor in my long-standing tendency to go down research rabbit holes, so it took me longer than expected to winnow my early drafts down to a manageable size. I thank Susan for her astute advice on how to do so and her patience with my occasional resistance, and my initial editor, the wonderful Wendy Wolf, for her support and insight in guiding me through the production of a previous book and the early stages of this one. Wendy had retired by the time I finished the manuscript and my new editor, Laura Tisdel, took over, providing strikingly perceptive suggestions for revision along with unstinting support for the project. Grateful thanks also to editorial assistant Carlos Zayas-Pons, who painstakingly shepherded the book (and me) through the production process.

I also thank my speakers' agent, Jodi Solomon, for her personal and intellectual support and her years of arranging speaking engagements that have allowed me to explore many of the themes in this book with diverse audiences. Their questions, comments, and personal stories—and Jodi's feedback—were always extremely helpful to me.

I have benefited so much from the astute comments and observations of the students I taught over my years at The Evergreen State College, as well as those I worked with while on exchange at Kobe University of Commerce and at the University of Hawaii and Hawaii Community College in Hilo. Many of my students conducted oral histories of their families and other community members, and almost all contributed interesting perspectives in our seminars, teaching me at least as much as I taught them. One former student, Alex Bertolucci, set up my first social media account for me and has for years patiently stepped in to help this technological dufus post comments and answer requests.

While writing this book I received an outpouring of support from colleagues, friends, and family members. My fellow board members, past and present, at the Council on Contemporary Families were especially generous in offering references and feedback. Sociologist Philip Cohen provided me with invaluable data and on several occasions took the trouble to perform special statistical analyses to answer specific questions I posed. Susan Brown and Wendy Manning at the National Center for Marriage and Family Research were always ready to share their research and expertise, as was Karen Guzzo of the Carolina Population Center. Historian Mary Beth Norton was generous in providing several sources.

Virginia Rutter and John Schmitt not only provided information about their own areas of expertise but carefully read and commented on several chapters. I also got helpful feedback on various chapters from Joshua Coleman, Sherry Frumkin, Colin McIntosh, Haley Swenson, and Michaela Wagar. Nika Fate-Dixon conducted several internet research searches for me, and I'm grateful for her exceptional skill at interpreting census forms and Excel tables.

I called frequently on the research and expertise of Daniel Carlson, David Cotter, Carolyn Cowan, Philip Cowan, Rebecca Davis, Paula England, Eli Finkel, Frank Furstenberg, Michael Garcia, Jennifer Glass, Benjamin Karney, Arielle Kuperberg, Melissa Milkie, Steven Mintz, Paul Ortiz, Joanna Pepin, Richard Petts, Jennifer Randles, Liana Sayer, Sarah Schoppe-Sullivan, Christia Spears-Brown, and Kristi Williams.

In addition, I benefited from information, commentary, or sources supplied by William Chopik, Andre Cimpian, Shawn Fremstad, Colin Gordon, Ellen Lamont, Susan Matt, Kelly Musick, Barbara Risman, Michael Rosenfeld, William Scarborough, Christine Schwartz, Pepper Schwartz, Pamela Smock, Jan Van Bavel, and Debra Umberson. People who helped me with specific questions about their research are cited in the relevant endnotes.

I am grateful for having had the opportunity to try out some of the ideas in this book at a 2018 appearance at PopTech and a 2023 keynote for the National Council on Family Relations, and I forecast some of my discussion of healthy versus unhealthy nostalgia in a 2018 article for the *Harvard Business Review.*

Library staff members at The Evergreen State College were unfailingly helpful in my research for this book. I am especially grateful for the extra attention given me by Jean Fenske, Liza Rognas, Jenna Rosen, and Ray Zill, along with the help I received from Paul McMillan, Jason Mock, and Ren Thomas.

Finally, I am thankful for the love and support of family members Kris Coontz, Panpim Thongsripong, Fred Riehle, Sharron Coontz, Robert and Marion McIntosh, Colin McIntosh, Brian McIntosh, Amanda Harvey, Jeff and Carolin Waddington, and above all my husband, Will Reissner, who patiently read and edited many successive drafts of each chapter. I was sustained during the writing by my good friends and walking companions Sherry Frumkin, Sarah Ryan, Terry Sickelbower, Cyndia Sieden, Debra Stephens, Laury Thorson, Michaela Wagar, and Mike Wagar. And few things can match the joy of the time with my grandson, Jaz Aran Coontz, to whom this book is dedicated. He may have slowed my writing down, but he always cheered me up.

Last but not least, I thank my wild mushroom mentor Paul Pryzbylowitz and razor-clam-digging expert Doug Miller for their generosity in letting me in on the secrets and the bounty of the Pacific Northwest's forests and beaches.

NOTES

Introduction

1. On the fallacy of thinking that getting more people married is the solution to child maladjustment, poverty, and crime, see chapters 7 and 8. For a recent book by two authors who are firmly convinced that marriage is a "social good" but nevertheless decisively rebut the claim of some pro-marriage commentators that we could end child poverty by promoting marriage, see Nicholas Wolfinger and Matthew McKeever, *Thanks for Nothing: The Economics of Single Motherhood Since 1980* (Oxford University Press, 2024). Rebecca Traister offers an incisive commentary in "The Return of the Marriage Plot: Why Everyone Is Suddenly So Eager for Men and Women to Get Hitched," *The Cut*, September 22, 2023, https://www.thecut.com/article/why-is-everyone-so-eager-for-men-and-women-to-get-married.html. On the strengths and assets of the never-married, see William Chopik, "Associations Among Relational Values, Support, Health, and Well-Being Across the Adult Lifespan," *Personal Relationships* 24 (2017), https://www.almendron.com/tribuna/wp-content/uploads/2018/02/chopik2017pr.pdf; and personal communication, July 2, 2024. See also Natalia Sarkisian and Naomi Gerstel, "Does Singlehood Isolate or Integrate?," *Journal of Social and Personal Relationships* 33 (2016), https://journals.sagepub.com/doi/full/10.1177/0265407515597564; and the writing of Bella DePaula, who summarizes the best-case research about how people thrive when they choose a single life "for positive reasons" in several books and this 2023 article: "Single and Flourishing: Transcending the Deficit Narratives of Single Life," *Journal of Family Theory and Review* 15, no. 3 (2023), https://doi.org/10.1111/jftr.12525.
2. Brienna Perelli-Harris, "Universal or Unique? Understanding Diversity in Partnership Experiences Across Europe," in Naomi Cahn et al., eds., *Unequal Family Lives: Causes and Consequences in Europe and the Americas* (Cambridge University Press, 2018); Michael Rosenfeld, "Couple Longevity in the Era of Same-Sex Marriage in the United States," *Journal of Marriage and*

Family 76, no. 5 (2014): 905–18. Although the study found that somewhat fewer married same-sex couples had parental approval than heterosexual ones (78 vs. 89 percent), the critical predictor of parental support was marriage. Parents were 26 percentage points more likely to be supportive of a child's partner, same sex or different sex, when the two were married than when they were cohabiting.

3. This analysis of Census Bureau data was generously performed for me by University of Maryland sociologist Philip Cohen. The exact figures were 87.1 in 1950 and 86.9 in 2023, not a significant difference. Personal communication, January 10, 2024. On divorce rates, see Jake Hays, "8 Facts About Divorce in the United States," Pew Research Center, October 16, 2025, https://www.pewresearch.org/short-reads/2025/10/16/8-facts-about-divorce-in-the-united-states/.
4. Carolina Aragão, "Among Young Adults Without Children, Men Are More Likely Than Women to Say They Want to Be Parents Someday," Pew Research Center, February 18, 2024, https://www.pewresearch.org/short-reads/2024/02/15/among-young-adults-without-children-men-are-more-likely-than-women-to-say-they-want-to-be-parents-someday/.
5. In the General Social Survey, taken every year since 1977, the greatest gains in support for feminist ideas about work, family, and marriage occurred from about 2000 to 2016. See David Cotter, "Patterns of Progress? Changes in Gender Ideology 1977–2016," Council on Contemporary Families, May 1, 2018, https://thesocietypages.org/ccf/2018/05/01/patterns-of-progress-changes-in-gender-ideology-1977-2016/.
6. For this and the following paragraphs, see Joanna Pepin and Philip Cohen, "Growing Uncertainty in Marriage Expectations Among U.S. Youth," *Socius* 10 (2024), https://doi.org/10.1177/23780231241241035; pepin_cohen_2024_growing_uncertainty_in_marriage_expectations_among_u_s_youth.pdf. My thanks to Joanna Pepin for generously sharing the original survey figures for each year with me. She warns that year-to-year variations should not be taken too literally, but the trends from 2019 to 2023 are unmistakable.
7. See Tyler Parry, *Jumping the Broom: The Surprising Multicultural Origins of a Black Wedding Ritual* (University of North Carolina Press, 2020). For a vivid account of the role of marriage in the lives of enslaved African Americans and in the aftermath of emancipation, including its costs as well as its benefits to the partners, see Tera Hunter, *Bound in Wedlock: Slave and Free Black Marriage in the Nineteenth Century* (Belknap, 2017). On the heartbreaking struggles of formerly enslaved African Americans to reunite with separated spouses and family members after the Civil War, see Judith Giesberg, *Last Seen: The Enduring Search by Formerly Enslaved People to Find Their Lost Families* (Simon & Schuster, 2025).

8. For a study of the struggles by gay and lesbian individuals and couples to win same-sex marriage, see Michael Rosenfeld, *The Rainbow After the Storm: Marriage Equality and Social Change in the U.S.* (Oxford University Press, 2021); Julia Raifman et al., "Difference-in-Differences Analysis of the Association Between State Same-Sex Marriage Policies and Adolescent Suicide Attempts," *JAMA Pediatrics* 171, no. 4 (2017), https://jamanetwork.com/journals/jamapediatrics/fullarticle/2604258.
9. Michael J. Rosenfeld, "Who Wants the Breakup? Gender and Breakup in Heterosexual Couples," in *Social Networks and the Life Course: Integrating the Development of Human Lives and Social Relational Networks*, eds. Duane Alwin, Diane Felmlee, and Derek Kreager, Springer, 201, 221–43.
10. For those interested in more comprehensive histories of marriage, sexuality, and gender, you might start with Steven Mintz and Susan Kellogg, *Domestic Revolutions: A Social History of American Family Life* (Free Press, 1989); John D'Emilio and Estelle Freedman, *Intimate Matters: A History of Sexuality in America* (University of Chicago Press, 2012); Nancy Cott, *Public Vows: A History of Marriage and the Nation* (Harvard University Press, 2000); Stephanie Coontz, *Marriage, a History: How Love Conquered Marriage* (Viking, 2005); Rebecca Davis, *Fierce Desires: A New History of Sex and Sexuality in America* (W. W. Norton & Company, 2024); Margot Canaday et al., eds., *Intimate States: Gender, Sexuality, and Governance in Modern US History* (University of Chicago Press, 2021). In addition, each chapter cites numerous books that provide more in-depth studies of the era under review there.
11. Richard Sima, "Why Catchy Songs Get Stuck in Your Head (and How to Stop It)," *Washington Post*, April 24, 2025, https://www.washingtonpost.com/wellness/interactive/2025/why-songs-get-stuck-in-your-head/.
12. J. K. McNulty, "Highlighting the Contextual Nature of Interpersonal Relationships," *Advances in Experimental Social Psychology* 54 (2016), 247–315, https://www.sciencedirect.com/science/article/abs/pii/S0065260116300168.
13. Luis Noé-Bustamante et al., "About One-in-Four U.S. Hispanics Have Heard of Latinx, but Just 3% Use It," Pew Research Center, August 11, 2020, https://www.pewresearch.org/hispanic/2020/08/11/about-one-in-four-u-s-hispanics-have-heard-of-latinx-but-just-3-use-it/; Justin McCarthy and Whitney Dupreé, "No Preferred Racial Term Among Most Black, Hispanic Adults," Gallup, August 4, 2021, https://news.gallup.com/poll/353000/no-preferred-racial-term-among-black-hispanic-adults.aspx. And a significant number of Hispanics say they find the term *Latinx* offensive: "The Use of 'LatinX' Among Hispanic Voters," Bendixen & Amandi International, https://www.politico.com/f/?id=0000017d-81be-dee4-a5ff-efbe74ec0000.

Chapter 1: The Many and Much Misunderstood "Traditional" Marriages

1. For this and other quotations from the Supreme Court ruling in *Obergefell v. Hodges*, see https://www.supremecourt.gov/opinions/14pdf/14-556_3204.pdf. On marriage as a way to rescue modern civilization, see Brad Wilcox, *Get Married: Why Americans Must Defy Elites, Forge Strong Families, and Save Civilization* (Broadside Books, 2024). For the *New York Times* review, see David Brooks, "To Be Happy, Marriage Matters More Than Career," *New York Times*, August 17, 2023, https://www.nytimes.com/2023/08/17/opinion/marriage-happiness-career.html.
2. Clementine Ford, *I Don't: The Case Against Marriage* (Allen & Unwin, 2023); and "Marriage Is an Inherently Misogynistic Institution—So Why Do Women Agree to It?," *Guardian*, October 30, 2023, https://www.theguardian.com/lifeandstyle/2023/oct/31/marriage-is-an-inherently-misogynistic-institution-so-why-do-women-agree-to-it.
3. For this and the next two paragraphs, see Robert P. Miller, ed., *Chaucer: Sources and Backgrounds* (Oxford University Press, 1977), 420–21; Dale Martin, *Sex and the Single Savior* (Westminster John Knox Press, 2006), 117; Diarmaid MacCulloch, *Lower Than the Angels: A History of Sex and Christianity* (Allen Lane, 2024). For the entire passage from Jerome quoted here, see part 9 of "Against Jovinianus (Book I)," New Advent, https://www.newadvent.org/fathers/30091.htm.
4. Katherine Harvey, "The Salacious Middle Ages," *Aeon*, January 23, 2018, https://aeon.co/essays/getting-down-and-medieval-the-sex-lives-of-the-middle-ages; Matthew Wills, "Green Sickness, the Disease of Virgins," *JSTOR Daily*, September 27, 2025, https://daily.jstor.org/green-sickness-the-disease-of-virgins/. For an example of the frank treatment of sex in much of secular society, see the hilariously bawdy fourteenth-century "The Miller's Tale" in Chaucer's *Canterbury Tales*.
5. For more on variations in marriage, see Stephanie Coontz, *Marriage, a History: How Love Conquered Marriage* (Viking, 2005), chapter 2; Katherine E. Starkweather and Raymond Hames, "A Survey of Non-Classical Polyandry," *Human Nature* 23 (2012), https://digitalcommons.unl.edu/anthropologyfacpub/50/; Sandra Hollimon, "The Archaeology of Nonbinary Genders in Native North American Societies," in *Handbook of Gender in Archaeology*, ed. Sarah Milledge Nelson (AltaMira Press, 2006).
6. See, for example, the articles in *Gender and Sexuality in Indigenous North America, 1400–1850*, eds. Sandra Slater and Fay A. Yarbrough (University of South Carolina Press, 2011); Kent Flannery and Joyce Marcus, *The Creation of Inequality* (Harvard University Press, 2012), 70–71, 181–83; Evelyn Blackwood, "Sexuality and Gender in Certain Native American Tribes: The Case of Cross-Gender Females," *Signs: Journal of Women in Culture and Society* 10, no. 1 (1984): 27–42, https://www.journals.uchicago.edu/doi/abs/10.1086/494112;

Sue-Ellen Jacobs et al., eds., *Two-Spirit People: Native American Gender Identity, Sexuality, and Spirituality* (University of Illinois Press, 1997); Harriet Whitehead, "The Bow and the Burden Strap," in *The Lesbian and Gay Studies Reader*, ed. Henry Abelove et al. (Routledge, 1993).

In her book *Yellow Woman and a Beauty of the Spirit* (Simon & Schuster, 1996), Laguna Pueblo author Leslie Marmon Silko claims that in the traditional Pueblo worldview, "we are all a mixture of male and female, and this sexual identity is changing constantly." On other variations in sexual behaviors and attitudes, see Kit Heyam, *Before We Were Trans: A New History of Gender* (Seal Press, 2023); Kevin P. Murphy et al., eds., *The Routledge History of American Sexuality* (Routledge, 2020); Susan Stryker, *Transgender History* (Seal Press, 2017); and Joanne Meyerowitz, *How Sex Changed: A History of Transsexuality in the United States* (Harvard University Press, 2004).

7. For a fascinating description of two-spirit and third-sex gender arrangements and norms in the Native American Illinois Confederacy, see Michaela Kleber, "'No Cause for Distrust': Gender Plurality in Illinois-French First Contacts," *Journal of American History* 111 (2024), https://doi.org/10.1093/jahist/jaae094.
8. For a brief summary of recent thinking about the timeline of human evolution, see Brian Handwerk, "An Evolutionary Timeline of Homo Sapiens," *Smithsonian Magazine*, February 2, 2021, https://www.smithsonianmag.com/science-nature/essential-timeline-understanding-evolution-homo-sapiens-180976807/. Most anthropologists and evolutionary scientists believe that the nearest equivalents to the communities our ancestors lived in for so many millennia are the technologically simple hunting-and-gathering societies observed by early explorers and studied by ethnographers since the nineteenth century. Few of these groups live in the same environments they confronted back then, and all have since been changed by contact with (and mistreatment by) more complex societies. But researchers have combined historical accounts with current ethnographic research, archaeological evidence, genealogical testing, and statistical modeling to develop what they believe is a reasonably good picture of how our Paleolithic ancestors lived.

   I have drawn on so much literature on band-level societies and likely Paleolithic living arrangements that it is pointless to try to provide separate endnotes for all my assertions, except where I am using an actual quote or referencing one particular page. The following books and articles have been among the most helpful: Kim Sterelny, *The Pleistocene Social Contract: Culture and Cooperation in Human Evolution* (Oxford University Press, 2021); Frank Marlowe, "Hunter-Gatherers and Human Evolution," *Evolutionary Anthropology* 14 (2005): 54; Joseph Henrich, "Human Cooperation: The Hunter-Gatherer Puzzle," *Current Biology* 28 (2018); Vicki Cummings et al., eds., *The Oxford Handbook of the Archaeology and Anthropology of Hunter-Gatherers*

(Oxford University Press, 2014); James Woodburn, "Egalitarian Societies," *Man*, New Series, 17, no. 3 (1982): 431–51; Jan Lucassen, *The Story of Work: A New History of Humankind* (Yale University Press, 2021); Gary Feinman and T. Douglas Price, eds., *Archaeology at the Millennium: A Sourcebook* (Kluwer Academic, 2001); Robert Sapolsky, *Behave: The Biology of Humans at Our Best and Worst* (Penguin, 2018); Brian Hayden, *Archeology: The Science of Once and Future Things* (W. H. Freeman, 1993); Stephanie Coontz, *Marriage, a History: How Love Conquered Marriage* (Viking, 2005), chapters 2 and 3; Nancy Bonvillain, *Women and Men: Cultural Constructs of Gender* (Rowman & Littlefield, 2021); Christopher Boehm, *Hierarchy in the Forest: The Evolution of Egalitarian Behavior* (Harvard University Press, 1999); Douglas Fry and Patrik Söderberg, "Lethal Aggression in Mobile Forager Bands and Implications for the Origins of War," *Science* 341 (2013); Marshall Sahlins, "What Kinship Is (Part One)," *Journal of the Royal Anthropological Institute* 17, no. 1 (2011), https://www.jstor.org/stable/23011568; David Graeber and David Wengrow, *The Dawn of Everything: A New History of Humanity* (Farrar, Straus and Giroux, 2021); Marja Ahola et al., "Far-Flung Ancient Communities Forged Bonds Through Broken Rings," *Psyche*, (August 29, 2022), https://psyche.co/ideas/far-flung-ancient-communities-forged-bonds-through-broken-rings; Kristen Hawkes, "Grandmothers and the Evolution of Human Longevity," *American Journal of Human Biology* 15 (2003); Nina Brown et al., eds., *Perspectives: An Open Invitation to Cultural Anthropology* (American Anthropology Association, 2017); Janet Carsten, *After Kinship* (Cambridge University Press, 2012); Christopher Boehm, "The Moral Consequences of Social Selection," *Behaviour* 151, no. 2–3 (2014): 167–83, https://doi.org/10.1163/1568539X-00003143; Kim Hill and A. M. Hurtado, "Cooperative Breeding in South American Hunter–Gatherers," *Proceedings: Biological Sciences* 276, no. 1674 (2009): 3863–70, https://www.jstor.org/stable/30245349. See also Kim Hill, "Altruistic Cooperation During Foraging by the Ache, and the Evolved Human Predisposition to Cooperate," *Human Nature* 13 (2002): 105–28, https://doi.org/10.1007/s12110-002-1016-3; Kim Hill et al., "Hunter-Gatherer Inter-Band Interaction Rates," *PLOS One* 9, no. 7 (2014), https://doi.org/10.1371/journal.pone.0102806.

9. Edward O. Wilson, "Human Decency Is Animal," *New York Times Magazine*, October 12, 1975, https://www.nytimes.com/1975/10/12/archives/human-decency-is-animal-hawks-and-baboons-are-not-usually-heroic.html.
10. For more on the views discussed in the following paragraphs, see Bruce Ellis, "The Evolution of Sexual Attraction: Evaluative Mechanisms in Women," in *The Adapted Mind: Evolutionary Psychology and the Generation of Culture*, ed. Jerome H. Barkow et al. (Oxford University Press, 1992); and David Buss, *Evolutionary Psychology: The New Science of the Mind* (Allyn and Bacon, 1999); along with the summaries and incisive critiques in David Buller, *Adapting*

Minds: Evolutionary Psychology and the Persistent Quest for Human Nature (MIT Press, 2005), especially chapter 5.

11. David Buller, *Adapting Minds*, 228; Elizabeth Cashdan, "Waist-to-Hip Ratio Across Cultures," *Current Anthropology* 49, no. 6 (2008), https://www.journals.uchicago.edu/doi/abs/10.1086/593036. For a more cautious exploration of the possible evolutionary pressures selecting for this widespread but far from universal preference, see Jeanne Bovet, "Evolutionary Theories and Men's Preferences for Women's Waist-to-Hip Ratio: Which Hypotheses Remain?," *Frontiers in Psychology* 10 (2019), https://pubmed.ncbi.nlm.nih.gov/31244708/.
12. Isabel Scott et al., "Human Preferences for Sexually Dimorphic Faces May Be Evolutionarily Novel," *Proceedings of the National Academy of Sciences of the United States of America* 111, no. 40 (2014): 14388–93, https://www.jstor.com/stable/43055114. The qualities that men and women *say* they want in a mate tend to differ widely by gender along the lines predicted by the male-hunter, female-reproducer theory, with men prioritizing the youth and physical attractiveness of potential partners and women looking for older partners with higher earnings. But when researchers Paul Eastwick and Eli Finkel compared such stated preferences with what males and females actually ended up preferring in a real-life dating scenario, they found few, if any, consistent differences by gender. In practice both men and women were attracted to similar things in the "opposite" sex—and were also more flexible in their actual preferences than their initial "wish list" suggested. See Paul W. Eastwick and Eli J. Finkel, "Sex Differences in Mate Preferences Revisited: Do People Know What They Initially Desire in a Romantic Partner?," *Journal of Personality and Social Psychology* 94 (2008), https://faculty.wcas.northwestern.edu/eli-finkel/documents/EastwickFinkel2008_JPSP.pdf. See also Paul Eastwick et al., "The Predictive Validity of Ideal Partner Preferences: A Review and Meta-Analysis," *Psychological Bulletin* 140, no. 3 (2013): 623–65, https://www.researchgate.net/publication/236183331_The_Predictive_Validity_of_Ideal_Partner_Preferences_A_Review_and_Meta-Analysis.

    My thanks to Eli Finkel for sending me these and other articles cited in the book. For some fun analyses of popular romance films for the extent to which they do and do not accord with scientific studies about how relationships work, see his podcast with Paul Eastman, *Love Factually*, https://www.lovefactuallypod.com/.
13. Catherine Panter-Brick, "Sexual Division of Labor: Energetic and Evolutionary Scenarios," *American Journal of Human Biology* 14, no. 5 (2002), https://doi.org/10.1002/ajhb.10074.
14. Randall Haas et al., "Female Hunters of the Early Americas," *Science Advances* 6, no. 45 (2020), https://www.science.org/doi/10.1126/sciadv.abd0310. See also Ann Gibbons, "Woman the Hunter: Ancient Andean Remains

Challenge Old Ideas of Who Speared Big Game," *Science* (November 4, 2020), https://www.science.org/content/article/woman-hunter-ancient-andean-remains-challenge-old-ideas-who-speared-big-game. Excavations from hunter-gatherer sites in Peru, eight thousand years old, reveal that both men and women had large upper-body muscles, probably from hauling nets, and lower body arthritis, associated with hauling heavy loads. But men had more damage to their elbow tendons, suggesting they did most of the spear throwing; see Jan Lucassen, *The Story of Work: A New History of Humankind* (Yale University Press, 2021), 34–35. See also Rebecca Wragg Sykes, "Sheanderthal," *Aeon* (January 12, 2021), https://aeon.co/essays/what-do-we-know-about-the-lives-of-neanderthal-women.

15. Most band-level societies put extraordinary effort into penalizing selfish acts. Hoarders are shamed. Braggarts and self-promoters are ridiculed. People who do not reciprocate generosity are shunned. And those who bully or take from others are ostracized or subjected to group punishment. This can sometimes even include being killed. See Polly Wiessner, "Leveling the Hunter: Constraints on the Status Quest in Foraging Societies," in *Food and the Status Quest: An Interdisciplinary Perspective*, eds. Polly Wiessner and Wulf Schiefenhövel (Berghahn Books, 1996); "Norm Enforcement Among the Ju/'hoansi Bushmen: A Case of Strong Reciprocity?," *Human Nature* 16, no. 2 (2005), https://pubmed.ncbi.nlm.nih.gov/26189619/; Stephanie Coontz, *Marriage, a History: How Love Conquered Marriage* (Viking, 2005), chapters 2 and 3; Christopher Boehm, "Emergency Decisions, Cultural-Selection Mechanics, and Group Selection," *Current Anthropology* 37 (1996): 774–77; and *Hierarchy in the Forest: The Evolution of Egalitarian Behavior* (Harvard University Press, 1999). While most researchers reject the idea that Paleolithic hunters and gatherers were warlike, there are examples of individual deaths that have been described as homicides but may have been a group-sanctioned execution in response to a serious violation of group norms. In a study of fifty "Pleistocene-type foraging societies," cultural anthropologist Christopher Boehm found that half of them admitted having conducted a morally based group killing of an individual. The most common reason for such capital punishment was that the individual was a habitually aggressive or violent bully. See Christopher Boehm, *Moral Origins: The Evolution of Virtue, Altruism, and Shame* (Basic Books, 2012); and "The Moral Consequences of Social Selection," *Behaviour* 151 (2014), https://www.jstor.org/stable/24526001. This is not to say that there was no interpersonal violence within or sometimes between bands if one moved into another's habitual territory without providing reciprocal benefits or took one-sided advantage of an alliance partnership. But for a refutation of the old-fashioned view that our Paleolithic human ancestors were routinely violent until the invention of civilized morality and police, see Robert Sapolsky, *Behave: The Biology of Humans*

at Our Best and Worst (Penguin, 2017), 306–27; Kim Hill and A. Magdalena Hurtado, *Ache Life History: The Ecology and Demography of a Foraging People* (Aldine de Gruyter, 1996); Douglas Fry and Patrik Söderberg, "Lethal Aggression in Mobile Forager Bands and Implications for the Origins of War," *Science* 341 (2013); and *War, Peace, and Human Nature: The Convergence of Evolutionary and Cultural Views*, ed. Douglas Fry (Oxford University Press, 2015). For a real-life case study of what happens when modern human boys are thrown back into "a state of nature"—completely contradicting the fictional ideas about aggressive, self-seeking human nature in *Lord of the Flies*—see Clay Risen, "Peter Warner, 90, Seafarer Who Discovered Shipwrecked Boys, Dies," *New York Times*, April 22, 2021, https://www.nytimes.com/2021/04/22/world/australia/peter-warner-dead.html.

16. Sarah Blaffer Hrdy, *Father Time: A Natural History of Men and Babies* (Princeton University Press, 2024), 185.
17. Sarah Blaffer Hrdy, *Mothers and Others: The Evolutionary Origins of Mutual Understanding* (Harvard University Press, 2011), chapters 3–9; Sarah Blaffer Hrdy, "Meet the Alloparents: Shared Child Care May Be the Secret of Human Evolutionary Success," *Natural History* (2009): 29, https://naturalhistorymag.com/features/09270/meet-the-alloparents. See also Eric Michael Johnson, "Raising Darwin's Consciousness: An Interview with Sarah Blaffer Hrdy on Mother Nature," *Scientific American*, March 16, 2012, https://www.scientificamerican.com/blog/primate-diaries/raising-darwins-consciousness-an-interview-with-sarah-blaffer-hrdy-on-mother-nature/.
18. Kim Hill et al., "Co-Residence Patterns in Hunter-Gatherer Societies Show Unique Human Social Structure," *Science* 331, no. 6022 (2011); Kim Hill et al., "Hunter-Gatherer Inter-Band Interaction Rates: Implications for Cumulative Culture," *PLOS One* 9 (2014), https://journals.plos.org/plosone/article?id=10.1371/journal.pone.0102806; Kristopher Smith et al., "Hunter-Gatherers Maintain Assortativity in Cooperation Despite High Levels of Residential Change and Mixing," *Current Biology* 28 (2018); Joseph Henrich, "Human Cooperation: The Hunter-Gatherer Puzzle," *Current Biology* 28, no. 19 (2018): R1143–45; Christopher Boehm et al., "Emergency Decisions, Cultural-Selection Mechanics, and Group Selection," *Current Anthropology* 37 (1996).
19. Brian A. Stewart et al., "Ostrich Eggshell Bead Strontium Isotopes Reveal Persistent Macroscale Social Networking Across Late Quaternary Southern Africa," *Proceedings of the National Academy of Sciences of the United States of America* 117, no. 12 (2020), https://www.pnas.org/doi/pdf/10.1073/pnas.1921037117; Polly Wiessner, "On Network Analyses: The Potential for Understanding (and Misunderstanding) !Kung Hxaro," *Current Anthropology* 39 (1998); Polly Wiessner, "Risk, Reciprocity, and Social Influences on !Kung San Economics," in *Politics and History in Band Societies*, eds. Eleanor Leacock and Richard Lee (Cambridge University Press, 1982); Polly Wiessner,

"Hunting, Healing, and Hxaro Exchange: A Long-Term Perspective on !Kung (Ju/'hoansi) Large-Game Hunting," *Evolution and Human Behavior* 23, no. 6 (2002).

20. Kim R. Hill et al., "Co-Residence Patterns in Hunter-Gatherer Societies Show Unique Human Social Structure," *Science* 331, no. 6022 (2011): 1286–89; Robert S. Walker and Drew H. Bailey, "Marrying Kin in Small-Scale Societies," *American Journal of Human Biology* 26, no. 3 (2014): 384–88.
21. Robert Walker et al., "Evolutionary History of Hunter-Gatherer Marriage Practices," *PLOS One* (2011), https://doi.org/10.1371/journal.pone.0019066; Menelaos Apostolou, "Sexual Selection Under Parental Choice: The Role of Parents in the Evolution of Human Mating," *Evolution and Human Behavior* 28 (2007): 403–9; and "Sexual Selection Under Parental Choice: Evidence from Sixteen Historical Societies," *Evolutionary Psychology* 10 (2012). The prevalence of arranged marriages suggests yet another problem with the claim that our contemporary mating impulses were laid down by sexual selection. The traits that parents desire in an in-law are typically quite different than those that young people desire in a sexual partner.
22. G. Robina Quale, *A History of Marriage Systems* (Greenwood Press, 1988); Pamela Stern and Richard Condon, "A Good Spouse Is Hard to Find," in *Romantic Passion: A Universal Experience?*, ed. William Jankowiak (Columbia University Press, 1995); Nancy Bonvillain, *Women and Men: Cultural Constructs of Gender* (Rowman & Littlefield, 2001), 23.
23. In addition to my previous references on band-level societies, see Robert Jarvenpa and Hetty Jo Brumbach, "Hunter-Gatherer Gender and Identity," in *The Oxford Handbook of the Archaeology and Anthropology of Hunter-Gatherers*, eds. Vicki Cummings et al. (Oxford University Press, 2014).
24. Journal of Father Paul Le Jeune, superior of the Jesuit mission in Quebec, quoted in Eleanor Leacock, "Montagnais Women and the Jesuit Program for Colonization," in *Women and Colonization*, eds. Mona Etienne and Eleanor Leacock (Praeger, 1980), 50. For a fascinating account of how male domination developed in this formerly egalitarian society, see Karen Anderson, *Chain Her by One Foot: The Subjugation of Native Women in Seventeenth-Century New France* (Routledge, 1991).
25. For a sampling of theories, see Kim Sterelny, "How Equality Slipped Away," *Aeon*, June 10, 2021, https://aeon.co/essays/for-97-of-human-history-equality-was-the-norm-what-happened; Samuel Bowles and Mattia Fochesato, "What We Can Learn from the Inequality Revolution in Prehistory," VoxEU-CEPR, January 3, 2025, https://cepr.org/voxeu/columns/what-we-can-learn-inequality-revolution-prehistory; Deborah Rogers et al., "The Spread of Inequality," *PLOS One* 6, no. 9 (2011), https://journals.plos.org/plosone/article?id=10.1371/journal.pone.0024683#s1; Brian Hayden, "Richman, Poorman, Beggarman, Chief: The Dynamics of Social Inequality," in *Archaeology at the Millennium*,

eds. Gary Feinman and T. Douglas Price (Kluwer Academic/Plenum Publishers, 2001); and Brian Hayden, "Social Complexity," in *The Oxford Handbook of the Archaeology and Anthropology of Hunter-Gatherers*, eds. Vicki Cummings et al. (Oxford University Press, 2014); Samuel Bowles et al., "The Emergence and Persistence of Inequality in Premodern Societies," *Current Anthropology* 51, no. 1 (2010); Douglas Kennett et al., "An Ecological Model for the Emergence of Institutionalized Social Hierarchies on California's Northern Channel Islands," in *Pattern and Process in Cultural Evolution*, ed. Stephen Shennan (University of California Press, 2009); Peter Richerson et al., "Was Agriculture Impossible During the Pleistocene but Mandatory During the Holocene? A Climate Change Hypothesis," *American Antiquity* 66, no. 3 (2001); Kent Flannery and Joyce Marcus, *The Creation of Inequality: How Our Prehistoric Ancestors Set the Stage for Monarchy, Slavery, and Empire* (Harvard University Press, 2012); Gary Feinman et al., "Assessing Grand Narratives of Economic Inequality Across Time," *Proceedings of the National Academy of Sciences* 122, no. 16 (2025): e2400698121, https://doi.org/10.1073/pnas.2400698121.

26. Some researchers have argued that the rapid proliferation of inegalitarian societies about ten thousand years ago resulted from the fact that they were so much more efficient at mobilizing labor and enforcing sustained productive efforts than leaderless band-level societies. People supposedly began to accept unaccustomed social inequalities in exchange for the higher standard of living and greater security from periodic famines that these societies provided. But anthropologist Deborah Rogers, computer scientist Omkar Deshpande, and evolutionary biologist Marcus Feldman have a different view. Using a complex demographic simulation to analyze the social, economic, and environmental changes that occur when a society begins to experience persistent inequalities in access to resources, they calculate that only a few societies would have had to develop systemic social and economic stratification in order to set off a snowball effect in surrounding territories—not because unequal societies are so advantageous that they inspire imitation, but because they breed conflict and competition for resources and status, creating an incentive for rulers and subjects alike to plunder, colonize, or simply flee to other territories. Band-level groups were especially vulnerable to being conquered or pushed out of their traditional territory. See Deborah Rogers et al., "The Spread of Inequality," *PLOS One* (September 21, 2011), https://journals.plos.org/plosone/article?id=10.1371/journal.pone.0024683#s1. See also Deborah Rogers, "Inequality: Why Egalitarian Societies Died Out," *New Scientist* (July 25, 2012), https://www.newscientist.com/article/dn22071-inequality-why-egalitarian-societies-died-out/#ixzz6BteMd9Ab.
27. Hrdy, *Father Time*, 238.
28. State v. Lash, 16 N.J.L. 380 (N.J. Sup. Ct. 1838). My thanks to law professor Linda McClain for this reference, which is available here: http://graphics8

.nytimes.com/packages/pdf/world/2012/FamilyLaw_Classhandout12_spring2012.pdf.

29. See my earlier book, *Marriage, a History: How Love Conquered Marriage*, for a detailed description of these maneuvers.
30. Luke 18:29–30; Luke 14:26; Luke 9:59–60; Matthew 12:46–49; Mark 3:31–35. On singlehood as more worthy, see Corinthians 7:32–35. Some of the following information first appeared, along with a discussion of the egalitarian values of early nineteenth-century American evangelicals, in Stephanie Coontz, "Family Values, Social Reciprocity, and Christianity," in *Human Families: Identities, Relationships, and Responsibilities, The Annual Publication of the College Theology Society* 2020, vol. 66, eds. Jacob Kohlhaas and Mary Doyle Roche (Orbis Books, 2021).

Chapter 2: The Paradox of Patriarchy and the Dark Side of Democracy

1. Veronica Chambers et al., "The Mrs. Files," *New York Times*, May 15, 2020, https://www.nytimes.com/2020/05/15/arts/mrs-women-identity.html; John Kelly, "Starting in the '70s, Married Women's First Names Were Included in Post References," November 23, 2019, https://www.washingtonpost.com/local/starting-in-the-1970s-womens-first-names-were-included-in-post-references/2019/11/23/73dc1eb2-0d59-11ea-bd9d-c628fd48b3a0_story.html.
2. Unless otherwise noted, the discussion of the evolution of "Mrs." is drawn from Amy Louise Erickson, "Mistresses and Marriage: or, a Short History of the Mrs," *History Workshop Journal* 78 (2014), http://www.jstor.org/stable/43299025; Una Stannard, *Mrs Man* (Germainbooks, 1977); Mary Beth Norton, *Founding Mothers and Fathers: Gendered Power and the Forming of American Society* (Knopf, 1996). See also Amy Erickson, "Mrs Man: Why Do Women Take Their Husbands' Surnames?," *Top of the Campops* (blog), Cambridge Group for the History of Population and Social Structure, University of Cambridge, July 11, 2024, https://www.campop.geog.cam.ac.uk/blog/2024/07/11/women-husbands-surnames/.
3. Nowadays, many women bristle when they are addressed as "ladies." But applying the term "ladies" to all women, not just aristocrats, was originally a democratic innovation, as was using the term "gentlemen" for an entire group of men, regardless of variations in their social rank.
4. Deborah Anthony, "Eradicating Women's Surnames: Law, Tradition, and the Politics of Memory," *Columbia Journal of Gender and Law* 37, no. 1 (2018): 9, https://journals.library.columbia.edu/index.php/cjgl/article/view/2783.
5. Amy Erickson, "The Marital Economy in Comparative Perspective," in *The Marital Economy in Scandinavia and Britain, 1400–1900*, eds. Maria Agren and Amy Erickson (Ashgate Publishing, 2004); and Erickson, "Mrs Man"; Stephanie Coontz, *Marriage, a History: How Love Conquered Marriage* (Vi-

king, 2005); Una Stannard, "Manners Make Laws: Married Women's Names in the United States," *Names* 32, no. 2 (1984): 114, https://ans-names.pitt.edu/ans/article/view/1041/1040.

6. Historian Mary Beth Norton generously ran a search for me while I could not get into my library during the pandemic lockdown and found that in the eighteenth century, women who were identified as Mrs. consistently had their first name mentioned. By the mid-nineteenth century, Mrs. John Doe was becoming more common, and by the late nineteenth century it was consistently the "Mrs. Man" form (personal communication, March 31, 2020).
7. Sofia Ling et al., "Marriage and Work," in *Making a Living, Making a Difference: Gender and Work in Early Modern European Society*, ed. Maria Agren (Oxford University Press, 2017), 91, 97; Cordelia Beattie and Matthew Stevens, *Married Women and the Law in Premodern Northwest Europe* (Boydell Press, 2013); Cathryn Spence, *Women, Credit and Debt in Early Modern Scotland* (Manchester University Press, 2016); and Amy Erickson, *Women and Property in Early Modern England* (Routledge, 1993).
8. Katie Barclay, *Love, Intimacy and Power: Marriage and Patriarchy in Scotland, 1650–1850* (Manchester University Press, 2011), 105.
9. Heather McLaughlin et al., "Sexual Harassment, Workplace Authority, and the Paradox of Power," *American Sociological Review* 77, no. 4 (2012): 625–47, https://journals.sagepub.com/doi/10.1177/0003122412451728.
10. Mary Beth Norton, *Separated by Their Sex: Women in Public and Private in the Colonial Atlantic World* (Cornell University Press, 2011), 2.
11. Gary B. Nash, *The Urban Crucible* (Harvard University Press, 1979), 43; William Hubbard, "The Happiness of a People," election sermon, May 3, 1676.
12. Quoted in Nash, *Urban Crucible*, 43.
13. See Robert Cleaver, *A Godly Form of Household Government* (1598), https://internetshakespeare.uvic.ca/doc/CleaverGodly_M/index.html; Benjamin Wadsworth, "The Well-Ordered Family," quoted in Stephanie Coontz, *The Social Origins of Private Life: A History of American Families, 1600–1900* (Verso Books, 1988), 100.
14. Linda Pollock, "'Teach Her to Live Under Obedience': The Making of Women in the Upper Ranks of Early Modern England," *Continuity and Change* 4, no. 2 (1989): 231–58; David Cressy, *Travesties and Transgressions in Tudor and Stuart England: Tales of Discord and Dissension* (Oxford University Press, 2000), 282–83; John Demos, *A Little Commonwealth: Family Life in Plymouth Colony* (Oxford University Press, 1999). One book often quoted to illustrate the subordination imposed upon women by European patriarchy is *Of Domesticall Duties*, based on a 1622 sermon by William Gouge and reprinted continuously in England and America for the next two centuries. Gouge declared that the husband is "king" in his own house and listed all the ways in which wives

were required to subordinate themselves. But in his introduction to the published version, Gouge admitted that his parishioners had taken "much exception" when he first preached this from the pulpit. Sounding more defensive than most contemporary misogynists, Gouge protested that he was no "hater of women" and had emphasized wives' duties so much only because, of all the many groups required to submit to others, wives were typically the "least likely" to do so. He also reminded his audience that he had advised men not to exercise the full command to which they were entitled, but instead to make their wives "a joynt Gourvernour of the family." William Gouge, "The Epistle Dedicatory," *Of Domesticall Duties* (London, 1622; facsimile ed., Theatrum Terrarum and Walter J. Johnson, 1976).

15. Dror Wahrman, *The Making of the Modern Self: Identity and Culture in Eighteenth-Century England* (Yale University Press, 2004); David Cressy, "Gender Trouble and Cross-Dressing in Early Modern England," *Journal of British Studies* 35, no. 4 (1996): 438–65. Think of Shakespeare's Portia, in his sixteenth-century play *The Merchant of Venice,* who disguises herself as a male lawyer and wins a case that all the male protagonists had considered hopeless.
16. Interestingly, in some areas of England, widows were paid more than married women for the same jobs because they had no partner to help them support their households. See Merry Wiesner-Hanks, *Women and Gender in Early Modern Europe,* 4th ed. (Cambridge University Press, 2019), 122, 124.
17. Ling et al., "Marriage and Work," 88; Coontz, *Marriage, a History*; Margaret Hunt, *Women in Eighteenth-Century Europe* (Pearson, 2010).
18. Jonathan Levy, *Ages of American Capitalism: A History of the United States* (Random House, 2021), 43.
19. Diane Bornstein, *The Lady in the Tower: Medieval Courtesy Literature for Women* (Archon Books, 1983), 106. Perhaps not coincidentally, this was the only fifteenth-century advice book known to have been written by a woman.
20. Alexandra Shepard, "Crediting Women in the Early Modern English Economy," *History Workshop Journal* 79 (2015); Alexandra Shepard, *Accounting for Oneself: Worth, Status, and the Social Order in Early Modern England* (Oxford University Press, 2015), 175. For a refutation of the common claim that women's reputations depended more on their sexual behavior than their diligence and reliability, see Garthine Walker, "Expanding the Boundaries of Female Honour in Early Modern England," *Transactions of the Royal Historical Society* 6 (1996): 235–45, https://www.jstor.org/stable/3679239; and Faramerz Dabhoiwala, "The Construction of Honour, Reputation and Status in Late Seventeenth- and Early Eighteenth-Century England," *Transactions of the Royal Historical Society* 6 (1996): 201–13, https://www.jstor.org/stable/3679236.
21. Dag Lindstrom et al., "Working Together," in *Making a Living, Making a Difference,* ed. Maria Agren (Oxford University Press, 2017); Jane Whittle, "En-

terprising Widows and Active Wives: Women's Unpaid Work in the Household Economy of Early Modern England," *History of the Family* 19, no. 3 (2014): 298, http://dx.doi.org/10.1080/1081602X.2014.892022; Laurel Ulrich, *Good Wives: Image and Reality in the Lives of Women in Northern New England, 1650–1750* (Knopf, 1982), 37–38; Bernard Capp, *When Gossips Meet: Women, Family, and Neighbourhood in Early Modern England* (Oxford University Press, 2003), 44–53.

22. Craig Muldrew, *The Economy of Obligation: The Culture of Credit and Social Relations in Early Modern England* (Macmillan Press, 1998), 125; Margaret Hunt, *The Middling Sort: Commerce, Gender and the Family in England, 1680–1780* (University of California Press, 1996), 22–23; Lisa Wilson, *Ye Heart of a Man: The Domestic Life of Men in Colonial New England* (Yale University Press, 1999); John Gillis, "Bringing Up Father: British Paternal Identities, 1700 to Present," *Masculinities* 3 (1995): 6, 16.
23. Elaine Chalus, "'To Serve My Friends': Women and Political Patronage in Eighteenth-Century England," in *Women, Privilege, and Power: British Politics, 1750 to the Present*, ed. Amanda Vickery (Stanford University Press, 2001).
24. On the business activities of eighteenth-century urban women, see Christine Wiskin, "Urban Businesswomen in Eighteenth-Century England," and Hannah Barker and Karen Harvey, "Women Entrepreneurs and Urban Expansion," in *Women and Urban Life in Eighteenth-Century England*, eds. Rosemary Sweet and Penelope Lane (Ashgate Publishing, 2003); and Linda Levy Peck, *Women of Fortune: Money, Marriage, and Murder in Early Modern England* (Cambridge University Press, 2018). See also Tom Almeroth-Williams, "London's Forgotten Businesswomen," University of Cambridge, https://www.cam.ac.uk/citywomen.

    For legal gains in that period, see Tim Stretton and Krista Kesselring, eds., *Married Women and the Law: Coverture in England and the Common Law World* (McGill, 2013); Peck, *Women of Fortune*; Allison Anna Tait, "The Beginning of the End of Coverture: A Reappraisal of the Married Woman's Separate Estate," *Yale Journal of Law and Feminism* 26 (2014): 166–216, https://openyls.law.yale.edu/server/api/core/bitstreams/4a6a146a-b587-4dcc-8065-8e876597c695/content.
25. Sara Horrell and Jane Humphries, "The Origins and Expansion of the Male Breadwinner Family," in *The Rise and Decline of the Male Breadwinner Family?*, ed. Angelique Janssens, *International Review of Social History*, Supplement 5 (Press Syndicate of the University of Cambridge, 1998), 25–64; Merry Wiesner-Hanks, *Women and Gender.*
26. Jeanne Boydston, "To Earn Her Daily Bread: Housework and Antebellum Working-Class Subsistence," *Radical History Review* 35 (1986); Joanna Bourke, "Housewifery in Working-Class England, 1860–1914," *Past and Present* 143 (1994).

27. Ingrid H. Tague, *Women of Quality: Accepting and Contesting Ideals of Femininity in England, 1690–1760* (Boydell Press, 2002), 44; Ulrich, *Good Wives*, 115–17.
28. For more on the lofty rhetoric about American wives and mothers, see Nancy Cott, *The Bonds of Womanhood: "Women's Sphere" in New England, 1780–1835* (Yale University Press, 1977); Mary Ryan, *Cradle of the Middle Class: The Family in Oneida County, New York, 1790–1865* (Cambridge University Press, 1983); and Mary Ryan, *The Empire of the Mother: American Writing About Domesticity, 1830–1860* (Routledge, 1985). The quote about the power of wives is from Sophia Hawthorne, wife of the novelist Nathaniel Hawthorne, cited in T. Walter Herbert, *Dearest Beloved: The Hawthornes and the Making of the Middle-Class Family* (University of California Press, 1993), 14.
29. Jan Lewis, "'Those Scenes for Which Alone My Heart Was Made': Affection and Politics in the Age of Jefferson and Hamilton," in *An Emotional History of the United States*, eds. Peter N. Stearns and Jan Lewis (New York University Press, 1998).
30. Arthur Cole, "The Tempo of Mercantile Life in Colonial America," *Business History Review* 33, no. 3 (1959): 277–99.
31. John Tosh, "Masculinities in an Industrializing Society: Britain, 1800–1914," *Journal of British Studies* 44, no. 2 (2005). For these and similar quotes from that era, see Cott, *The Bonds of Womanhood*, 67–68; Kirk Jeffrey, "The Family as Utopian Retreat from the City: The Nineteenth-Century Contribution," *Soundings: An Interdisciplinary Journal* 55, no. 1 (1972).
32. Cott, *Bonds of Womanhood*, 64; John Tosh, *A Man's Place: Masculinity and the Middle-Class Home in Victorian England* (Yale University Press, 1999), 33.
33. Catherine E. Kelly, *In the New England Fashion: Reshaping Women's Lives in the Nineteenth Century* (Cornell University Press, 1999), 40, 47. For more on the cult of "passionlessness," see Cott, *Bonds of Womanhood*. On how Black women at times utilized and at times critiqued the concept, see Darlene Clark Hine, "Rape and the Inner Lives of Black Women in the Middle West," *Signs* 14, no. 4 (1989); Evelyn Brooks Higginbotham, *Righteous Discontent: The Women's Movement in the Black Baptist Church, 1880–1920* (Harvard University Press, 1994); and April R. Haynes, *Riotous Flesh: Women, Physiology, and the Solitary Vice in Nineteenth-Century America* (University of Chicago Press, 2015).
34. Jeanne Boydston, *Home and Work: Housework, Wages, and the Ideology of Labor in the Early Republic* (Oxford University Press, 1990), 152–53.
35. G. R. Searle, *Morality and the Market in Victorian Britain* (Clarendon Press, 1998), 156.
36. Boydston, *Home and Work*, 148–52; Francesca Cancian and Stacey Oliker, *Caring and Gender* (Pine Forge Press, 2000), 24. Grant is quoted in E. Anthony Rotundo, *American Manhood: Transformations in Masculinity from the*

Revolution to the Modern Era (Basic Books, 1993), 107. The final quote is from John Tosh, *A Man's Place*, 56.

37. Richard Godbeer, *The Overflowing of Friendship: Love Between Men and the Creation of the American Republic* (Johns Hopkins University Press, 2009). See also John Gilbert McCurdy, *Citizen Bachelors: Manhood and the Creation of the United States* (Cornell University Press, 2009).
38. On how the Black abolitionist William Johnson and others popularized the more inclusive phrase "human rights," see Bennett Parten, "Not a Mere Rhetorical Flourish," *History News Network*, August 20, 2024, https://www.hnn.us/article/not-a-mere-rhetorical-flourish. On Black voting rights, see Van Gosse, *The First Reconstruction: Black Politics in America from the Revolution to the Civil War* (University of North Carolina Press, 2021). See also Paul Ortiz, *An African American and Latinx History of the United States* (Beacon Press, 2018), 18; Gillian Brockell, "More Than a Century Before the 19th Amendment, Women Were Voting in New Jersey," *Washington Post*, August 4, 2020, https://www.washingtonpost.com/graphics/2020/local/history/new-jersey-women-vote-1776-suffrage/.
39. For the scornful quote about "indiscriminate" voting, see Rosemarie Zagarri, *Revolutionary Backlash: Women and Politics in the Early American Republic* (University of Pennsylvania Press, 2007), 33.
40. Quoted in Catherine Hall, *Lucky Valley: Edward Long and the History of Racial Capitalism* (Cambridge University Press, 2024). My first discussion of how democracy spurred racist biological excuses for inequality appeared in my 1988 book, *The Social Origins of Private Life*. I owe a huge debt to historians such as Duncan MacLeod, George Fredrickson, Gordon Wood, Willie Lee Rose, and other authors I cite on pages 158–59 of that book. For a more recent version of my arguments, see "American History Is a Parade of Horrors—and Also Heroes," *Los Angeles Times*, August 14, 2022, https://www.latimes.com/opinion/story/2022-08-14/stephanie-coontz-slavery-shame-american-history-abolition.

    In recent years, debates over whether the heritage of the American Revolution is an honorable one of democracy and human rights or a shameful one of racial oppression and settler colonialism have become ever more heated. Both things can be true. The ideals revolutionary leaders espoused did indeed bequeath us a great legacy of egalitarian thought and inspired an unprecedented and courageous cross-racial abolition movement. But the cognitive dissonance created by founders' failure to act on those ideals led many people to rationalize their support for slavery and attacks on Indigenous Americans with a racist ideology that left an equally powerful and extremely destructive legacy. Interestingly, the vice president of the Confederacy offered a similar analysis to mine, though one informed by very different values, in his "Cornerstone Address" of March 21, 1861, defending the need for secession. On the one hand, he admitted what one-sided admirers of America's founders generally deny—that the Constitution "secured every essential guarantee" of slavery. But he also recognized what one-sided critics of Enlightenment thinkers often fail to see—that their embrace of equality as an ideal had convinced growing numbers of people to see slavery as "evil," a "violation of the laws of nature." Secession for the United States, he argued, was the only way to perpetually defend the "great truth" that inequality, not equality, was a "law of nature" and "slavery—subordination to the superior race—[the] natural and normal condition" of Black men and women: https://www.ucl.ac.uk/USHistory/Building/docs/Cornerstone.htm. Recent books on the contradictory legacy of the American Revolution include: Eric Foner, *Our Fragile Freedoms: Essays* (W. W. Norton & Company, 2025); Joseph Ellis, *The Great Contradiction: The Tragic Side of the American Founding* (Knopf, 2025); and Jill Lepore, *These Truths: A History of the United States* (W. W. Norton & Company, 2018), plus her *We the People: A History of the U.S. Constitution* (Liveright, 2025). See also the following pioneering works on this topic, including Nell Irvin Painter, *The History of White People* (W. W. Norton & Company, 2010); Karen E. Fields and Barbara J. Fields, *Racecraft: The Soul of Inequality in American Life* (Verso, 2014); and Jacqueline Jones, *A Dreadful Deceit: The Myth of Race from the Colonial Era to Obama's America* (Basic Books, 2013). On how the concepts of race and "heathenness" were used in different ways, but also reinforced each other, see Kathryn Gin Lum, *Heathen: Religion and Race in American History* (Harvard University Press, 2022). On the economics, politics, and rationalizations of Native American dispossession, see Claudio Saunt, *Unworthy Republic: The Dispossession of Native Americans and the Road to Indian Territory* (W. W. Norton & Company, 2020); Jeffrey Ostler, *Surviving Genocide: Native Nations and the United States from the American Revolution to Bleeding Kansas* (Yale University Press, 2019); and Ned Blackhawk, *The Rediscovery of America: Native Peoples and the Unmaking of U.S. History* (Yale University Press, 2023). For a recent moving account of how Black families coped with the oppression of slavery and racism, including their experience after emancipation, see Brenda E. Stevenson, *What Sorrows Labour in My Parent's Breast? A History of the Enslaved Black Family* (Rowman & Littlefield, 2023).

41. On the claims that "Dame Nature," not mere men, imposed inequality on women, see Zagarri, *Revolutionary Backlash*, chapter 5, and Coontz, *The Social Origins of Private Life*, 133–56.
42. See the description of this notion in Matthew D. Hammond and Andrei Cimpian, "'Wonderful but Weak': Children's Ambivalent Attitudes Toward Women," *Sex Roles* 84, no. 7 (2021): 76–90.
43. Zagarri, *Revolutionary Backlash*, 177.

44. Zagarri, *Revolutionary Backlash*, 177. For more on the class and race double standards referred to in the next paragraph, see John D'Emilio and Estelle B. Freedman, *Intimate Matters: A History of Sexuality in America* (Harper and Row, 1988).
45. Stannard, *Mrs Man*, 20.
46. John Stuart Mill, "Early Essays on Marriage and Divorce (1832)," in *Essays on Sex Equality*, ed. Alice S. Rossi (University of Chicago Press, 1970), 65–88, https://englishiva1011.pbworks.com/f/MARRDIVR.PDF; Stannard, *Mrs Man*, 10.
47. The information in this and the previous paragraph are from Stannard, *Mrs Man*, 11 and 17. On President Tyler's widow, Julia Gardiner, signing her letters "Mrs. Ex President Tyler, see "Our White House," National Children's Book and Literary Alliance, 2025, entry on Julia Gardiner, https://ourwhitehouse.org/julia-gardiner-tyler/.

Chapter 3: How the Gender Legacy of Democracy Holds Women Back

1. Richard Fox and Jennifer Lawless, "The Invincible Gender Gap in Political Ambition," *PS: Political Science & Politics* 57, no. 2 (2024), https://www.cambridge.org/core/journals/ps-political-science-and-politics/article/invincible-gender-gap-in-political-ambition/547D8E289D82299856644844269E2FC9#r11.
2. Gijsbert Stoet and David C. Geary, "The Gender-Equality Paradox in Science, Technology, Engineering, and Mathematics Education," *Psychological Science* 29, no. 4 (2018), https://doi.org/10.1177/0956797617741719. See also Maria Charles and Karen Bradley, "Equal but Separate? A Cross-National Study of Sex Segregation in Higher Education," *American Sociological Review* 67, no.4 (2002), https://doi.org/10.2307/3088946; Maria Charles and David B. Grusky, *Occupational Ghettos: The Worldwide Segregation of Women and Men* (Stanford University Press, 2005).
3. Christina Hoff Sommers, "The Myth of the Gender Wage Gap," Prager University, https://assets.ctfassets.net/qnesrjodfi80/2lC4ZMGBBaaAO8U26IOIc6/7c7b0d9c794405a39d8705ce2808e0c1/sommers-the_myth_of_the_gender_wage_gap-transcript.pdf; and "The Gender Wage Gap Myth," American Enterprise Institute, February 3, 2014, https://www.aei.org/articles/the-gender-wage-gap-myth/. See also Erin Cech, "The Self-Expressive Edge of Occupational Sex Segregation," *American Journal of Sociology* 119, no. 3 (2013), https://www.journals.uchicago.edu/doi/abs/10.1086/673969.
4. Erik Mac Giolla and Petri J. Kajonius, "Sex Differences in Personality Are Larger in Gender Equal Countries," *International Journal of Psychology* 54 (2019), https://pubmed.ncbi.nlm.nih.gov/30206941/; Thomas Breda et al., "Gender Stereotypes Can Explain the Gender-Equality Paradox," *Proceedings*

of the National Academy of Sciences 117, no. 49 (2020): 31063–69, https://doi.org/10.1073/pnas.2008704117.

5. Jong-Eun Roselyn Lee et al., "Does the Mask Govern the Mind?: Effects of Arbitrary Gender Representation on Quantitative Task Performance in Avatar-Represented Virtual Groups," *Cyberpsychology, Behavior, and Social Networking* 17, no. 4 (2014), https://doi.org/10.1089/cyber.2013.0358. See also Felix Chang et al., "Stereotype Threat in Virtual Learning Environments: Effects of Avatar Gender and Sexist Behavior on Women's Math Learning Outcomes," *Cyberpsychology, Behavior, and Social Networking* 22, no. 10 (2019), https://doi.org/10.1089/cyber.2019.0106.
6. This and the following experiment are cited in Daniel Gilbert, *Stumbling on Happiness* (Vintage Books, 2006), 228–29. For similar examples of how cultural and even political stereotypes can influence how we interpret our feelings, see Gilbert, *Stumbling on Happiness*, 229–32.
7. Rachel Connor et al., "Ambivalent Sexism in the Twenty-First Century," in *The Cambridge Handbook of the Psychology of Prejudice*, eds. Chris Sibley and Fiona Barlow (Cambridge University Press, 2017); Peter Glick and Susan Fiske, "An Ambivalent Alliance: Hostile and Benevolent Sexism as Complementary Justifications for Gender Inequality," *American Psychologist* 56, no. 2 (2001), https://doi.org/10.1037/0003-066X.56.2.109.
8. Nurit Shnabel et al., "Help to Perpetuate Traditional Gender Roles: Benevolent Sexism Increases Engagement in Dependency-Oriented Cross-Gender Helping," *Journal of Personality and Social Psychology* 110, no. 1 (2016): 55, https://doi.org/10.1037/pspi0000037.
9. Kristen Jones et al., "Negative Consequence of Benevolent Sexism on Efficacy and Performance," *Gender in Management: An International Journal* 29, no. 3 (2014): 171–89, https://doi.org/10.1108/GM-07-2013-0086; M. Dumont et al., "Be Too Kind to a Woman, She'll Feel Incompetent: Benevolent Sexism Shifts Self-Construal and Autobiographical Memories Toward Incompetence," *Sex Roles* 62 (2010): 545–53, https://doi.org/10.1007/s11199-008-9582-4.
10. On the 1973 polls, see Alice Eagly et al., "Gender Stereotypes Have Changed: A Cross-Temporal Meta-Analysis of US Public Opinion Polls from 1946 to 2018," *American Psychologist* 75, no. 3 (2020), https://doi.org/10.1037/amp0000494. On women being less suited for politics, see Tom Smith et al., *General Social Surveys, 1972–2018*, gssdataexplorer.norc.org. Thanks to Joanna Pepin, University of Toronto, for summarizing the NORC findings for me.
11. Eagly et al., "Gender Stereotypes Have Changed." See also Deborah Prentice and Erica Carranza, "What Women and Men Should Be, Shouldn't Be, Are Allowed to Be, and Don't Have to Be: The Contents of Prescriptive Gender Stereotypes," *Psychology of Women Quarterly* 26, no. 4 (2002): 269–81, https://doi.org/10.1111/1471-6402.t01-1-00066.

12. Eagly et al., "Gender Stereotypes Have Changed," 6. On the tendency of patriarchal cultures to see men as more self-sacrificing than women, see Jane Collier, "Victorian Visions," in *Gender Matters: Rereading Michelle Z. Rosaldo*, eds. Alejandro Lugo and Bill Maurer (University of Michigan Press, 2000), 157.
13. As I show in chapter 4, it was only in the second half of the nineteenth century that attaining manhood began to be defined by the rejection of feminine traits rather than the rejection of childish ones. For more on the dilemmas of masculine identity, see my interview with Meagan Day, "The Trump-Era Gender Wars, Brought to You by Neoliberalism," *Jacobin*, August 15, 2025, https://jacobin.com/2025/08/gender-roles-sexism-jobs-class.
14. Eagly et al., "Gender Stereotypes Have Changed"; Janet Spence and Camille Buckner, "Instrumental and Expressive Traits, Trait Stereotypes, and Sexist Attitudes," *Psychology of Women Quarterly* 24, no. 1 (2000): 44–62, https://doi.org/10.1111/j.1471-6402.2000.tb01021.x.
15. Jill E. Yavorsky, "Uneven Patterns of Inequality: An Audit Analysis of Hiring-Related Practices by Gendered and Classed Contexts," *Social Forces* 98, no. 2 (2019), https://www.jstor.org/stable/26862400; Catalyst, "Women in Management: Quick Take," August 11, 2020, https://web.archive.org/web/20200812131714/https://www.catalyst.org/research/women-in-management/.
16. For more on race and ethnic differences see Robert Livingston et al., "Can an Agentic Black Woman Get Ahead? The Impact of Race and Interpersonal Dominance on Perceptions of Female Leaders," *Psychological Science* 23, no. 4 (2012), https://doi.org/10.1177/0956797611428079; Ashleigh Rosette and Robert Livingston, "Failure Is Not an Option for Black Women: Effects of Organizational Performance on Leaders with Single Versus Dual-Subordinate Identities," *Journal of Experimental Social Psychology* 48, no. 5 (2012), https://doi.org/10.1016/j.jesp.2012.05.002; Kieran Snyder and Aileen Lee, "No More 'Abrasive,' 'Opinionated,' or 'Nice': Why Managers Need to Stop Giving Women and People of Color Feedback on Their Personality," *Fortune*, June 15, 2022, https://fortune.com/2022/06/15/performance-reviews-bias-gender-race-language-textio-kieran-snyder-aileen-lee/; Kieran Snyder, "The Abrasiveness Trap: High-Achieving Men and Women Are Described Differently in Reviews," *Fortune*, August 26, 2014, https://fortune.com/2014/08/26/performance-review-gender-bias/; Shelley Correll, "Reducing Gender Biases in Modern Workplaces: A Small Wins Approach to Organizational Change," *Gender & Society* 31, no. 6 (2017), https://www.gsb.stanford.edu/faculty-research/publications/reducing-gender-biases-modern-workplaces-small-wins-approach; Alice Eagly, "Once More: The Rise of Female Leaders," American Psychological Association, September 8, 2020, https://www.apa.org/research/action/female-leaders; Joan Williams et al., "Double Jeopardy?

Gender Bias Against Women of Color in Science," WorkLife Law, 2014, https://www.worklifelaw.org/publications/Double-Jeopardy-Report_v6_full_web-sm.pdf.

17. Laurie Rudman and Peter Glick, "Feminized Management and Backlash Toward Agentic Women: The Hidden Costs to Women of a Kinder, Gentler Image of Middle Managers," *Journal of Personality and Social Psychology* 77, no. 5 (1999): 1004–10, https://doi.org/10.1037/0022-3514.77.5.1004.
18. This shift occurred among White and nonwhite children alike, and independently of parental education or income. See Lin Bian et al., "Gender Stereotypes About Intellectual Ability Emerge Early and Influence Children's Interests," *Science* 355, no. 6323 (2017): 389–91, https://www.science.org/doi/10.1126/science.aah6524. My thanks to Lin Bian and Andrei Cimpian for discussing their findings with me: personal communication, May 17, 2021.
19. Tresa Undem and Ann Wang, "The State of Gender Equality for US Adolescents," Plan International, 2018 https://www.planusa.org/docs/state-of-gender-equality-summary-2018.pdf; Barbara Risman and Elizabeth Seale, "Betwixt and Be Tween: Gender Contradictions Among Middle Schoolers," in *Families as They Really Are*, ed. Barbara Risman (W. W. Norton & Company, 2010).
20. For more on the emotional and cognitive tasks of relationship management, and how they fall unequally on women, see Nicky James, "Emotional Labour: Skill and Work in the Social Regulation of Feelings," *Sociological Review* 37, no. 1 (1989), https://doi.org/10.1111/j.1467-954X.1989.tb00019.x; Allison Daminger, "The Cognitive Dimension of Household Labor," *American Sociological Review* 84, no. 4 (2019): 609–33, https://doi.org/10.1177/000312241985900; Jean Duncombe and Dennis Marsden, "Love and Intimacy: The Gender Division of Emotion and 'Emotion Work': A Neglected Aspect of Sociological Discussion of Heterosexual Relationships," *Sociology* 27, no. 2 (1993), https://doi.org/10.1177/0038038593027002003. On the different ways these tasks are divided in male-female, female-female, and male-male relationships, and the consequences of that for relationship satisfaction, see Michael Garcia and Debra Umberson, "Marital Strain and Psychological Distress in Same-Sex and Different-Sex Couples," *Journal of Marriage and Family* 81, no. 5 (2019), https://onlinelibrary.wiley.com/doi/abs/10.1111/jomf.12582; Debra Umberson et al., "Intimacy and Emotion Work in Lesbian, Gay, and Heterosexual Relationships," *Journal of Marriage and Family* 77, no. 2 (2015), https://doi.org/10.1111/jomf.12178; Yiwen Wang and Debra Umberson, "Dyadic Coping and Marital Quality in Same-Sex and Different-Sex Marriages," *Journal of Social and Personal Relationships* 40, no. 3 (2023), https://doi.org/10.1177/02654075221123096; Stephanie Coontz, "How to Make Your Marriage Gayer," *New York Times*, February 13, 2020, https://www.nytimes.com/2020/02/13/opinion/sunday/marriage-housework-gender-happiness.html.

As Missouri State University sociologist Alicia Walker points out, "Many men don't realize how much relational management their partner handles until it's pointed out. Men typically don't recognize relational management as work. They simply see it as something a woman does when she cares about you." Alicia M. Walker, "The Silent Labor of Love: How Women Become Relational Managers in Marriage," *Society Pages*, May 13, 2025, https://thesocietypages.org/ccf/2025/05/13/the-silent-labor-of-love-how-women-become-relational-managers-in-marriage/.

Chapter 4: Separate Spheres, Soulmate Love & Sexual Tension

1. Marist Poll, "2/10: 'It's Destiny!' Most Americans Believe in Soul Mates," Marist College, February 10, 2011, https://maristpoll.marist.edu/polls/210-its-destiny-most-americans-believe-in-soul-mates/; Jamie Ballard, "Do Americans Believe in the Idea of Soulmates?," YouGov, February 10, 2021, https://today.yougov.com/topics/society/articles-reports/2021/02/10/soulmates-poll-survey-data; Peter Moore, "America the Romantic: Most Believe in Love at First Sight," YouGov, April 3, 2015, https://today.yougov.com/topics/society/articles-reports/2015/04/03/america-romantic-most-believe-love-first-sight; Darren K. Carlson, "Over Half of Americans Believe in Love at First Sight," Gallup, February 14, 2001, https://news.gallup.com/poll/2017/over-half-americans-believe-love-first-sight.aspx.

   For a vivid illustration of the increase, see "Soul Mate," Google Books Ngram Viewer, https://books.google.com/ngrams/graph?content=soul+mate&year_start=1800&year_end=2008&corpus=15&smoothing=3&direct_url=t1%3B%2Csoul%20mate%3B%2Cc0#t1%3B%2Csoul%20mate%3B%2Cc1.
2. For more on this and other myths about what makes relationships work, see Eli Finkel et al., "Online Dating: A Critical Analysis from the Perspective of Psychological Science," *Psychological Science in the Public Interest* 13, no. 1 (2012), especially pages 50–51 on soulmates, https://doi.org/10.1177/1529100612436522; and Gil Freedman et al., "Ghosting and Destiny: Implicit Theories of Relationships Predict Beliefs About Ghosting," *Journal of Social and Personal Relationships* 36, no. 3 (2019), https://doi.org/10.1177/0265407517748791.
3. Quoted in Elaine Hatfield and Richard L. Rapson, *Love & Sex: Cross-Cultural Perspectives* (Allyn & Bacon, 1996), 44. See also chapter 1 of Stephanie Coontz, *Marriage, a History* (Viking, 2005).
4. This understanding of marital harmony was much like what was until recently the norm in many countries around the world, where members of the older generation still describe a good marriage as one based on mutual consideration and respect for each other's performance of their particular gender obligations, in contrast to the younger generation's emphasis on intimacy and shared leisure activities. For examples, see Jennifer Hirsch, "'Love Makes a Family': Globalization, Companionate Marriage, and the Modernization of

Gender Inequality"; and L. A. Rebbun, "The Strange Marriage of Love and Interest: Economic Change and Emotional Intimacy in Northeast Brazil, Private and Public," in *Love and Globalization: Transformations of Intimacy in the Contemporary World*, eds. Mark Padilla et al. (Vanderbilt University Press, 2007).

5. Quoted in Francesca Beauman, *Matrimony, Inc.* (Pegasus Books, 2020), 5.
6. Hannah Webster Foster, *The Coquette; Or, The History of Eliza Wharton; A Novel; Founded on Fact* (1797), published online at https://digital.library.upenn.edu/women/foster/coquette/coquette.html.
7. Charlotte was supposedly buried at Trinity Church near Wall Street but excavations at the church have provided no evidence for the claim that this was a true story. See "The Mystery of Charlotte Temple," Trinity Church, December 16, 2008, https://trinitywallstreet.org/stories-news/mystery-charlotte-temple.
8. Clare Lyons, *Sex Among the Rabble: An Intimate History of Gender & Power in the Age of Revolution, Philadelphia, 1730–1830* (University of North Carolina Press, 2012), 189; Richard Godbeer, *Sexual Revolution in Early America* (Johns Hopkins University Press, 2002), 265.
9. T. S. Arthur, *Advice to Young Men on Their Duties and Conduct in Life* (Phillips, Sampson & Company, 1850), 169, https://d.lib.msu.edu/ssb/1.
10. Nathan Hale, *Freud and the Americans: The Beginnings of Psychoanalysis in the United States, 1876–1917* (Oxford University Press, 1971), 46.
11. John Ruskin, "Lecture II. Lilies. Of Queens' Gardens," *Sesame and Lilies*, The Project Gutenberg eBook, transcribed from the 1894 George Allen edition by David Price, https://www.gutenberg.org/files/1293/1293-h/1293-h.htm.
12. E. Anthony Rotundo, *American Manhood: Transformations in Masculinity from the Revolution to the Modern Era* (Basic Books, 1991), 158; O. S. Fowler, *Love and Parentage: Applied to the Improvement of Offspring, Including Important Directions and Suggestions to Lovers and the Married Concerning the Strongest Ties and the Most Momentous Relations of Life* (Fowlers and Wells, 1851). First published in 1844, this was its thirteenth edition.
13. For examples of the similarities in men's and women's idealization of love, family life, and domesticity, see Laura McCall, "'Not So Wild a Dream': The Domestic Fantasies of Literary Men and Women, 1820–1860"; and Donald Yacovone, "'Surpassing the Love of Women': Victorian Manhood and the Language of Fraternal Love," in *A Shared Experience: Men, Women, and the History of Gender*, eds. Laura McCall and Donald Yacovone (New York University Press, 1998).
14. Unless otherwise noted, the quotes in this and the following paragraphs can be found in Ellen Rothman, *Hands and Hearts: A History of Courtship in America* (Basic Books, 1984); and Karen Lystra, *Searching the Heart: Women, Men, and Romantic Love in Nineteenth-Century America* (Oxford University

Press, 1989). See also Peter N. Stearns, *American Cool: Constructing a Twentieth-Century Emotional Style* (New York University Press, 1994), 80.

15. Karen Lystra, *Love and the Working Class: The Inner Worlds of Nineteenth Century Americans* (Oxford University Press, 2024), 94.
16. Lucia McMahon, *Mere Equals: The Paradox of Educated Women in the Early American Republic* (Cornell University Press, 2012), 101; Lystra, *Searching the Heart*, 190; Rothman, *Hands and Hearts*, 107–10.
17. Lystra, *Searching the Heart*, 22–23, 45, 50.
18. Peter N. Stearns and Mark Knapp, "Men and Romantic Love: Pinpointing a 20th-Century Change," *Journal of Social History* 24, no. 4 (1993): 769–95, https://doi.org/10.1353/jsh/26.4.769.
19. Historian Helen Lefkowitz Horowitz argues that there were four distinct sexual cultures in nineteenth-century America, rather than one overarching "Victorian" one, in *Rereading Sex: Battles over Sexual Knowledge and Suppression in Nineteenth-Century America* (Knopf, 2002). For a lively description of several alternative sexual subcultures and ideas in that era, see Rebecca Davis, *Fierce Desires: A New History of Sex and Sexuality in America* (W. W. Norton & Company, 2024). See also Joanne Passet, *Sex Radicals and the Quest for Women's Equality* (University of Illinois Press, 2003); Carol Faulkner, *Unfaithful: Love, Adultery, and Marriage Reform in Nineteenth-Century America* (University of Pennsylvania Press, 2019); John D'Emilio and Estelle B. Freedman, "Since Intimate Matters: Recent Developments in the History of Sexuality in the United States," *Journal of Women's History* 25, no. 4 (2013), https://dx.doi.org/10.1353/jowh.2013.0044; Regina Kunzel, "The Power of Queer History," *American Historical Review* 123, no. 5 (2018), https://doi.org/10.1093/ahr/rhy202.
20. Katherine Hijar, "Brothels for Gentlemen: Nineteenth-Century American Brothel Guides, Gentility, and Moral Reform," *Common Place: The Journal of Early American Life*, 18.1 (2018), https://commonplace.online/article/brothels-for-gentlemen/. See also Sean Wilentz, *Chants Democratic: New York City and the Rise of the American Working Class, 1788–1850* (Oxford University Press, 1984).
21. Rebecca Edwards, *New Spirits: Americans in the Gilded Age, 1865–1905* (Oxford University Press, 2006), 132–33. For a longer discussion of the sexual exploitation of Native American, Mexican, Chinese, and Black women during this era, reflecting the race and ethnic double standard held even by many men who accepted a single standard of moral behavior toward women of their own race and class, see John D'Emilio and Estelle Freedman, *Intimate Matters: A History of Sexuality in America* (Harper & Row, 1988), 84–108.
22. Cott, *Bonds of Womanhood*, 72; Herbert, *Dearest Beloved*, 74–75; Lystra, *Searching the Heart*, 235; Kelly, *New England Fashion*, 126; Tague, *Women of Quality*, 40.

23. Cott, *Bonds of Womanhood*, 77. See also Martha Tomhave Blauvelt, *The Work of the Heart: Young Women and Emotion 1780–1830* (University of Virginia Press, 2007).
24. Many of the quotes about sexuality in the following paragraphs come from notes I have taken over the years on more than two dozen marriage and medical manuals that were widely circulated in America between the 1830s and the 1890s. For more easily accessible selections, along with an insightful analysis of their real-life significance, see "Part One" of Steven Seidman, *Romantic Longings: Love in America, 1830–1980*; along with Anita Clair Fellman and Michael Fellman, *Making Sense of Self: Medical Advice Literature in Late Nineteenth-Century America* (University of Pennsylvania Press, 1981); and Hale, *Freud and the Americans*, 33–46. John S. Haller Jr. and Robin M. Haller, *The Physician and Sexuality in Victorian America* (University of Illinois Press, 1974) is also an excellent source, although I believe that what they describe as an increasingly strident insistence on female "passionlessness" after the 1870s reflected a conservative backlash as evidence to the contrary mounted. Primary sources I quote from include William Acton, *The Functions and Disorders of the Reproductive Organs* (1857; repr., Creative Media Partners, 2015); William Alcott, *The Young Wife, Or Duties of Woman the Marriage Relation* (George W. Light, 1837; repr., Arno Press, 1972); James Ashton, *The Book of Nature: Containing Information for Young People Who Think of Getting Married . . .* (Wallis and Ashton, 1861); John Cowan, *The Science of a New Life* (Fowler & Wells, 1869); O. S. Fowler, *Private Lectures on Perfect Men, Women and Children, in Happy Families* (E. W. Austin, 1880); Henry Guernsey, *Plain Talks on Avoided Subjects* (F. A. Davis, 1882); William Jay, *Thoughts on Marriage* (James Loring, 1833); John Harvey Kellogg, *Ladies' Guide in Health and Disease* (W. D. Condit, 1884), and *Plain Facts for Old and Young* (Segner and Condit, 1881); Robert Dale Owen, *Moral Philosophy* (1830); Alice B. Stockham, *Tokology: A Book for Every Woman*, rev. ed. (Sanitary Publishing Co., 1887); R. T. Trall, *Sexual Physiology. A Scientific and Popular Exposition of the Fundamental Problems in Sociology* (Miller, Wood & Co., 1866). For a witty (though one-sided, as the author admits) compendium of some of the most outlandish Victorian gender and sexual beliefs, see Therese Oneill, *Unmentionable: The Victorian Lady's Guide to Sex, Marriage, and Manners* (Little, Brown and Company, 2016).
25. D'Emilio and Freedman, *Intimate Matters*, 70–71; Seidman, *Romantic Longings*, 26–29.
26. Seidman, *Romantic Longings*, 18–19; see also Fellman and Fellman, *Making Sense of Self.*
27. For a balanced discussion of the difficulties facing women negotiating sexual relations with their husbands in this period, see Jesse Battan, "The 'Rights' of Husbands and the 'Duties' of Wives: Power and Desire in the

American Bedroom, 1850–1910," *Journal of Family History* 24 (1999), https://doi.org/10.1177/036319909902400203. For the complaint about lack of sex education, see Rufus Griswold, "Some Observations on the Physiology of Coitus from the Female Side of the Matter," *Clinical News* (1880); repr. in *The Medical Gazette: A Weekly Journal of Medicine, Surgery, and the Collateral Sciences*, vol. 7 (Bermingham & Company, 1880), 592.

28. Katherine Davis, *Factors in the Sex Life of Twenty-Two Hundred Women* (Harper & Brothers, 1929; repr., Arno Press, 1972), 68–69, 155–64, 219, and chapter 12.
29. Judith Walzer Leavitt, "Under the Shadow of Maternity: American Women's Responses to Death and Debility Fears in Nineteenth-Century Childbirth," *Feminist Studies* 12, no. 1 (1986).
30. Michael R. Haines et al., "Early Fertility Decline in the United States: Tests of Alternative Hypotheses Using New County-Level and Individual-Level Census Data," Working Paper No. 2020-03 (Minnesota Population Center, University of Minnesota, May 2020), https://assets.ipums.org/_files/mpc/wp2020-03.pdf. For year-by-year figures, see "Total Fertility Rate in the United States from 1800 to 2020," Statistics, Statista, https://www.statista.com/statistics/1033027/fertility-rate-us-1800-2020/.
31. Molly Farrell, "Ben Franklin Put an Abortion Recipe in His Math Textbook," *Slate*, May 5, 2022, https://slate.com/news-and-politics/2022/05/ben-franklin-american-instructor-textbook-abortion-recipe.html; Mary Fissell, *Pushback: The 2,500-Year Fight to Thwart Women by Restricting Abortion* (Seal Press, 2025).
32. Excellent studies of birth control and abortion in nineteenth-century America include: James Mohr, *Abortion in America: The Origins and Evolution of National Policy, 1800–1900* (Oxford University Press, 1978); Linda Gordon, *Woman's Body, Woman's Right: A Social History of Birth Control in America* (Grossman, 1976), and *The Moral Property of Women: A History of Birth Control Politics in America* (University of Illinois Press, 2002); Leslie J. Reagan, *When Abortion Was a Crime: Women, Medicine, and Law in the United States, 1867–1973* (University of California Press, 1997); Andrea Tone, ed., *Controlling Reproduction: An American History* (Rowman & Littlefield, 1996), 100. See also Lauren MacIvor Thompson, "Held: Legal Authority and the Abuse of History," *Perspectives* 61, no. 4 (2023): 21, https://www.historians.org/wp-content/uploads/2024/07/Perspectives_61N4.pdf; and Joshua Zeitz, "The Supreme Court's Faux 'Originalism,'" *Politico*, June 26, 2022, https://www.politico.com/news/magazine/2022/06/26/conservative-supreme-court-gun-control-00042417.
33. Allison McCann and Amy Schoenfeld Walker, "Tracking Abortion Laws Across the Country," *New York Times*, accessed July 7, 2025, https://www.nytimes.com/interactive/2024/us/abortion-laws-roe-v-wade.html.

34. The Comstock Act has been modified by court decisions but never repealed. So in the wake of the Supreme Court's 2022 repeal of *Roe v. Wade*, twenty state attorneys general used this same act to threaten pharmacies with prosecution if they continued selling the "abortion pill," the combination of medications used to terminate an early pregnancy up to eleven weeks after the first day of a woman's last period.
35. For this and the following paragraph, see Amy Sohn, *The Man Who Hated Women: Sex, Censorship, and Civil Liberties in the Gilded Age* (Farrar, Straus, and Giroux, 2021); Amy Werbel, *Lust on Trial: Censorship and the Rise of American Obscenity in the Age of Anthony Comstock* (Columbia University Press, 2018); Nicholas Syrett, *The Trials of Madame Restell: Nineteenth-Century America's Most Infamous Female Physician and the Campaign to Make Abortion a Crime* (New Press, 2023); Reagan, *When Abortion Was a Crime*, especially 61–68.
36. C. W. Malchow, M.D., *The Sexual Life: A Scientific Treatise Designed for Advanced Students and the Professions*, 5th ed. (C. V. Mosby Company, 1921), 123; Ryan Hurt and Paul Nelson, "*The Sexual Life* by Charles W. Malchow," *Ramsey County History* 55, no. 3 (2020): 12–25, https://publishing.rchs.com/wp-content/uploads/2020/12/RCHS_Fall2020_HurtNelson.pdf.
37. Henry Seidel Canby, *The Age of Confidence: Life in the Nineties* (Farrar & Rinehart, Inc., 1934), 160.
38. Claudia Goldin, "The Quiet Revolution That Transformed Women's Employment, Education, and Family," *American Economic Review* 96, no. 2 (2006), https://www.aeaweb.org/articles?id=10.1257/000282806777212350; Patricia Albjerg Graham, "Expansion and Exclusion: A History of Women in American Higher Education," *Signs* 3, no. 4 (1978): 759–73, https://www.journals.uchicago.edu/doi/10.1086/493536.
39. Kim England and Kate Boyer, "Women's Work: The Feminization and Shifting Meanings of Clerical Work," *Journal of Social History* 43, no. 2 (2009), https://doi.org/10.1353/jsh.0.0284.
40. The classic account is Gail Bederman, *Manliness and Civilization: A Cultural History of Gender and Race in the United States, 1880–1917* (University of Chicago Press, 1995). For this and the following paragraphs, see also Arnaldo Testi, "The Gender of Reform Politics: Theodore Roosevelt and the Culture of Masculinity," *Journal of American History* 81, no. 4 (1995), https://doi.org/10.2307/2081647; Julia Grant, "A 'Real Boy' and Not a Sissy: Gender, Childhood, and Masculinity, 1890–1940," *Journal of Social History* 37, no. 4 (2004): 829–51, https://doi.org/10.1353/jsh.2004.0046; Richard Godbeer, *The Overflowing of Friendship: Love Between Men and the Creation of the American Republic* (Johns Hopkins University Press, 2009); Donald Yacovone, "Abolitionists and the 'Language of Fraternal Love'"; Clyde Griffen, "Reconstructing Masculinity from the Evangelical Revival to the Waning of Progressivism:

A Speculative Synthesis," in *Meanings for Manhood: Constructions of Masculinity in Victorian America*, eds. Mark Carnes and Clyde Griffen (University of Chicago Press, 1990); and Cassandra Good, *Founding Friendships: Friendships Between Men and Women in the Early American Republic* (Oxford University Press, 2015), 91. The new admiration for "masculine" physical strength and personal forcefulness was reflected in a "muscular Christianity" movement that emerged in mid-nineteenth-century England and soon spread among Protestants in America. Artistic portrayals of Jesus discarded the long flowing locks, meek countenance, and slender figure of traditional Christian iconography, making him look almost literally like the body builders who were increasingly admired in popular culture. See Rachel McBride Lindsey, "'The Mirror of All Perfection': Jesus and the Strongman in America, 1893–1920," *American Quarterly* 68, no. 1 (2016), https://doi.org/10.1353/aq.2016.0005.

41. There is nothing wrong with enjoying genre novels. Because such novels have predictable themes and endings, readers can count on them to resolve emotional tensions or satisfy particular fantasies. My personal comfort fiction is the private detective novel with a heroine who pursues justice, solves mysteries, defends herself without needing male protection, and has a healthy love life but anchors her identity in her work more than her love. Readers of romance novels may be more interested in seeing passion and ambiguity reconciled with intimacy and safety. For a variety of perspectives on the needs that romance novels meet, see Tania Modleski, *Loving with a Vengeance: Mass-Produced Fantasies for Women*, 2nd ed. (Routledge, 2008); Janice Radway, *Reading the Romance: Women, Patriarchy, and Popular Literature*, 2nd ed. (University of North Carolina Press, 1991); and Eva Illouz, *Hard-Core Romance: Fifty Shades of Grey, Best-Sellers, and Society* (University of Chicago Press, 2014). It's important to note that romance novels have diversified in the past forty years. The females are less passive than in the past. Female *Star Trek* fans, many of them heterosexual, pioneered "slash fiction," writing stories about sexuality and love between Captain Kirk and Mr. Spock. Some writers emphasize sex-positive Christian values; others describe bondage, sadism, and masochism. All treat women's sexual awakenings as positive. Unlike the seduction novels of the late eighteenth and early nineteenth centuries, women who have sex before marriage generally end up happy instead of dead. For more on recent variations, see Alexandra Alter, "The Changing Face of Romance Novels," *New York Times*, July 7, 2018, https://www.nytimes.com/2018/07/07/books/romance-novels-diversity.html; and Jayashree Kamblé et al., eds., *The Routledge Research Companion to Popular Romance Fiction* (Routledge, 2020). My thanks to William Gleason, chair of the English Department at Princeton University, for pointing me to some of these recent sources. A documentary about the contemporary romance industry, *Love Between the Covers*, argues that readers feel empowered by these

books and points out that the immense popularity of the genre provides a lucrative and satisfying career for many female authors: *Love Between the Covers*, directed by Laurie Kahn (2015), https://www.lovebetweenthecovers.com. For a more critical reading, see Susan Ostrov Weisser, *The Glass Slipper: Women and Love Stories* (Rutgers University Press, 2013).

42. The noted Zambian and American author Namwali Serpell calls these the "hit me" books. As Serpell describes their plots, the female protagonist is modern and independent-minded enough to embrace feminism and other social liberation movements and to have experimented with same-sex desire. She has been getting by on her own but has not yet reached her financial or professional goals. She becomes involved with an older, powerful, usually wealthy man who supports her efforts but remains emotionally distant. Eventually the two engage in some type of mutually satisfying BDSM (Bondage, Discipline, Sadism, Masochism), sometimes at her initiation. He ends up falling so deeply in love that it evens out or actually reverses the earlier power relationship. As Serpell describes the ending, "Both choose to submit, she to dominance, he to romance." Full disclosure: I was only able to force myself to make it through one of these books. The generalizations about the genre appear in Namwali Serpell, "Hit Me, Baby," *New York Review of Books*, November 23, 2023, https://www.nybooks.com/articles/2023/11/23/hit-me-baby-namwali-serpell.
43. On the lack of such a separate female emotional culture in colonial America, see Nancy Cott, "Eighteenth-Century Family and Social Life Revealed in Massachusetts Divorce Records," in *A Heritage of Her Own: Toward a New Social History of American Women*, eds. Nancy Cott and Elizabeth Pleck (Simon & Schuster, 1979), 116 and note 36. On women's equation of love and caring with intimate emotional revelation, a counterpoint to the association of desire with male stoicism and inscrutability, see Francesca Cancian, *Love in America: Gender and Self-Development* (Cambridge University Press, 1987).

Chapter 5: From Spiritual Soulmates to Sexual Playmates

1. In an 1839 memoir about his travels in America (*A Diary in America V2*), the British Royal Navy officer Frederick Marryat recalled asking a young woman who had just stumbled whether she had hurt her leg. "She turned from me evidently much shocked, or much offended; and . . . I begged to know what was the reason of her displeasure. After some hesitation, she said . . . the word *leg* was never mentioned before ladies." And in an 1869 book, *Vulgarisms and Other Errors of Speech*, Pennsylvania author Richard Meade Bache informed readers that "many women in this country, in speaking of their sex's legs to persons of the other sex, call them distinctively *limbs*, and there drop the subject." For other examples, see Merriam-Webster, https://www.merriam-webster.com/words-at-play/do-you-say-leg-or-limb.

2. "Sex O'Clock in America," *Current Opinion* 55, no. 2 (1913), 113, https://archive.org/details/sim_current-opinion_1913-08_55_2/page/112/mode/2up; Agnes Repplier, "The Repeal of Reticence," *Atlantic*, March 1914, 298, https://cdn.theatlantic.com/media/archives/1914/03/113-3/132218193.pdf.
3. The poem is quoted in Rebecca Jo Plant, *Mom: The Transformation of Motherhood in Modern America* (University of Chicago Press, 2012), 92. For an extensive treatment of the sentimentalization of mother love in the nineteenth century, see May Ryan, *The Empire of the Mother: American Writing About Domesticity* (copublished by the Institute for Research in History and the Haworth Press, 1982).
4. Personal communication, March 23, 2023. For a critical examination of our contemporary resistance to "too close" parent-child relations, see Coleman's *Rules of Estrangement: Why Adult Children Cut Ties and How to Heal the Conflict* (Harmony, 2021).
5. For other examples of the idealization of intense mother-son love, see Plant, *Mom*, 89–92 and notes 14 and 15 on page 215.
6. E. Anthony Rotundo, "Romantic Friendship: Male Intimacy and Middle Class Youth in the Northern United States, 1800–1900," *Journal of Social History* 23, no. 1 (1989), https://doi.org/10.1353/jsh/23.1.1; Richard Godbeer, *The Overflowing of Friendship: Love Between Men and the Creation of the American Republic* (Johns Hopkins University Press, 2009); Carroll Smith-Rosenberg, *Disorderly Conduct: Visions of Gender in Victorian America* (Oxford University Press, 1985), 53–76; John D'Emilio and Estelle Freedman, *Intimate Matters: A History of Sexuality in America* (Harper & Row, 1988), 125–27.
7. W. A. Newman Dorland, *The American Illustrated Medical Dictionary* (W. B. Saunders & Co., 1902); *Funk & Wagnalls New Standard Dictionary of the English Language* (Funk & Wagnalls, 1913). Thanks to Janis Walworth, at the time director of the Center for Gender Sanity in Bellingham, Washington, for providing me with photos of these definitions of heterosexuality from her personal collection of old dictionaries back in the early 2000s. For more on this history, see Jonathan Ned Katz, *The Invention of Heterosexuality* (Plume, 1996); and Hanne Blank, *Straight: The Surprisingly Short History of Heterosexuality* (Beacon Press, 2012), 20.
8. The classic account of the rise of dating is Beth Bailey's aptly named *From Front Porch to Back Seat: Courtship in Twentieth-Century America* (Johns Hopkins University Press, 1988).
9. Automotive Training Centres, https://www.autotrainingcentre.com/blog/top-cars-decade-1910s; Dan Schlenoff, "The Reliable Motor Vehicle, 1916," *Scientific American*, January 1, 2016, https://www.scientificamerican.com/article/automobiles-the-reliable-motor-vehicle-1916-slide-show/.
10. Dix quoted in James R. McGovern, "The American Woman's Pre-World War I Freedom in Manners and Morals," *Journal of American History* 55, no. 2

(1968), 324, https://doi.org/10.2307/1899561; Alexander Black, "Is the Young Person Coming Back?," *Harper's Monthly Magazine* (August 1924), 342, https://harpers.org/archive/1924/08/is-the-young-person-coming-back/.

11. Coed quoted in Paula Fass, *The Damned and the Beautiful: American Youth in the 1920s* (Oxford University Press, 1977), 307. For more on petting parties, see Linton Weeks, "When 'Petting Parties' Scandalized the Nation," NPR History Department, May 26, 2015, https://www.npr.org/sections/npr-history-dept/2015/05/26/409126557/when-petting-parties-scandalized-the-nation.
12. Alan Mattay, "'Down with the Flapper': *The Defender*'s Anti-Flapper Campaign," UNLV Public History, November 5, 2016; Emily Sparks, "The 'Dangerous Chance of Being a Flapper': The Black Flapper's Challenge to Respectability in *The Chicago Defender*, 1920–1929" (master's thesis, Case Western Reserve University, 2018), http://rave.ohiolink.edu/etdc/view?acc_num=case1523038600884478. For pictures of Black flappers of the day, see https://kalamu.com/neogriot/2014/08/03/history-african-american-flappers-and-jazz-age-women/; Maria Montserrat Feu López, "The U.S. Hispanic Flapper: *Pelonas* and *Flapperismo* in U.S. Spanish-Language Newspapers, 1920–1929," *Studies in American Humor* 1, no. 2 (2015), 192–217; Vicki Ruiz, "The Flapper and the Chaperone," in Donna Gabaccia, ed., *Seeking Common Ground: Multidisciplinary Studies of Immigrant Women in the United States* (Greenwood Press, 1992); Judy Yung, "'It Is Hard to Be Born a Woman but Hopeless to Be Born a Chinese': The Life and Times of Flora Belle Jan," *Frontiers: A Journal of Women Studies* 18, no. 3 (1997); Fleur Yano and Saralyn Daly, *Unbound Spirit: Letters of Flora Belle Jan* (University of Illinois Press, 2009). For an in-depth biography of Anna May Wong, covering both her immersion in the "modern" sexual and gender norms of 1920s–1940s Hollywood and the racist discrimination she faced, see Yunte Huang, *Daughter of the Dragon: Anna May Wong's Rendezvous with American History* (Liveright, 2023). See also Anthony Chan, *Perpetually Cool: The Many Lives of Anna May Wong* (Scarecrow Press, 2003).
13. Repplier, "Repeal of Reticence," 298–99.
14. Erica Ryan, *Red War on the Family: Sex, Gender, and Americanism in the First Red Scare* (Temple University Press, 2015), 155–60.
15. For a review of some of the leading sex radicals of the period, see Christina Simmons, "Women's Power in Sex Radical Challenges to Marriage in the Early-Twentieth-Century United States," *Feminist Studies* 29, no. 1 (2003); and Nancy Cott, "Marriage Crisis and All That Jazz," in Kristin Celello and Hanan Kholoussy, eds., *Domestic Tensions, National Anxieties: Global Perspectives on Marriage, Crisis, and Nation* (Oxford University Press, 2016), 58. See also Coontz, *Marriage, a History*, 198, 202–4.
16. Sidney Howard, *The Silver Cord* (Samuel French, 1926), 90–91. *New York Times* critic Brooks Atkinson's rave review appeared in *The New York Times*

on December 21, 1926, https://timesmachine.nytimes.com/timesmachine/1926/12/21/118879176.pdf.

17. For this and the following paragraph, see Lillian Schlissel, *Three Plays by Mae West: Sex, The Drag, The Pleasure Man* (Routledge, 1997); Allison McNearney, "How Mae West's Play 'Sex' Scandalized Broadway—and Landed Her in Jail," *Daily Beast*, October 15, 2021, https://www.thedailybeast.com/how-mae-wests-play-sex-scandalized-broadwayand-landed-her-in-jail. See also Marybeth Hamilton, "Mae West Live: SEX, The Drag, and 1920s Broadway," *Drama Review* 36, no. 4 (1992), https://www.jstor.org/stable/1146217.
18. For more on the surprisingly widespread acceptance of gender nonconformance and the visibility of gay subcultures, see George Chauncey, *Gay New York: Gender, Urban Culture, and the Making of the Gay Male World, 1890–1940* (Basic Books, 2004); Sharon Ullman: *Sex Seen: The Emergence of Modern Sexuality in America* (University of California Press, 1997); Andrew L. Erdman, *Blue Vaudeville: Sex, Morals, and the Mass Marketing of Amusement, 1895–1915* (McFarland & Co., 2004); Chad Heap, *Slumming: Sexual and Racial Encounters in American Nightlife, 1885–1940* (University of Chicago Press, 2009); Sarah Pruitt, "How Gay Culture Blossomed During the Roaring Twenties," *History*, June 10, 2019, https://www.history.com/news/gay-culture-roaring-twenties-prohibition; Natalie Zarrelli, "In the Early 20th Century, America Was Awash in Incredible Queer Nightlife," *Atlas Obscura*, April 14, 2016, https://www.atlasobscura.com/articles/in-the-early-20th-century-america-was-awash-in-incredible-queer-nightlife.
19. "Anthony Comstock," in *The Concise Oxford Companion to American Literature*, https://www.oxfordreference.com/display/10.1093/oi/authority.20110803095630124.
20. For more details on the growing resistance to the Comstock Act, see Amy Werbel, *Lust on Trial: Censorship and the Rise of American Obscenity in the Age of Anthony Comstock* (Columbia University Press, 2018). On how the female sex radicals Comstock persecuted over the years helped build mass support for legalization of birth control and opposition to censorship, see Amy Sohn, *The Man Who Hated Women: Sex, Censorship, and Civil Liberties in the Gilded Age* (Farrar, Straus, and Giroux, 2021).
21. Quoted in Erica Ryan, *When the World Broke in Two: The Roaring Twenties and the Dawn of America's Culture Wars* (Praeger, 2018), 122. I am indebted to her work for several of the factoids and quotes in the following paragraphs.
22. For more on these parallels, see Adam Hochschild, *American Midnight: The Great War, a Violent Peace, and Democracy's Forgotten Crisis* (Mariner Books, 2022); and Nancy MacLean, *Behind the Mask of Chivalry: The Making of the Second Ku Klux Clan* (Oxford University Press, 1994, and thirtieth anniversary edition, 2024). The thirtieth anniversary edition includes a new preface also commenting on some of these parallels. For the Donald Trump campaign

quotes, see https://www.cnn.com/videos/politics/2015/06/28/donald-trump-mexico-immigration-wall-intv-tappersotu.cnn#:~:text=Trump:%20'Killers%20and%20rapists'%20are%20crossing%20the%20border%20%7C%20CNN%20Politics.

23. Ryan, *Red War on the Family* and *When the World Broke*; Linda Gordon, *The Second Coming of the KKK: The Ku Klux Klan of the 1920s and the American Political Tradition* (Liveright, 2017); Kathleen Blee, *Women of the Klan: Racism and Gender in the 1920s* (University of California Press, 1991), 85–86.
24. Henry Ford based his articles on a forgery that claimed to be "The Protocols of the Elders of Zion" and is still being cited by contemporary anti-Semites. For more on this, see Binjamin Segel, *A Lie and a Libel: The History of the Protocols of the Elders of Zion*, trans. and ed. Richard S. Levy (University of Nebraska Press, 1996); Svetlana Boym, "Conspiracy Theories and Literary Ethics: Umberto Eco, Danilo Kis and *The Protocols of Zion*," *Comparative Literature* 51, no. 2 (1999), https://doi.org/10.2307/1771244; and "Anti-Semitism: History of the 'Protocols of the Elders of Zion,'" Jewish Virtual Library, https://www.jewishvirtuallibrary.org/the-ldquo-protocols-of-the-elders-of-zion-rdquo.
25. Joe Schwarcz, "QAnon's Adrenochrome Quackery," *Pseudoscience*, McGill University Office for Science and Society, February 10, 2022, https://www.mcgill.ca/oss/article/pseudoscience/qanons-adrenochrome-quackery; Kevin Roose, "What Is QAnon, the Viral Pro-Trump Conspiracy Theory?," *New York Times*, September 3, 2021, https://www.nytimes.com/article/what-is-qanon.html. On the supposed Catholic plot, see Blee, *Women of the Klan*, 87.
26. Naisha Mercury and Valerie Ernat, "Restrictions on the Right to Travel for Out-of-State Abortion Care," The Network for Public Health Law, April 2025, https://www.networkforphl.org/wp-content/uploads/2025/05/Restrictions-on-the-Right-to-Travel-for-Out-of-State-Abortion-Care-1.pdf. As of April 2025, legislators in twelve states had even introduced bills that would allow authorities to prosecute abortion patients as murderers. At this writing, none had passed. But to keep up with all the current attacks on abortion and birth control, subscribe to Jessica Valenti's passionate and painstakingly researched newsletter, *Abortion, Every Day*, Substack, https://jessica.substack.com/.
27. Adam Laats, *Fundamentalism and Education in the Scopes Era: God, Darwin, and the Roots of America's Culture Wars* (Palgrave Macmillan, 2010), 3–4.
28. Mississippi House Bill 1193, https://legiscan.com/MS/text/HB1193/2025.
29. Julissa Cruz, "Marriage: More Than a Century of Change," National Center for Family & Marriage Research (2013), https://www.bgsu.edu/content/dam/BGSU/college-of-arts-and-sciences/NCFMR/documents/FP/FP-13-13.pdf.
30. Frederic Thompson explained his strategy in "Amusing the Million," *Everybody's Magazine*, 1908, reprinted in Louis Parascandola and John Parascan-

dola, eds., *A Coney Island Reader: Through Dizzy Gates of Illusion* (Columbia University Press, 2014), 103–8. For more on the mass amusement parks, see John Kasson, *Amusing the Million: Coney Island at the Turn of the Century* (Hill & Wang, 1979).

31. Floyd Dell, *Love in the Machine Age: A Psychological Study of the Transition from Patriarchal Society* (Farrar & Rinehart, 1930), 6–7, 117–82, 364.
32. For a lively description of the changing conventions of dating during this era, see Beth Bailey's classic *From Front Porch to Back Seat*.
33. For more on the scandal that ensued, followed by the rapid expansion of unmarried cohabitation, see Elizabeth Pleck, *Not Just Roommates: Cohabitation After the Sexual Revolution* (University of Chicago Press, 2012).
34. Godbeer, *The Overflowing of Friendship*, 5 and passim. For an argument that even mutual masturbation was acceptable among many young men who went on to court women and live seemingly contentedly in heterosexual marriages, see Rebecca Davis, *Fierce Desires: A New History of Sex and Sexuality in America* (W. W. Norton & Company, 2024), 97–98. On nineteenth-century same-sex affection, see Rotundo, "Romantic Friendship"; Graham Robb, *Strangers: Homosexual Love in the Nineteenth Century* (W. W. Norton & Company, 2003), 107.
35. Rachel Hope Cleves, "'What, Another Female Husband?': The Prehistory of Same-Sex Marriage in America," *Journal of American History* 101, no. 4 (2015), http://www.jstor.org/stable/44285272. For stories of other such couples in a slightly later time period, see Emily Skidmore, *True Sex: The Lives of Trans Men at the Turn of the Twentieth Century* (New York University Press, 2017). For a fascinating history of how attitudes toward men and women who chose to live as the "opposite sex" from that of their birth identity have changed over time, see Jen Manion, *Female Husbands: A Trans History* (Cambridge University Press, 2020).
36. John Ibson, *Picturing Men: A Century of Male Relationships in Everyday American Photography* (Smithsonian Institution Press, 2002).
37. Regina Kunzel, "The Uneven History of Modern American Sexuality," *Modern American History* 1, no. 1 (2018), 99, https://doi.org/10.1017/mah.2017.13; Chauncey, *Gay New York*. See also John D'Emilio and Estelle Freedman, "Since Intimate Matters: Recent Developments in the History of Sexuality in the United States," *Journal of Women's History* 25, no. 4 (2013): 88–100.
38. For the references in this and the next paragraph, see Tiffany Field, "Touch for Socioemotional and Physical Well-Being: A Review," *Developmental Review* 30, no. 4 (2010), https://doi.org/10.1016/j.dr.2011.01.001; "American Adolescents Touch Each Other Less and Are More Aggressive Toward Their Peers as Compared with French Adolescents," *Adolescence* 34, no. 136 (1999); and "Preschoolers in America Are Touched Less and Are More Aggressive Than Preschoolers in France," *Early Child Development and Care* 151, no. 1

(1999). See also Andrew Reiner, "The Power of Touch, Especially for Men," *New York Times*, December 5, 2017, https://www.nytimes.com/2017/12/05/well/family/gender-men-touch.html; and Tiffany Field, "Violence and Touch Deprivation in Adolescents," *Adolescence* 37, no. 148 (2002), https://pubmed.ncbi.nlm.nih.gov/12564826/.

39. Bailey, *Front Porch to Back Seat*, 20–21. On the persistence of the idea that men should ask and pay for dates, even among people who otherwise report a preference for egalitarian gender relationships, see Ellen Lamont, *The Mating Game: How Gender Still Shapes How We Date* (University of California Press, 2020).
40. For other examples of these contradictory messages, see Bailey, *Front Porch to Back Seat*; Art Unger, *Datebook's Complete Guide to Dating* (Prentice-Hall, 1960); Marina Zayats, "A Time Travel Through Dating and 'Pick-Up' Guides," September 6, 2015, https://medium.com/@marinazet/a-time-travel-through-dating-and-pick-up-guides-8bd9d339fa20; Rebecca Davis, "What's New About Consent," in Stephanie Coontz and Paula England, eds., "Defining Consent," Council on Contemporary Families Symposium, October 22, 2019, https://thesocietypages.org/ccf/2020/03/03/whats-new-about-consent/.

Chapter 6: Nostalgia for the 1950s

1. Public Religion Research Institute, "Challenges in Moving Toward a More Inclusive Democracy: Findings from the 2022 American Values Survey," October 27, 2022, https://prri.org/research/challenges-in-moving-toward-a-more-inclusive-democracy-findings-from-the-2022-american-values-survey/.
2. Stephanie Coontz, *The Way We Never Were: American Families and the Nostalgia Trap* (Basic Books, 1992).
3. For references on the dynamics and impact of personal nostalgia, see Clay Routledge, *Nostalgia: A Psychological Resource* (Routledge Press, 2016); Cheung Wing-Yee et al., "Back to the Future: Nostalgia Increases Optimism," *Personality and Social Psychology Bulletin* 39, no. 11 (2013): 1484–96, https://doi.org/10.1177/0146167213499187; Erica G. Hepper et al., "Time Capsule: Nostalgia Shields Psychological Wellbeing from Limited Time Horizons," *Emotion* 21, no. 3 (2021): 644–64, https://doi.org/10.1037/emo0000728; Jacob Juhl et al., "Nostalgia Promotes Help Seeking by Fostering Social Connectedness," *Emotion* 21, no. 3 (2021): 631–43, https://doi.org/10.1037/emo0000720; John Tierney, "What Is Nostalgia Good For? Quite a Bit, Research Shows," *New York Times*, July 8, 2013, http://www.nytimes.com/2013/07/09/science/what-is-nostalgia-good-for-quite-a-bit-research-shows.html; Art Markman, "What Does Nostalgia Do?," *Psychology Today*, November 1, 2013, https://www.psychologytoday.com/blog/ulterior-motives/201311/what-does-nostalgia-do; Jeanette Leardi, "The Incredible Powers of Nostalgia,"

Huffington Post, October 5, 2013, http://www.huffingtonpost.com/2013/10/05/benefits-of-nostalgia_n_4031759.html.

4. Two excellent sources on the history of nostalgia are Susan Matt, *Homesickness: An American History* (Oxford University Press, 2011); and Thomas Dodman, *What Nostalgia Was: War, Empire, and the Time of a Deadly Emotion* (University of Chicago Press, 2018). See also Carolyn Kiser Anspach, "Medical Dissertation on Nostalgia by Johannes Hofer, 1688," *Bulletin of the Institute of the History of Medicine* 2, no. 6 (1934): 376–91; Julie Beck, "When Nostalgia Was a Disease," *Atlantic,* August 14, 2013, https://www.theatlantic.com/health/archive/2013/08/when-nostalgia-was-a-disease/278648/; Michael Roth, "Dying of the Past: Medical Studies of Nostalgia in Nineteenth-Century France," *History and Memory* 3, no. 1 (1991): 5–29, http://www.jstor.org/stable/25618609.
5. Some perceptive Americans saw the connections. John Howard Payne, the composer of "Home, Sweet Home," wrote of the Cherokee removal that White people's "eyes of avarice" refused to see the "heart strings" that bound Cherokees to their "sacred home." And Colonel Richard Irving Dodge attributed the horrendous death rates among "resettled" Indians to "nostalgia" resulting from loss of their ancestral lands. President Andrew Jackson, by contrast, scorned the Indians' seeming unwillingness to follow the White man's example of leaving their birthplaces to supposedly "better their condition in an unknown land." Matt, *Homesickness,* 40, 41, 111, and see her other examples of homesickness among displaced Africans and Native Americans.
6. Stephanie Coontz, "Taking the Nostalgia of Trump Supporters Seriously," Insights, Berggruen Institute, July 31, 2016, https://stephaniecoontz.com/node/374; Julian Jacobs, "A Portrait of the Automation Susceptible Individual: Skills-Biased Technological Change and the American Conscience," SSRN, August 24, 2021, https://papers.ssrn.com/sol3/papers.cfm?abstract_id=3965751. For empathetic interviews with Trump supporters in an impoverished White county in Kentucky, see Arlie Russell Hochschild, *Stolen Pride: Loss, Shame, and the Rise of the Right* (The New Press, 2024).
7. Diana Elliott et al., "Historical Marriage Trends from 1890–2010: A Focus on Race Differences," Working Paper No. 2012-12 (United States Census Bureau, Social, Economic, and Housing Statistics Division, May 1, 2012), https://www.census.gov/content/dam/Census/library/working-papers/2012/demo/SEHSD-WP2012-12.pdf; Centers for Disease Control, *100 Years of Marriage and Divorce Statistics: United States, 1867–1967,* National Center for Health Statistics, December 1973, https://www.cdc.gov/nchs/data/series/sr_21/sr21_024.pdf.
8. Elliott et al., "Historical Marriage Trends"; Deirdre Bloome and Shannon Ang, "Marriage and Union Formation in the United States: Recent Trends

Across Racial Groups and Economic Backgrounds," *Demography* 57, no. 5 (2020), https://pubmed.ncbi.nlm.nih.gov/32914334/.

9. Philip Cohen, "Family Diversity Is the New Normal for America's Children," *Society Pages*, Council on Contemporary Families, September 15, 2014, https://thesocietypages.org/ccf/2014/09/15/family-diversity-is-the-new-normal-for-americas-children/.

10. Joseph Veroff et al., *The Inner American: A Self-Portrait from 1957 to 1976* (Basic Books, 1981); Douglas Miller and Marion Nowak, *The Fifties: The Way We Really Were* (Doubleday, 1977), 154.

11. For more on this and the other favorable trends for working-class men in the postwar era that I describe in the chapter, see Andrew Cherlin, *Labor's Love Lost: The Rise and Fall of the Working-Class Family in America* (Russell Sage Foundation, 2014); Carter Price and Kathryn Edwards, "Trends in Income from 1975 to 2018," Working Paper No. WR-A516-1 (RAND Education and Labor, September 14, 2020), https://www.rand.org/pubs/working_papers/WRA516-1.html; Chad Stone et al., "A Guide to Statistics on Historical Trends in Income Inequality," Center on Budget and Policy Priorities, January 13, 2020, https://www.cbpp.org/research/poverty-and-inequality/a-guide-to-statistics-on-historical-trends-in-income-inequality; Frank Levy, "Incomes, Families, and Living Standards," in Robert Litan et al., eds., *American Living Standards: Threats and Challenges* (Brookings Institution, 1988); Shawn Fremstad, "Talking About Poverty in a Jobs and Economy Framework," Center for Economic and Policy Research, September 2011, https://cepr.net/documents/publications/poverty-2011-09.pdf; Frank Levy and Richard Michel, "An Economic Bust for the Baby Boom," *Challenge* 29, no. 1 (1986): 33–39, https://doi.org/10.1080/05775132.1986.11471067; Steven Ruggles, "Patriarchy, Power, and Pay: The Transformation of American Families, 1800–2015," *Demography* 52, no. 6 (2015): 1797–1823, http://link.springer.com/article/10.1007%2Fs13524-015-0440-z; Eva Bertram, "Net Gains and Losses: A Modern Labor Market and a New Deal Welfare State," Third Way, February 8, 2013, https://www.thirdway.org/report/net-gains-and-losses-a-modern-labor-market-and-a-new-deal-welfare-state; Henry Farber, "Employment Insecurity: The Decline in Worker-Firm Attachment in the United States," Working Paper No. 172 (Center for Economic Policy Studies, Princeton University, January 2008), https://www.princeton.edu/~ceps/workingpapers/172farber.pdf; Jacob Hacker, *The Great Risk Shift: The New Economic Insecurity and the Decline of the American Dream* (Oxford University Press, 2008), 27–33; Colin Gordon, "The Wage Crunch in Perspective," *Dissent*, June 9, 2014, http://www.dissentmagazine.org/blog/the-wage-crunch-in-perspective; Andrew Sum et al., *Vanishing Dreams Revisited: The Deteriorating Economic Fortunes of Young Workers and Young Families from 1973–2008* (Children's Defense Fund, 2010).

12. Pavlina Tcherneva, "Reorienting Fiscal Policy: A Bottom-Up Approach," *Journal of Post Keynesian Economics* 37, no. 1 (2014): 64–66, https://www.tandfonline.com/doi/abs/10.2753/PKE0160-3477370105. For other striking illustrations of the difference in income gains then and since the 1970s, see the charts here: http://www.motherjones.com/files/averagehouseholdincome.jpg, and http://www.motherjones.com/files/changeinshare.jpg; Eduardo Porter, "Black Workers Stopped Making Progress on Pay. Is It Racism?," *New York Times*, June 28, 2021, https://www.nytimes.com/2021/06/28/business/economy/black-workers-racial-pay-gap.html; William Spriggs, "The Unfinished March for Jobs," Economic Policy Institute, November 20, 2013, https://www.epi.org/publication/unfinished-march-jobs-fiscal-policy-shift/; David Leonhardt, "The Black-White Wage Gap Is as Big as It Was in 1950," *New York Times*, July 5, 2020. See also Sylvia Allegretto, "The Rich Are Not Rich Enough in America," Center for Economic and Policy Research, July 15, 2025, https://cepr.net/publications/the-rich-are-not-rich-enough-in-america/.
13. United States Census Bureau, "Income of Families and Persons in the United States: 1960," Report No. P60-37, January 17, 1962, https://www.census.gov/library/publications/1962/demo/p60-037.html; Paulette Perhach, "Renting Forever and Trying to Create a Strong Financial Future," *New York Times*, May 19, 2024, https://www.nytimes.com/2024/05/19/business/renting-forever-investing.html.
14. For more on the discrimination against women in the 1950s and 1960s, and their much more widespread dissatisfaction than is commonly recognized, see Stephanie Coontz, *A Strange Stirring: The Feminine Mystique and American Women at the Dawn of the 1960s* (Basic Books, 2011).
15. Frank F. Furstenberg Jr., "The Recent Transformation of the American Family: Witnessing and Exploring Social Change," in Marcia Carlson and Paula England, eds., *Social Class and Changing Families in an Unequal America* (Stanford University Press, 2022); Frank F. Furstenberg et al., "The Teenage Marriage Controversy: Bringing Back the Shotgun Wedding," *National Affairs* 90 (1988), http://www.nationalaffairs.com/public_interest/detail/the-teenage-marriage-controversy-bringing-back-the-shotgun-wedding.
16. Young women who resisted were sometimes even threatened with being made wards of the state. For more on coerced adoption, see Ann Fessler, *The Girls Who Went Away: The Hidden History of Women Who Surrendered Children for Adoption in the Decades Before Roe v. Wade* (Penguin, 2006); and Gabrielle Glaser, *American Baby: A Mother, a Child, and the Shadow History of Adoption* (Viking, 2021). For the number of babies born each year since 1945, see "Live Births and Birth Rates, by Year," Infoplease, https://www.infoplease.com/us/population/live-births-and-birth-rates-year. On the number of voluntary adoptions per year recently, see Olga Khazan, "The New

Question Haunting Adoption," *Atlantic*, October 19, 2021, https://www.theatlantic.com/politics/archive/2021/10/adopt-baby-cost-process-hard/620258/.

17. Eric Berkowitz, *Sex and Punishment* (Counterpoint Press, 2012), 392, note 9.
18. Ruggles, "Patriarchy, Power, and Pay."
19. John E. Snell et al., "The Wifebeater's Wife: A Study of Family Interaction," *Archives of General Psychiatry* 11, no. 2 (1964): 107–12, https://jamanetwork.com/journals/jamapsychiatry/article-abstract/488595. See also "Psychiatry: The Wife Beater & His Wife," *Time*, September 25, 1964, https://time.com/archive/6813927/psychiatry-the-wife-beater-his-wife/.
20. Elizabeth Pleck, *Domestic Tyranny: The Making of American Social Policy Against Family Violence from Colonial Times to the Present* (University of Illinois Press, 2004); Linda Gordon, *Heroes of Their Own Lives: The Politics and History of Family Violence* (University of Illinois Press, 2002). For one story of incest in the 1950s, see the memoir of Marilyn Van Derbur, "Miss America" of 1958, *Miss America by Day* (Oak Hill Ridge Press, 2003). She first publicly exposed the incest in "The Darkest Secret," *People*, June 10, 1991 (retrieved January 11, 2016).
21. Suzanne Kahn, *Divorce, American Style: Fighting for Women's Economic Citizenship in the Neoliberal Era* (University of Pennsylvania Press, 2021), 27.
22. Lillian Rubin, *Worlds of Pain: Life in the Working-Class Family* (Basic Books, 1977). For more on marital discontents in the 1950s, see Elaine Tyler May, *Homeward Bound: American Families in the Cold War Era* (Basic Books, 1988), especially chapter 8; and Kristin Celello, *Making Marriage Work: A History of Marriage and Divorce in the Twentieth-Century United States* (University of North Carolina Press, 2009).
23. For examples of such chicanery, see former federal Justice Department prosecutor Brendan Ballou's *Plunder: Private Equity's Plan to Pillage America* (Hatchett, 2023), along with the references in note 31.
24. Richard Rothstein, *The Color of Law: A Forgotten History of How Our Government Segregated America* (Liveright, 2017); Kenneth Jackson, *Crabgrass Frontier: The Suburbanization of the United States* (Oxford University Press, 1985); Colin Gordon, *Patchwork Apartheid: Private Restriction, Racial Segregation, and Urban Inequality* (Russell Sage Foundation, 2023). It's worth noting, however, that New Deal jobs programs in the 1930s had employed African Americans at rates the same or above their percentage of the population, paying them the same rates as Whites. For more on the benefits of the New Deal for Blacks, despite its limits, see Adolph Reed Jr., "The New Deal Wasn't Intrinsically Racist," *New Republic*, November 26, 2019, https://newrepublic.com/article/155704/new-deal-wasnt-intrinsically-racist.
25. In recent decades, by contrast, de-unionization has simultaneously increased the average racial wage disadvantage of Black men and women and depressed

the wages of most White working-class men compared to the highest-earning Whites. See William Collins and Gregory Niemesh, "Unions and the Great Compression of Wage Inequality in the US at Mid-Century," *Economic History Review* 72, no. 2 (2019): 691–715, https://onlinelibrary.wiley.com/doi/10.1111/ehr.12744; Heidi Shierholz et al., "Workers Want Unions, but the Latest Data Point to Obstacles in Their Path," Economic Policy Institute, January 23, 2024, https://www.epi.org/publication/union-membership-data/; Henry Farber et al., "Unions and Inequality over the Twentieth Century: New Evidence from Survey Data," *Quarterly Journal of Economics* 136, no. 3 (2021), https://academic.oup.com/qje/article/136/3/1325/6219103; Jake Rosenfeld and Meredith Kleykamp, "Organized Labor and Racial Wage Inequality in the United States," *American Journal of Sociology* 117, no. 5 (2012): 1460–1502, https://www.ncbi.nlm.nih.gov/pmc/articles/PMC4300995/; Jake Grumbach and Ruth Berins Collier, "The Deep Structure of Democratic Crisis," *Boston Review*, January 2, 2022, https://bostonreview.net/articles/the-deep-structure-of-democratic-crisis/; Nicole Fortin et al., "Labor Market Institutions and the Distribution of Wages: The Role of Spillover Effects," Working Paper No. 28375 (National Bureau of Economic Research, January 2021), https://www.nber.org/system/files/working_papers/w28375/w28375.pdf. See also Clark Merrefield, "Research Sheds Light on How Labor Unions Reduced Income Inequality from WWII Through the 1970s," *Journalist's Resource*, October 4, 2021, https://journalistsresource.org/economics/inequality-labor-unions/.

26. *The Papers of Dwight David Eisenhower*, vol. 15, chap. 13: "A New Phase of Political Experience," repr. in Teaching American History, "Letter from Dwight D. Eisenhower to Edgar Newton Eisenhower (1954)," https://teachingamericanhistory.org/document/letter-to-edgar-newton-eisenhower/.

27. The high-speed mainframe computers first constructed in government-funded universities in the 1960s weren't all built to the same standards, so new protocols had to be designed to allow far-separated computer networks to communicate with one another. That effort was spearheaded first by researchers working under the direction of the US Advanced Research Projects Agency (ARPA) and later by the US military and NSFNet, a network of scientific and academic computers funded by the National Science Foundation. Only in 1995 was the main transmission line of the Internet turned over to commercial providers. None of the socially connected platforms we use today would have been possible if the expansion of computing had been done by private competitors without the capital or incentive to finance such coordination. See Michael Moyer, "Yes, Government Researchers Really Did Invent the Internet," *Scientific American*, July 23, 2012, https://blogs.scientificamerican.com/observations/yes-government-researchers-really-did-invent-the-internet/; Richard John, "From Franklin to Facebook," in Steven

Conn, ed., *To Promote the General Welfare: The Case for Big Government* (Oxford University Press, 2012).

28. David Leonhardt, "The Rich Really Do Pay Lower Taxes Than You," *New York Times*, October 6, 2019, https://www.nytimes.com/interactive/2019/10/06/opinion/income-tax-rate-wealthy.html.
29. A May 2025 study by Nature Climate Change calculates that the world's wealthiest 10 percent have caused two-thirds of observed global warming since 1990, thus contributing heavily to climate extremes such as heat waves and droughts, https://iiasa.ac.at/news/may-2025/worlds-wealthiest-10-caused-two-thirds-of-global-warming-since-1990. For more on the outsize contributions of the wealthy to energy and pollution costs, see Beatrice Barros and Richard Wilk, "The Outsized Carbon Footprints of the Super-Rich," *Sustainability: Science, Practice and Policy* 17, no. 1 (2021): 316–22, https://doi.org/10.1080/15487733.2021.1949847; Jared Starr et al., "Assessing U.S. Consumers' Carbon Footprints Reveals Outsized Impact of the Top 1%," *Ecological Economics* 205, issue C (2023), https://doi.org/10.1016/j.ecolecon.2022.107698. See also Chuck Collins, *Burned by Billionaires: How Concentrated Wealth and Power Are Ruining Our Lives and Planet* (The New Press, 2025). It's worth noting that progressive taxation was not as radical a departure from America's founding principles as some people claim. James Madison, "the Father of the Constitution," advocated laws to "reduce extreme wealth toward a state of mediocrity, and raise extreme indigence toward a state of comfort." Thomas Jefferson suggested that legislators "tax the higher portions of property in geometrical progression as they rise." On the founding fathers' support for measures to protect against wealth inequality, despite their blindness on the issues of slavery, racism, and female subordination, see Philip Kurland and Ralph Lerner, eds., *The Founders' Constitution* (University of Chicago Press, 1987), vol. 1, 596; Robert Rutland et al., eds., *Papers of James Madison*, vol. 14 (University Press of Virginia, 1983), 197–98; and Andrew Lipscombe and Albert Bergh, eds., *Writings of Thomas Jefferson*, vol. 19 (Thomas Jefferson Memorial Association, 1905), 18.
30. Federal Reserve Bank of St. Louis, "Real Gross Domestic Product," FRED, https://fred.stlouisfed.org/series/A191RL1Q225SBEA.
31. In 1982, the Securities and Exchange Commission assured corporate boards that stock buybacks were perfectly legal. This practice allows a company to buy back half of its shares and then essentially tear them up. By doing so, a company can double the value of the remaining half, enriching shareholders, who then reward stock-owning executives with massive raises, all without increasing the total value or output of the company at all. This has become a windfall for the wealthiest 10 percent of the population who own 89 percent of all stock—see Robert Frank, "The Wealthiest 10% of Americans Own a Record 89% of All U.S. Stocks," CNBC, October 18, 2021, https://www.cnbc.com/2021/10/18/the-wealthiest-10percent-of-americans-own-a-record

-89percent-of-all-us-stocks.html—and for the CEOs who then get rewarded by shareholders. One 2018 study estimated that from 2015 to 2017, retail companies spent 79 percent of their net profits on buybacks. The authors calculate that if Starbucks had directed the money it spent on share repurchases to employee compensation, it could have given every worker a yearly raise of $7,000, while Lowe's, CVS, and Home Depot could have given each worker a raise of $18,000. See Irene Tung and Katy Milani, "Curbing Stock Buybacks: A Crucial Step to Raising Worker Pay and Reducing Inequality," Roosevelt Institute, July 31, 2018, https://rooseveltinstitute.org/publications/curbing-stock-buybacks-crucial-step-raising-worker-pay-reduce-inequality/. For more on this, see William Lazonick, "Profits Without Prosperity," *Harvard Business Review*, September 2014, https://hbr.org/2014/09/profits-without-prosperity; Brad Dress, "CEOs Average Pay in 2021 Was 324 Times Higher Than Employees: Report," *Hill*, July 20, 2022, https://thehill.com/policy/finance/3567014-ceos-average-pay-in-2021-was-324-times-higher-than-employees-report/; Lawrence Mishel and Julia Wolfe, "CEO Compensation Has Grown 940% Since 1978," Economic Policy Institute, August 14, 2019, https://www.epi.org/publication/ceo-compensation-2018/.

32. And that ratio was after a rare *dip* in CEO compensation! Josh Bivens et al., "CEO Pay Declined in 2023: But It Has Soared 1,085% Since 1978 Compared with a 24% Rise in Typical Workers' Pay," Economic Policy Institute, September 19, 2024, https://www.epi.org/publication/ceo-pay-in-2023/. See also Taylor Telford, "CEO Pay Fell Last Year Despite a Strong Stock Market, Study Finds," *Washington Post*, October 16, 2024, https://www.washingtonpost.com/business/2024/10/16/ceo-executive-pay-compensation/.
33. Carnival Corporation, "Notice of Annual Meetings of Shareholders and Proxy Statement," 2025, https://www.carnivalcorp.com/wp-content/uploads/2024/08/Carnival-Corporation-plc-2025-Notice-of-Annual-Meetings-and-Proxy-Statement-1.pdf.
34. Price and Edwards, "Trends in Income." The median wage of full-time prime-age White male workers would have been $109,000 instead of $57,000, and for Black men $83,000 instead of $45,000. For White women, $61,000 instead of $47,000, and for Black women $59,000 instead of $40,000.
35. On the mixed but increasingly ubiquitous messages about sexual display and experimentation in 1950s culture, see Stephanie Coontz, "Golden Oldies," in Yona McDonough, ed., *The Barbie Chronicles* (Touchstone, 1999); and Elaine Tyler May, *Homeward Bound: American Families in the Cold War Era* (Basic Books, 1988).
36. For more on the discontents of 1950s housewives and the reactions of their daughters, see Coontz, *A Strange Stirring.*
37. For more on the Powell memo, see https://web.archive.org/web/20120104052451/http://www.pbs.org/wnet/supremecourt/personality/sources

_document13.html, and also available at https://www.thwink.org/sustain/articles/017_PowellMemo/PowellMemoReproduction.pdf; Steven Higgs, "A Call to Arms for Class War: From the Top Down," *Counterpunch*, May 11, 2012, https://www.counterpunch.org/2012/05/11/a-call-to-arms-for-class-war-from-the-top-down/. Powell recommended that the campaign target communists, socialists, environmentalists, liberal clergy, professors, and anyone who referred to "tax incentives" as tax "breaks," which he said was a sure sign of antibusiness bias. He urged businesses to fund think tanks to promote "free enterprise" and to monitor textbooks, TV networks, and university faculties to root out "socialistic" criticism of business priorities. For more details on the influence of the Powell memo, see the following book and article, which appeared as this book was heading into production: David Sirota and Jared Jacang Maher, *Master Plan: The Hidden Plot to Legalize Corruption in America* (Lever Books, 2025), and "The Ad Campaign for Capitalism," The American Prospect, October 13, 2025, https://prospect.org/2025/10/13/lewis-powell-memo-nader-chamber-commerce-master-plan/.

38. Jane Mayer, *Dark Money: The Hidden History of the Billionaires Behind the Rise of the Radical Right* (Doubleday, 2016), and "The Big Money Behind the Big Lie," *New Yorker*, August 9, 2021, https://www.newyorker.com/magazine/2021/08/09/the-big-money-behind-the-big-lie; Nancy MacLean, *Democracy in Chains: The Deep History of the Radical Right's Stealth Plan for America* (Viking, 2017). For more details on the campaign against the New Deal, see Colin Gordon, "Growing Apart," https://scalar.usc.edu/works/growing-apart-a-political-history-of-american-inequality/wall-street-and-main-street-the-rise-of-finance?path=differences-that-matter; John Schmitt, "Inequality as Policy, the United States Since 1979," Center for Economic and Policy Research, October 2009, https://www.cepr.net/documents/publications/inequality-policy-2009-10.pdf; Lawrence Mishel and Josh Bivens, "Identifying the Policy Levers Generating Wage Suppression and Wage Inequality," Economic Policy Institute, May 13, 2021, https://files.epi.org/uploads/215903.pdf; Lazonick, "Profits Without Prosperity"; David Howell, "From Decent to Lousy Jobs: New Evidence on the Decline of American Job Quality, 1979-2017," Washington Center for Equitable Growth, August 2019, https://equitablegrowth.org/working-papers/from-decent-to-lousy-jobs-new-evidence-on-the-decline-in-american-job-quality-1979-2017/; Elizabeth Fones-Wolf, *Selling Free Enterprise: The Business Assault on Labor and Liberalism, 1945–60* (University of Illinois Press, 1994); Lee Drutman, "How Corporate Lobbyists Conquered American Democracy," *Atlantic*, April 20, 2015, https://www.theatlantic.com/business/archive/2015/04/how-corporate-lobbyists-conquered-american-democracy/390822/. For insight on how financial deregulation has allowed speculators to basically "loot" the economy, destroying productive firms and creating unemployment, see Kim Phillips-

Hein, "Conspicuous Destruction," *New York Review of Books*, October 19, 2023, https://www.nybooks.com/articles/2023/10/19/conspicuous-destruction-plunder-brendan-ballou/. See also Joseph Stiglitz, "Whither America?," *Project Syndicate*, January 12, 2019, https://www.project-syndicate.org/commentary/trump-capitol-insurrection-revealed-america-s-challenges-by-joseph-e-stiglitz-2021-01.

39. For the ways that the principles advocated by Powell have pervaded—and, Adam Cohen argues, perverted—recent Supreme Court rulings, see Adam Cohen, *Supreme Inequality: The Supreme Court's Fifty-Year Battle for a More Unjust America* (Penguin Press, 2020). See also Tim Lau, "Citizens United Explained," Brennan Center for Justice, December 12, 2019, https://www.brennancenter.org/our-work/research-reports/citizens-united-explained; Maria Pino and Julia Fishman, "Fifteen Years Later, *Citizens United* Defined the 2024 Election," Brennan Center for Justice, January 14, 2025, https://www.brennancenter.org/our-work/research-reports/fifteen-years-later-citizens-united-defined-2024-election; and Liz Tracey, "*Citizens United v. Federal Election Commission*: Annotated," *JSTOR Daily*, January 24, 2025, https://daily.jstor.org/citizens-united-v-federal-election-commission-annotated/.

40. Schlafly's campaign prevented the ERA from gaining additional ratifications before the deadline set by Congress. It has since gained enough additional ratifications, but the deadline has so far not been renewed.

41. For the Falwell quote, see Randall Balmer, review of Darren E. Grem, *The Blessings of Business: How Corporations Shaped Conservative Christianity*, in *American Historical Review* 122, no. 3 (2017): 866. For the very different values of evangelical Christians in the early Republic, see Donald Dayton with Douglas Strong, *Rediscovering an Evangelical Heritage* (Baker Academic, 2014). For more on the origins and evolution of the business-Christian coalition, see Kevin Kruse, *One Nation Under God: How Corporate America Invented Christian America* (Basic Books, 2015). For a discussion of the tensions between the economically conservative but more socially liberal corporations and those businesses that endorse anti-feminist and anti-diversity issues and the anti-union and anti-regulation cause, see Peter Coy, "Anti-Woke Businesses Push Back," *New York Times*, July 3, 2022.

42. My account of this period focuses on the alliance between those who oppose the New Deal and those who object to the social liberalization. For a more extensive discussion of the many other forces contributing to the decline of the New Deal Order and the loss of confidence in traditional liberalism, see Paul Starr, *American Contradiction: Revolution and Revenge from the 1950s to Now* (Yale University Press, 2025).

43. Price and Edwards, "Trends in Income"; quoting Kathryn A. Edwards and Carter C. Price in "A $2.5 Trillion Question: What if Incomes Grew Like

GDP Did?," Commentary, Rand, October 6, 2020, https://www.rand.org/blog/2020/10/a-25-trillion-question-what-if-incomes-grew-like-gdp.html: "The difference between 1975 and 2018, in terms of the share of income taken home by the bottom 90 percent, is 17 percentage points—or $2.5 trillion in a single year. Over the whole 43 years, it's $47 trillion. That's so large, it becomes difficult to interpret. But that's what happens when incomes at the bottom grow at a rate that's about 20 percent of GDP, and top incomes grow at 300 percent of GDP over four decades." See also Nick Hanauer and David Rolf, "The Top 1% of Americans Have Taken $50 Trillion from the Bottom 90%—and That's Made the U.S. Less Secure," *Time*, September 14, 2020, https://time.com/5888024/50-trillion-income-inequality-america/. See also https://www.businessinsider.com/wealthiest-1-percent-stole-50-trillion-working-americans-what-means-2020-9. For other good summaries of the different trends during the New Deal and Great Society Era and those since the mid-1970s, see Chad Stone et al., "A Guide to Statistics on Historical Trends in Income Inequality," Center on Budget and Policy Priorities, January 13, 2020, https://www.cbpp.org/research/poverty-and-inequality/a-guide-to-statistics-on-historical-trends-in-income-inequality; and Dana Milbank, "Democrats Don't Have a Working-Class Problem. America Does," *Washington Post*, November 29, 2024, https://www.washingtonpost.com/opinions/2024/11/29/democrats-working-people/.

44. Ana Hernandez Kent, "The State of U.S. Household Wealth," Federal Reserve Bank of St. Louis, 2025, https://www.stlouisfed.org/community-development/publications/the-state-of-us-household-wealth.

45. Jonathan Vespa, "The Changing Economics and Demographics of Young Adulthood: 1975–2016," Current Population Reports, US Census Bureau, April 2017, https://www.census.gov/content/dam/Census/library/publications/2017/demo/p20-579.pdf; and Bivens et al., "CEO Pay Declined in 2023." For more on the decline in job quality, real wages, and economic security since the early 1970s, see Ruggles, "Patriarchy, Power, and Pay"; David Autor with Michael Klein, "Econofact Chat: The Future of Work," November 19, 2021, https://econofact.org/wp-content/uploads/2021/12/EFChats-Transcript-David-Autor-FutureofWork.pdf; Robert Rank et al., *Poorly Understood: What America Gets Wrong About Poverty* (Oxford University Press, 2021), 134; Colin Gordon, "Growing Apart"; Patricia Cohen, "Bump in U.S. Incomes Doesn't Erase 50 Years of Pain," *New York Times*, September 16, 2017, https://www.nytimes.com/2017/09/16/business/economy/bump-in-us-incomes-doesnt-erase-50-years-of-pain.html; Price and Edwards, "Trends in Income"; Sheldon Danziger and Cecilia Elena Rouse, eds., *The Price of Independence: The Economics of Early Adulthood* (Russell Sage, 2007), 8; inequality.org, "Wealth Inequality in the United States," https://inequality.org/facts

/wealth-inequality/; Juliana Menasce Horowitz et al., "Trends in U.S. Income and Wealth Inequality," Pew Research Center, August 17, 2020, https://www.pewresearch.org/social-trends/2020/01/09/trends-in-income-and-wealth-inequality/; Ron Ivey and Tim Shirk, "Ending America's Antisocial Contract," *American Affairs* 5, no. 3 (2021), https://americanaffairsjournal.org/2021/08/ending-americas-antisocial-contract/; Josh Bivens and Lawrence Mishel, *Understanding the Historic Divergence Between Productivity and a Typical Worker's Pay: Why It Matters and Why It's Real* (Economic Policy Institute, 2015).

46. Fatih Guvenen, "Stagnation in Lifetime Incomes: An Overview of Trends and Potential Causes," The Hamilton Project, February 2018, https://www.brookings.edu/wp-content/uploads/2018/02/es_2272018_stagnation_lifetime_incomes_guvenen_policy_proposal.pdf.
47. Nelson Schwartz, *The Velvet Rope Economy: How Inequality Became Big Business* (Doubleday, 2020).
48. An "industry note" memo on "equity strategy" from Citigroup, October 16, 2005, https://delong.typepad.com/plutonomy-1.pdf, accessed September 19, 2025. The memo has been deleted from its original site but can be found here: https://www.sourcewatch.org/images/8/86/CITIGROUP-OCTOBER-16-2005-PLUTONOMY-MEMO.pdf (accessed December 27, 2025). It is also mentioned here: Angela Barnes, "Want Wealth? Invest in the Uber-Rich," *Globe and Mail*, October 2, 2006, https://www.theglobeandmail.com/report-on-business/want-wealth-invest-in-the-uber-rich/article1106279/(accessed September 19, 2025).
49. On upper-class spending, see Rachel Ensign, "The U.S. Economy Depends More Than Ever on Rich People," *Wall Street Journal*, February 23, 2025, https://www.wsj.com/economy/consumers/us-economy-strength-rich-spending-2c34a571?page=1. On the hierarchy of service and amenities at Disneyland—which once advertised itself as a place where "Everyone Is a V.I.P."—see Daniel Currell, "Disney Used to Be for Everyone. Not Anymore," *New York Times*, August 31, 2025, https://www.nytimes.com/2025/08/28/opinion/disney-world-economy-middle-class-rich.html. For the study of air rage, see Katherine DeCelles and Michael Norton, "Physical and Situational Inequality on Airplanes Predicts Air Rage," *Proceedings of the National Academy of Sciences* 113, no. 20 (2016), https://www.pnas.org/doi/full/10.1073/pnas.1521727113.
50. Ian Haney López, "Can Democracy Survive Racism as a Strategy?," Protect Democracy Project, July 9, 2021, https://protectdemocracy.org/project/endgame/#section-4, and *Dog Whistle Politics: How Coded Racial Appeals Have Reinvented Racism and Wrecked the Middle Class* (Oxford University Press, 2015). President Ronald Reagan, for example, made implicit racism

a central part of his campaign to delegitimize anti-poverty measures, claiming that an "underclass" of "undeserving" people was taking advantage of taxpayer-funded social welfare programs such as Medicaid and food stamps that actually serve more White people than minorities. In some speeches, the racism was shockingly explicit, as when Reagan asked White audiences to picture themselves "waiting in line to buy hamburger" while a "strapping young buck" ahead of them used food stamps to buy a T-bone steak. As Heather McGhee puts it in her 2021 book, *The Sum of Us: What Racism Costs Everyone and How We Can Prosper Together* (One World, 2021), decades of racist stereotypes and fear campaigns helped lobbyists and politicians roll back pro-worker regulations and defeat expansions of the social safety net. People of color have paid the highest price for these defeats, but McGhee points out that most White people didn't "win." Instead, she says, "for the most part they lost right along with the rest of us."

51. Erin Hatton, "The Rise of the Permanent Temp Economy," *New York Times*, January 26, 2013, https://archive.nytimes.com/opinionator.blogs.nytimes.com/2013/01/26/the-rise-of-the-permanent-temp-economy/, and *The Temp Economy: From Kelly Girls to Permatemps in Postwar America* (Temple University Press, 2011).
52. Stephanie Coontz, Paula England, and Virginia Rutter, eds., "Defining Consent," Council on Contemporary Families Symposium, October 22, 2019, https://sites.utexas.edu/contemporaryfamilies/files/2019/10/defining-consent-symposium-2019.pdf; Council on Criminal Justice, "Trends in Assault," https://counciloncj.org/wp-content/uploads/2024/07/assault-fact-sheet.pdf.
53. Christia Spears Brown, "Media Messages to Young Girls: Does 'Sexy Girl' Trump 'Girl Power'?," Council on Contemporary Families, September 3, 2020, https://sites.utexas.edu/contemporaryfamilies/2020/09/02/girls-media-messaging-brief-report/; Matt Richtel, "It's Time to Talk About Pornography, Scholars Say," *New York Times*, December 16, 2024, https://www.nytimes.com/2024/12/12/science/pornography-adolescents-teenagers.html; Barbara Risman and Elizabeth Seale, "Betwixt and Be Tween: Gender Contradictions in Middle School, in Risman, *Families as They Really Are* (W. W. Norton & Company, 2009); Tressa Undem and Ann Wang, "The State of Gender Equality for U.S. Adolescents, 2018," PLAN International, https://planusa-org-staging.s3.amazonaws.com/public/uploads/2021/08/state-of-gender-equality-summary-2018.pdf. For a sobering argument about how the pornographic industry has mainstreamed degrading images of women and violent behaviors while insisting to girls that presenting oneself as a sexual object is "empowering," see Sophie Gilbert, "What Porn Taught a Generation of Women," *Atlantic*, April 15 2025, https://www.theatlantic.com/magazine/archive/2025/05/porn-american-pop-culture-feminism/682114/.

54. Betsey Stevenson and Justin Wolfers, "Bargaining in the Shadow of the Law," *Quarterly Journal of Economics* 121 (2006), https://users.nber.org/~jwolfers/Papers/bargaining_in_the_shadow_of_the_law.pdf.
55. The original article is reprinted here: https://fbaum.unc.edu/teaching/articles/DiIulioTheWeeklyStandard1995.pdf. For more examples of the hysteria about family change as the cause of murder rates, see David Blankenhorn, *Fatherless America: Confronting Our Most Urgent Social Problems* (Basic Books, 1995), 30; Patrick Fagan, "The Real Root Causes of Violent Crime: The Breakdown of Marriage, Family, and Community," The Heritage Foundation, March 17, 1995, https://www.heritage.org/crime-and-justice/report/the-real-root-causes-violent-crime-the-breakdown-marriage-family-and; John Dilulio, "The Coming of the Super-Predators," *Weekly Standard*, November 27, 1995. For more recent claims, see Lee Habeeb, "Meet the Man Leading the Charge on America's Boy Crisis," *Newsweek*, July 14, 2020, https://www.newsweek.com/meet-man-leading-charge-americas-boy-crisis-opinion-1517782; Emilie Kao, "The Crisis of Fatherless Shooters," The Heritage Foundation, March 14, 2018, https://www.heritage.org/marriage-and-family/commentary/the-crisis-fatherless-shooters; Jake Thomas, "Utah GOP Senator Mike Lee Blames Mass Shootings on 'Fatherlessness,'" *Newsweek*, May 22, 2022, https://www.newsweek.com/utah-gop-senator-mike-lee-blames-mass-shootings-fatherlessness-1710243.
56. "Historical Living Arrangements of Children," US Census Bureau, https://www.census.gov/data/tables/time-series/demo/families/children.html. See also Gretchen Livingston and Kim Parker, "A Tale of Two Fathers," Pew Research Center, June 15, 2011, https://www.pewresearch.org/social-trends/2011/06/15/a-tale-of-two-fathers/.
57. For this and the next paragraph, see https://counciloncj.org/homicide-trends-report/; https://www.statista.com/statistics/251884/murder-offenders-in-the-us-by-age/; http://bjs.ojp.usdoj.gov/content/homicide/homtrnd.cfm; Matthew Friedman et al., "Crime Trends: 1990–2016," Brennan Center for Justice, April 18, 2017, https://www.brennancenter.org/sites/default/files/publications/Crime%20Trends%201990-2016.pdf; United States Department of Justice, Federal Bureau of Investigation, 2021; "Deaths by Homicide per 100,000 Resident Population in the U.S. from 1950 to 2019," Statista, https://www.statista.com/statistics/187592/death-rate-from-homicide-in-the-us-since-1950/; "Crime Data Explorer: Trend of Violent Crime from 2010 to 2020," retrieved on July 30, 2021, https://crime-data-explorer.fr.cloud.gov/pages/explorer/crime/crime-trend.
58. Emily Badger and Ben Blatt, "Murders Surged in the Pandemic. Now in Many Cities That Surge Is Gone," *New York Times*, November 2, 2024, https://www.nytimes.com/2024/11/02/upshot/murder-decline-pandemic-cities.html; Isabelle Taft and Kate Selig, "Murder Rates Keep Falling Across

U.S., but Fear of Crime Persists," *New York Times*, December 30, 2024, https://www.nytimes.com/2024/12/30/us/murders-decline-crime-concerns.html. My deep appreciation for the generosity of sociologist Philip Cohen, who compared data from the FBI Crime Data Explorer 2024 with Census Bureau Population to double-check the claims in the *New York Times* article and told me he thought that overall it was safer to say the lowest rates in twenty years than the article's claim of the lowest rate in fifty years. The rape and assault figures are based on the National Crime Victimization Survey (NCVS), a self-report survey administered each year. Alexandra Thompson and Susannah N. Tapp, "Criminal Victimization, 2021," September 22, 2023, https://bjs.ojp.gov/content/pub/pdf/cv21.pdf. See also Ames Grawert, "FBI Data Confirms Drop in Most Crimes in 2023, Especially Murders," Brennan Center for Justice, September 26, 2024, https://www.brennancenter.org/our-work/analysis-opinion/fbi-data-confirms-drop-most-crimes-2023-especially-murders. A fascinating analysis from Brookings of homicide spikes in different cities suggests that they tend to take place in cities with high rates of concentrated poverty—neighborhoods where 30 percent or more of the population live below the poverty line—when some kind of societal "shock" leads to big increases in the number of teenage boys who drop out of school and/or in the number of men who lose or are unable to find jobs in those low-income neighborhoods. The authors point to evidence that in cities where authorities manage to keep teens in school and maintain access to employment for youth, such spikes can be avoided. See Rohit Acharya and Rhett Morris, "Why Did U.S. Homicides Spike in 2020 and Then Decline Rapidly in 2023 and 2024?," Brookings Institution, December 16, 2024, https://www.brookings.edu/articles/why-did-u-s-homicides-spike-in-2020-and-then-decline-rapidly-in-2023-and-2024/.

59. "Since 1990, would you say murder rates in U.S. cities have . . . ?" Survey Results, YouGov, July 30, 2025, https://today.yougov.com/topics/politics/survey-results/daily/2025/07/30/94e10/2. For the chart on murder rates and other excellent data on crime, see Jeff Asher, "How 2025 Could Feature the Lowest US Murder Rate Ever Recorded," May 12, 2025, https://jasher.substack.com/p/how-2025-could-feature-the-lowest, and his subsequent updates on the continuing drop in crime through 2025. Follow him at https://jasher.substack.com/.

Chapter 7: Has Marriage Become a Luxury Good?

1. Roni Caryn Rabin, "Put a Ring on It? Millennial Couples Are in No Hurry," *New York Times*, May 29, 2018, https://www.nytimes.com/2018/05/29/well/mind/millennials-love-marriage-sex-relationships-dating.html; Arielle Kuperberg, "Premarital Cohabitation and Direct Marriage in the United States:

1956–2015," *Marriage & Family Review* 55, no. 5 (2019), https://libres.uncg.edu/ir/uncg/f/A_Kuperberg_Premarital_2019.pdf.

2. Wendy Manning and Lisa Carlson, "Trends in Cohabitation Prior to Marriage," National Center for Family & Marriage Research, https://www.bgsu.edu/ncfmr/resources/data/family-profiles/manning-carlson-trends-cohabitation-marriage-fp-21-04.html.
3. Fenaba Addo et al., "The Changing Nature of the Association Between Student Loan Debt and Marital Behavior in Young Adulthood," *Journal of Family and Economic Issues* 40 (2019): 86–101, https://doi.org/10.1007/s10834-018-9591-6. Young people of every race, ethnicity, and sexual orientation tend to "think about marital timing in terms of 'checkpoints,' circumstances or conditions such as financial security, college education, and/or personal maturity." Aaron Hoy and Sachita Pokhrel, "When to Marry, if at All? A Qualitative Exploration of How Sexual Minority Young Adults in the US Think About Marital Timing," *Qualitative Report* 29 no. 1 (2024): 337–54, https://doi.org/10.46743/2160-3715/2024.6457.
4. Andrew Cherlin, "Marriage Has Become a Trophy," *Atlantic*, March 20, 2018, https://www.theatlantic.com/family/archive/2018/03/incredible-everlasting-institution-marriage/555320/, and "Degrees of Change: An Assessment of the Deinstitutionalization of Marriage Thesis," *Journal of Marriage and Family* 82, no. 1 (2020): 73, https://doi.org/10.1111/jomf.12605.
5. Nikki Graf, "Key Findings on Marriage and Cohabitation in the U.S.," Pew Research Center, November 6, 2019, https://www.pewresearch.org/fact-tank/2019/11/06/key-findings-on-marriage-and-cohabitation-in-the-u-s/.
6. Heather Rackin and Christina Gibson-Davis, "Low-Income Childless Young Adults' Marriage and Fertility Frameworks," *Journal of Marriage and Family* 79, no. 4, 1096–1110, https://doi.org/10.1111/jomf.12405; Pamela Smock et al., "'Everything's There Except Money': How Money Shapes Decisions to Marry Among Cohabitors," *Journal of Marriage and Family* 67, no. 3 (2005): 680–96, http://www.jstor.org/stable/3600197.
7. My thanks to Karen Benjamin Guzzo, currently director of University of North Carolina's Population Center, for having her then-colleagues at Bowling Green State University's National Center for Family & Marriage Research calculate these figures for me. Personal communication, April 16, 2022.
8. Kelly Raley, "Cohabitating Couples with Lower Education Levels Marry Less. Is This Because They Do Not Want To?," *PRC Research Brief* 1, no. 3 (2016), http://doi.org/10.15781/T2DV1CN96.
9. Wendy Wang and Kim Parker, "Record Share of Americans Have Never Married," Pew Research Center, September 14, 2014, https://www.pewresearch.org/social-trends/2014/09/24/record-share-of-americans-have-never-married/.

10. US Census Bureau, "America's Families and Living Arrangements: 2021," November 29, 2021, Table A1: *Marital Status of People 15 Years and Over, by Age, Sex, and Personal Earnings: 2021*, https://www.census.gov/data/tables/2021/demo/families/cps-2021.html.
11. Arne L. Kalleberg, *Good Jobs, Bad Jobs: The Rise of Polarized and Precarious Employment Systems in the United States, 1970s—2000s* (Russell Sage Foundation, 2011); Daniel Schneider et al., "What Explains the Decline in First Marriage in the United States?," *Journal of Marriage and Family* 80, no. 4 (2018), https://www.jstor.org/stable/26647602; Daniel Schneider et al., "Job Quality and the Educational Gradient in Entry into Marriage and Cohabitation," *Demography* 56, no. 2 (2019), https://doi.org/10.1007/s13524-018-0749-5; Kristen Harknett and Arielle Kuperberg, "Education, Labor Markets, and the Retreat from Marriage," *Social Forces* 90, no. 1 (2011): 41–63, https://doi.org/10.1093/sf/90.1.41.
12. William J. Goode, *World Revolution and Family Patterns* (Free Press, 1970), and *World Changes in Divorce Patterns* (Yale University Press, 1993); Paul M. de Graaf and Matthijs Kalmijn, "Change and Stability in the Social Determinants of Divorce: A Comparison of Marriage Cohorts in the Netherlands," *European Sociological Review* 22, no. 5 (2006), https://doi.org/10.1093/esr/jcl010; Juho Härkönen and Jaap Dronkers, "Stability and Change in the Educational Gradient of Divorce. A Comparison of Seventeen Countries," *European Sociological Review* 22, no. 5 (2006), https://doi.org/10.1093/esr/jcl011.
13. Jaap Dronkers, "The Changing Impact of Education on Divorce and Break-Up Risk," Institute for Family Studies, October 20, 2015, https://ifstudies.org/blog/the-changing-impact-of-education-on-divorce-and-break-up-risk; R. Kelly Raley et al., "The Growing Racial and Ethnic Divide in U.S. Marriage Patterns," *Future Child* 25, no. 2 (2015), https://doi.org/10.1353/foc.2015.0014; Wendy Wang, "The Link Between a College Education and a Lasting Marriage," Pew Research Center, December 4, 2015, https://www.pewresearch.org/fact-tank/2015/12/04/education-and-marriage/.
14. The quotes here and in the next paragraph are from Brad Wilcox, "When Marriage Disappears, the New Middle America," 2010 State of Our Unions Report, The National Marriage Project, https://nationalmarriageproject.org/2010-state-our-unions; http://stateofourunions.org/2010/when-marriage-disappears.php; and W. Bradford Wilcox et al., "One Nation, Divided: Culture, Civic Institutions, and the Marriage Divide," in "Marriage and Child Wellbeing Revisited," *Future of Children* 25, no. 2 (2015).
15. Glenn Stanton, *The Ring Makes All the Difference: The Hidden Costs of Cohabitation and the Strong Benefits of Marriage* (Moody Publishers, 2011); W. Bradford Wilcox, "Don't Be a Bachelor: Why Married Men Work Harder, Smarter, and Make More Money," *Washington Post*, April 2, 2015, https://www.washingtonpost.com/news/inspired-life/wp/2015/04/02/dont-be-a-bachelor-why-married-men-work-harder-and-smarter-and-make-more

-money/; Ben Christenson, "Want to Be Rich and Happy? Get Married," *Federalist*, February 13, 2024, https://thefederalist.com/2024/02/13/want-to-be-rich-and-happy-get-married/.

16. Lynn Prince Cooke, "The Pathology of Patriarchy and Family Inequalities," in Cahn et al., eds., *Unequal Family Lives: Causes and Consequences in Europe and the Americas* (Cambridge University Press, 2018), 249–50. Sometimes it's just pure coincidence, since men's wages tend to start rising at the same age that they tend to move into marriage. See Alexandra Kilewald and Ian Lindberg, "New Evidence Against a Causal Marriage Wage Premium," *Demography* 54 (2017): 1007–28, https://link.springer.com/article/10.1007/s13524-017-0566-2. It's equally unrealistic to expect that getting married will transform a person's well-being. One study of nearly seventeen thousand people found that almost 80 percent of those who married had reported the same levels of well-being four years *before* their marriage as they reported four years afterward. Anthony Mancini et al., "Stepping Off the Hedonic Treadmill: Individual Differences in Response to Major Life Events," *Journal of Individual Differences* 32 (2011), https://doi.org/10.1027/1614-0001/a000047. See also Virginia Rutter, "Revisit: The Trouble with Averages," Council on Contemporary Families, October 25, 2017, https://thesocietypages.org/ccf/2017/10/25/revisit-the-trouble-with-averages/. On how less-educated, lower-income cohabitors are less likely to marry than more educated and presumably more financially stable couples even when they start with equal intentions to wed, see Raley, "Cohabitating Couples with Lower Education Levels Marry Less."
17. Philip N. Cohen, "Who Are You Gonna Marry? That One Big Assumption Marriage Promotion Gets Totally Wrong," *Family Inequality*, May 8, 2018, https://familyinequality.wordpress.com/2018/05/08/who-are-you-gonna-marry/, and "Partner Prospects and the Marriage Promotion Fallacy," *Family Inequality*, September 30, 2023, https://familyinequality.wordpress.com/2023/09/30/partner-prospects-and-the-marriage-promotion-fallacy/; Wendy Wang, "The Best and Worst Cities for Women Looking to Marry," Pew Research Center, October 2, 2014, http://www.pewresearch.org/fact-tank/2014/10/02/the-best-and-worst-cities-for-women-looking-to-marry/.
18. Philip N. Cohen, *The Family: Diversity, Inequality, and Social Change*, 4th ed. (W. W. Norton & Company, 2024), 96–97; Christina Cross, *Inherited Inequality: Why Opportunity Gaps Persist Between Black and White Youth Raised in Two-Parent Families* (Harvard University Press, 2025). For references to the footnote on this page, see John Schmitt and Kris Warner, "Ex-Offenders and the Labor Market," Center for Economic and Policy Research, November 2010, https://cepr.net/documents/publications/ex-offenders-2010-11.pdf; John Tierney, "Prison and the Poverty Trap, *New York Times*, February 18, 2013; https://www.nytimes.com/2013/02/19/science/long-prison-terms-eyed-as-contributing-to-poverty.html; and Devah Pager et al., "Sequencing

Disadvantage: Barriers to Employment Facing Young Black and White Men with Criminal Records," *ANNALS of the American Academy of Political and Social Science* 623, no. 1 (2009), https://doi.org/10.1177/0002716208330793.

19. Tara Watson and Sara McLanahan, "Marriage Meets the Joneses: Relative Income, Identity, and Marital Status," *Journal of Human Resources* 46, no. 3 (2011): 482–517, https://doi.org/10.3368/jhr.46.3.482.
20. Schneider et al., "What Explains the Decline in First Marriage in the United States?" Another study of young adults from 1997 to 2011 found a strong association between income inequality and the likelihood of unwed births. The higher the income inequality in any particular locality, the less likely men and women were to marry before having a first child, possibly due to the lack of middle-skilled jobs paying wages above the poverty line. Andrew Cherlin et al., "Nonmarital First Births, Marriage, and Income Inequality," *American Sociological Review* 81, no. 4 (2016), https://pmc.ncbi.nlm.nih.gov/articles/PMC5699507/. For an understanding of the dynamics that lead women to embrace motherhood outside of marriage (though unwed childbearing has been falling among low-income women, especially among teenagers), see Gabrielle Raley, "Avenue to Adulthood: Teenage Pregnancy and the Meaning of Motherhood in Poor Communities," in Stephanie Coontz et al., eds., *American Families: A Multicultural Reader*, 2nd ed. (Routledge, 2008); Ellen Scott et al., "'I Try Not to Depend on Anyone but Me': Welfare-Reliant Women's Perspectives on Self-Sufficiency, Work, and Marriage," *Sociological Inquiry* 77, no. 4 (2007), https://doi.org/10.1111/j.1475-682X.2007.00210.x; Catherine Kenny, "Father Doesn't Know Best? Parents' Control of Money & Children's Food Insecurity," *Journal of Marriage and Family* 70, no. 3 (2008): 654–69; Kathryn Edin and Maria Kefalas, *Promises I Can Keep: Why Poor Women Put Motherhood Before Marriage* (University of California Press, 2005).
21. See Stephanie Coontz, "The Moynihan Family Circus," Book Forum, May 31, 2015, republished on Portside, July 23, 2015, https://portside.org/2015-07-23/moynihan-family-circus.
22. Daniel Carlson and Ben Lennox Kail, "Socioeconomic Variation in the Association of Marriage with Depressive Symptoms," *Social Science Research* 71 (2018), https://doi.org/10.1016/j.ssresearch.2017.12.008.
23. Unless otherwise noted, information about the impact of poverty-related stress on marriage formation and intimate relationships is drawn from the following: Benjamin Karney, "Socioeconomic Status and Intimate Relationships," *Annual Review of Psychology* 72 (2021), https://www.annualreviews.org/doi/abs/10.1146/annurev-psych-051920-013658; Benjamin Karney et al., "Supporting Healthy Relationships in Low-Income Couples," *Policy Insights from the Behavioral and Brain Sciences* 51 (2018), https://marriage.psych.ucla.edu/wp-content/uploads/sites/213/2020/05/2372732217747890.pdf; April Buck and Lisa Neff, "Stress Spillover in Early Marriage: The Role of Self-

Regulatory Depletion," *Journal of Family Psychology* 26 (2012), https://pubmed.ncbi.nlm.nih.gov/22866931/; Hannah Williamson et al., "Financial Strain and Stressful Events Predict Newlyweds' Negative Communication Independent of Relationship Satisfaction," *Journal of Family Psychology* 27 (2013), https://pubmed.ncbi.nlm.nih.gov/23421833/; Lisa Neff and Benjamin Karney, "Stress and Reactivity to Daily Relationship Experiences: How Stress Hinders Adaptive Processes in Marriage," *Journal of Personality and Social Psychology* 97 (2009), https://pubmed.ncbi.nlm.nih.gov/19686000/; Linda Burton et al., "The Role of Trust in Low-Income Mothers' Intimate Unions," *Journal of Marriage and Family* 7 (2009), https://pubmed.ncbi.nlm.nih.gov/19966929/. On erratic work schedules and income flows, see Lauren Bauer et al., "Low-Income Workers Experience—by Far—the Most Earnings and Work Hours Instability," Brookings Institution, January 9, 2025, https://www.brookings.edu/articles/low-income-workers-experience-by-far-the-most-earnings-and-work-hours-instability/.

24. A study of how families coped with the COVID shutdowns found that one of the strongest predictors that a family would sustain or even improve its functioning during this stressful period was if the couple reported feeling appreciated and acknowledged by each other. Allen Barton et al., "Family Resiliency in the Aftermath of COVID-19 Pandemic: A Latent Profile Analysis," *Journal of Marriage and Family* 85, no. 5 (2023): 1125–37, https://doi.org/10.1111/jomf.12929. Psychologist John Gottman argues that when partners don't recognize and respond positively to each other's "bids for connection," that is a particularly strong predictor of later divorce. John Gottman and Julie Gottman, "The Natural Principles of Love," *Journal of Family Theory and Review* 9 (2017), https://doi.org/10.1111/jftr.12182.
25. Williamson et al., "Financial Strain and Stressful Events"; Thomas Bradbury and Benjamin Karney, "Understanding and Altering the Longitudinal Course of Marriage," *Journal of Marriage and Family* 66, no. 4 (2004), https://www.jstor.org/stable/3600163.
26. To illustrate the impact of scarcity on judgment and observational abilities, researchers divided a group of subjects into two groups on the basis of their self-reported income and then divided each of the two different economic groups into two, giving each half one of two different scenarios to test their reasoning abilities. In one, the problem involved a decision about a car repair issue that involved a $300 expense. The high-income and low-income groups who got this problem did equally well in solving it. But the other half of each group got a different problem, just as mathematically easy, but this time involving a $3,000 expense. The requirement to imagine coming up with so much money in the context of their real-world inability to do so left the lower-income group so stressed that they took longer to decide and gave less rational answers. Next the researchers gave the same people a concentration

test where they had to hit a button as soon as a flower appeared. The half of the high-income group and the half of the low-income group who had been given the low-money problem performed equally well, hitting the right key about 83 percent of the time, as did the high-income group that had completed that high-money problem. But the low-income group that had just completed the stressful money-imagining experiment hit the right key only 63 percent of the time. That decline in performance corresponded to a thirteen- to fourteen-point drop in IQ, a difference, the authors point out, that can move a person from average to borderline deficient. Sendhil Mullainathan and Eldar Shafir, *Scarcity: Why Having Too Little Means So Much* (Times Books, 2013), 49–52. The South Dakota Statewide Family Engagement Center has developed a powerful way of helping affluent Americans "get" just how stressful poverty is: Morgan VonHaden and Jessica Olson, "Poverty Escape Room Brings Home the Realities Low-Income Families Face," Spotlight on Poverty and Opportunity, February 26, 2025, https://spotlightonpoverty.org/spotlight-exclusives/poverty-escape-room-brings-home-the-realities-low-income-families-face/. And the Better Life Lab that Haley Swenson describes in her afterword to this book has created an enlightening interactive "game" to illustrate the hard choices and complicated outcomes that people in poverty must make: Jasmine Heyward, "Why Did a Think Tank Make a Text-Based Game?," New America, March 12, 2025, https://www.newamerica.org/better-life-lab/blog/why-did-a-think-tank-make-a-text-based-game/.

27. Benjamin R. Karney, "Socioeconomic Status and Intimate Relationships," *Annual Review of Psychology* 72 (2021), https://pmc.ncbi.nlm.nih.gov/articles/PMC8179854/.
28. Daniel Schneider et al., "Intimate Partner Violence in the Great Recession," *Demography* 53 (2016), https://pubmed.ncbi.nlm.nih.gov/27003136/.
29. Adrianne Brown and Karen Guzzo, "Trends in Non-Marriage Among Men, 2005–2019," National Center for Family & Marriage Research, https://doi.org/10.25035/ncfmr/fp-22-01. Unfortunately, as this book went to press, there were no comparable figures on education and marriage rates of Native American men or women.
30. On Black and Indian marriage and divorce rates, see Gordon Limb and Kevin Shafer, "American Indian Fragile Families and the Marriage Initiative: A Replication Study," *Advances in Social Work* 19, no. 1 (2019), https://doi.org/10.18060/22605; Ana Swanson, "Who Gets Divorced in America in 7 Charts," *Washington Post*, April 6, 2016, https://www.washingtonpost.com/news/wonk/wp/2016/04/06/who-gets-divorced-in-america-in-7-charts/; Dedrick Asante-Muhammad et al., "Racial Wealth Snapshot: Native Americans," February 14, 2022, https://ncrc.org/racial-wealth-snapshot-american-indians-native-americans/.

31. Unless otherwise noted, the information about Black marriage values and patterns comes from the following works, many of which also discuss the strengths and coping mechanisms that allow many Black marriages to thrive despite the pressures I describe here: M. Belinda Tucker, "Marital Values and Expectations in Context: Results from a 21-City Survey," in Linda Waite et al., eds., *The Ties That Bind: Perspectives on Marriage and Cohabitation* (Aldine de Gruyter, 2000); "Why Has Marriage Declined Among Black Americans," Scholars Strategy Network, October 26, 2013; https://scholars.org/brief/why-has-marriage-declined-among-black-americans; Antoinette Landor and Shardé McNeil Smith, "Systemic Racism and Romantic Relationships," in Brian G. Ogolsky, ed., *The Sociocultural Context of Romantic Relationships* (Cambridge University Press 2023); Christiana Awosan and Kenneth Hardy, "Coupling Processes and Experiences of Never-Married Heterosexual Black Men and Women: A Phenomenological Study," *Journal of Marital and Family Therapy* 43, no. 3 (2017), 463–81, https://doi.org/10.1111/jmft.12215; Allen W. Barton and Chalandra M. Bryant, "Financial Strain, Trajectories of Marital Processes, and African American Newlyweds' Marital Instability," *Journal of Family Psychology* 30, no. 6 (2016), 657, https://doi.org/10.1037/fam0000190; Linda M. Burton and M. Belinda Tucker, "Romantic Unions in an Era of Uncertainty: A Post-Moynihan Perspective on African American Women and Marriage," *Annals of the American Academy of Political and Social Science* 621, no. 1 (2009): 132–48, https://www.jstor.org/stable/40375836; Carolyn Cutrona et al., "Neighborhood Context and Financial Strain as Predictors of Marital Interaction and Marital Quality in African American Couples," *Personal Relationships* 10, no. 3 (2003): 389–409, https://doi.org/10.1111/1475-6811.00056; Justin Lavner et al., "Racial Discrimination and Relationship Functioning Among African American Couples," *Journal of Family Psychology* 32, no. 5 (2018): 686–91, https://doi.org/10.1037/fam0000415. For a helpful historical discussion of the dangers of attributing changes in the Black family primarily to cultural factors, see Donna Franklin and Angela James, *Ensuring Inequality: The Structural Transformation of the Black Family*, rev. ed. (Oxford University Press, 2015).
32. Patrick Sharkey, "Neighborhoods and the Black-White Mobility Gap," Economic Mobility Project, Pew Charitable Trusts, July 2009, https://www.pewtrusts.org/~/media/legacy/uploadedfiles/wwwpewtrustsorg/reports/economic_mobility/pewsharkeyv12pdf. Wealth, which is a better predictor of people's security than income, is a strong predictor of marriage and of ongoing marital stability. Racial differences in wealth are even more pronounced than racial differences in income, and researchers estimate that differences in wealth account for about 30 percent of the gap in marriage entry between Blacks and Whites. See Daniel Schneider, "Wealth and the Marital Divide," *American Journal of Sociology* 117, no. 2 (2011), https://www

.journals.uchicago.edu/doi/abs/10.1086/661594; Alicia Eads and Laura Tach, "Wealth and Inequality in the Stability of Romantic Relationships," *Russell Sage Foundation Journal of the Social Sciences* 2, no. 6 (2016), https://doi.org/10.7758/RSF.2016.2.6.10.

33. For more on the distinctive family processes of Black families, including the cultural, religious, and community processes that foster strength and resilience, see Dawne M. Mouzon, "'Blacks Don't Value Marriage as Much as Other Groups': Family Patterns and Persisting Inequality," in *What White People Think They Know (and People of Color Aren't Totally Clear on Either): Questioning Conventional Wisdom About Race*, eds. Cherise Harris and Nikki Khanna (Sage Publications, 2013); Chalandra M. Bryant, "Studying Marital Relationships Using Family Systems as a Guide," in *Black Families: A Systems Approach*, ed. Anthony Jones (Cognella Press, 2020); Deirdre Bloome and Shannon Ang, "Marriage and Union Formation in the United States: Recent Trends Across Racial Groups and Economic Backgrounds," *Demography* 57, no. 5 (2020), https://doi.org/10.1007/s13524-020-00910-7; Tera R. Hurt, "Toward a Deeper Understanding of the Meaning of Marriage Among Black Men," *Journal of Family Issues* 34, no. 7 (2013): 859–84, https://doi.org/10.1177/0192513X12451737; Landor and Smith, "Systemic Racism and Romantic Relationships"; TeKisha Rice et al., "Racial Discrimination and Romantic Relationship Dynamics Among Black Americans," *Journal of Family Theory and Review* 15, no. 4 (2023), https://doi.org/10.1111/jftr.12535; Linda Burton et al., "The Role of Trust in Low-Income Mothers' Intimate Unions," *Journal of Marriage and Family* 71, no. 5 (2009), https://www.jstor.org/stable/27752528; and the classic work by Robert Hill, *The Strengths of Black Families*, new edition with updated afterword (University Press of America, 2003).

34. Jennifer Lundquist, "When Race Makes No Difference: Marriage and the Military," *Social Forces* 83, no. 2 (2004), https://doi.org/10.1353/sof.2005.0017, and "The Black–White Gap in Marital Dissolution Among Young Adults: What Can a Counterfactual Scenario Tell Us?," *Social Problems* 53, no. 3 (2006), https://doi.org/10.1525/sp.2006.53.3.421.

35. Jay Teachman and Lucky Tedrow, "Divorce, Race, and Military Service: More Than Equal Pay and Equal Opportunity," *Journal of Marriage and Family* 70, no. 4 (2008), https://doi.org/10.1111/j.1741-3737.2008.00544.x.

36. Ana Swanson, "Who Gets Divorced in America in 7 Charts"; Dedrick Asante-Muhammad et al., "Racial Wealth Snapshot: Native Americans."

37. For horrifying examples of the massacres and other atrocities that resulted in intergenerational trauma, see Margaret Jacobs, *After One Hundred Winters: In Search of Reconciliation on America's Stolen Lands* (Princeton University Press, 2021). On the trauma caused by the removal of Native children to boarding schools, see David Wallace Adams, *Education for Extinction: American Indians and the Boarding School Experience, 1875–1928*, 2nd ed. (Univer-

sity Press of Kansas, 2020); "Trigger Points: Current State of Research on History, Impacts, and Healing Related to the United States' Indian Industrial/Boarding School Policy," Native American Rights Fund, November 2019, https://www.narf.org/nill/documents/trigger-points.pdf; K. Tsianina Lomawaima et al., "Native American Boarding School Stories," *Journal of American Indian Education* 57, no. 1 (2018), https://doi.org/10.5749/jamerindieduc.57.1.0001. I thank Carolyn Liebler, associate professor of sociology, University of Minnesota, for providing me with research guidance and comments on this question. For details of the physical and sexual abuse to which children were subjected, see also Dana Hedgpeth and Emmanual Martinez, "More Schools That Forced American Indian Children to Assimilate Revealed," *Washington Post*, August 30, 2023, https://www.washingtonpost.com/nation/2023/08/30/indian-boarding-schools/; Sari Horwitz et al., "In the Name of God," *Washington Post*, May 29, 2024, https://www.washingtonpost.com/investigations/interactive/2024/sexual-abuse-native-american-boarding-schools/; "The Native American Boarding School System," *New York Times*, August 30, 2023, https://www.nytimes.com/interactive/2023/08/30/us/native-american-boarding-schools.html; Dana Hedgpeth et al., "More Than 3,100 Students Died at Schools Built to Crush Native American Cultures," *Washington Post*, December 22, 2024, https://www.washingtonpost.com/investigations/interactive/2024/native-american-deaths-burial-sites-boarding-schools. And for a moving personal account of the trauma, see Mary Annette Pember, *Medicine River: A Story of Survival and the Legacy of Indian Boarding Schools* (Pantheon, 2025).

38. For this and the following two paragraphs, see Isabel Sawhill and Katherine Guyot, "Women's Work Boosts Middle Class Incomes but Creates a Family Time Squeeze That Needs to Be Eased," Brookings Institution, May 2020, https://www.brookings.edu/articles/womens-work-boosts-middle-class-incomes-but-creates-a-family-time-squeeze-that-needs-to-be-eased/; and "The Middle Class Time Squeeze," Brookings Institution, August 2020, https://www.brookings.edu/wp-content/uploads/2020/08/The-Middle-Class-Time-Squeeze_08.18.2020.pdf.

39. Urban Institute calculations from the Survey of Financial Characteristics of Consumers 1962, the Survey of Changes in Family Finances 1963, and the Survey of Consumer Finances 1983–2022, "Nine Charts About Wealth Inequality in America," April 25, 2024, https://apps.urban.org/features/wealth-inequality-charts.

40. Comparative cross-cultural studies reveal that this is an international pattern: Competitive and intensive child-rearing rises as economic inequality increases. See Matthias Doepke and Fabrizio Zilibotti, *Love, Money, and Parenting: How Economics Explains the Way We Raise Our Kids* (Princeton University Press, 2019). On American trends, see Melissa Milkie and Catharine

Warner, "Status Safeguarding: Mothers' Work to Secure Children's Place in the Status Hierarchy," in *Intensive Mothering: The Cultural Contradictions of Modern Motherhood*, ed. Linda Rose Ennis (Demeter Press, 2014), 66–85; and Melissa Milkie et al., "Gendered Pressures," *Journal of Comparative Family Studies* 52, no. 2 (2021), https://www.jstor.org/stable/27092301; Patrick Ishizuka, "Social Class, Gender, and Contemporary Parenting Standards in the United States: Evidence from a National Survey Experiment," *Social Forces* 98, no. 1 (2019), https://doi.org/10.1093/sf/soy107; Garey Ramey and Valerie Ramey, "The Rug Rat Race," Working Paper No. 15284 (National Bureau of Economic Research, August 2009), https://www.nber.org/system/files/working_papers/w15284/w15284.pdf.

41. Sawhill and Guyot, "The Middle Class Time Squeeze."

Chapter 8: The New "Rules of Engagement"

1. The phrase "deinstitutionalization of marriage" was first used by sociologist Andrew Cherlin. I am using a looser and in some ways more far-reaching definition of deinstitutionalization than many sociologists, emphasizing the decrease in the rewards society offers to those who wed and the penalties it imposes on those who don't, as well as the lessening of control over what roles individuals can and can't play in a marriage, and how restricted their options are for exiting marriage. For a more traditional sociological discussion of the concept, see Andrew Cherlin, "The Deinstitutionalization of American Marriage," *Journal of Marriage and Family* 66, no. 4 (2004), https://doi.org/10.1111/j.0022-2445.2004.00058.x, and "Degrees of Change: An Assessment of the Deinstitutionalization of Marriage Thesis," *Journal of Marriage and Family* 82, no. 1 (2020), https://doi.org/10.1111/jomf.12605; and Sean Lauer and Carrie Yodanis, "The Deinstitutionalization of Marriage Revisited: A New Institutional Approach to Marriage," *Journal of Family Theory & Review* 2, no. 2 (2010), https://doi.org/10.1111/j.1756-2589.2010.00039.x.
2. Nancy Cott, *Public Vows: A History of Marriage and the Nation* (Harvard University Press, 2000), 212–13. On the American cases, see Carl Esbeck and Jonathon Hartog, eds., *Disestablishment and Religious Dissent: Church-State Relations in the New American States, 1776–1833* (University of Missouri Press, 2019).
3. Philip N. Cohen, "Turning the Tide on Marriage Is Not the Same as Coasting Downstream on Teen Pregnancy," *Family Inequality*, November 25, 2023, https://familyinequality.wordpress.com/2023/11/05/turning-the-tide-on-marriage-is-not-the-same-as-coasting-downstream-on-teen-pregnancy/ and https://familyinequality.files.wordpress.com/2023/11/25-countries.png.
4. Natalie Bankey, "Median Age at First Marriage: Geographic Variation, 2023," Family Profiles, 2025, National Center for Family & Marriage Research, https://www.bgsu.edu/content/dam/BGSU/college-of-arts-and-sciences

/NCFMR/documents/FP/fp-25-09-med-age-1stmar-geo-var-2025-04-16-kkp.pdf.

5. See the references in Coontz, *Marriage, a History*, 227.
6. Evelyn Lehrer, "Are Individuals Who Marry at an Older Age Too Set in Their Ways to Make Their Marriages Work?," Council on Contemporary Families, January 29, 2009, https://contemporaryfamilies.utah.edu/publications/posts/2009/january/marrying-at-older-ages.php.
7. Philip Cohen, "Science Says: Get Married at Age Whatever You Want," *Family Inequality*, May 29, 2022, https://familyinequality.wordpress.com/2022/05/29/science-says-get-married-at-age-whatever-you-want-and-these-are-the-odds-of-divorce/.
8. For an in-depth examination of the different ways twenty-one young couples dealt with the difficulties of reconciling their egalitarian aspirations with their structural and cultural constraints, see Jaclyn Wong, "Competing Desires: How Young Adult Couples Negotiate Moving for Career Opportunities," *Gender & Society* 31, no. 2 (2017), 171–96, https://doi.org/10.1177/0891243217695520.
9. Philip N. Cohen, *The Family: Diversity, Inequality, and Social Change*, 4th ed. (W. W. Norton & Company, 2024), 225.
10. Sharon Sassler and Amanda Miller, "Assessing the Deinstitutionalization of Marriage Thesis: Changes in the Meaning of Cohabitation over the Relationship Life Course," *Journal of Marriage and Family* 85, no. 2 (2023), https://doi.org/10.1111/jomf.12883.
11. Galena Rhodes and Scott Stanley, "Before 'I Do,'" The National Marriage Project, 2014, https://nationalmarriageproject.org/sites/g/files/jsddwu1276/files/2025-06/SOCI221_NMP_BeforeIDoReport.pdf.
12. Unless otherwise noted, most of the information about hookups is drawn from the following: Jessie Ford and Paula England, "Hookups, Sex, and Relationships at College," *Contexts*, December 22, 2014, https://contexts.org/blog/hookups-sex-and-relationships-at-college/; Arielle Kuperberg and Joseph Padgett, "The Date's Not Dead After All: New Findings on Hooking Up, Dating and Romantic Relationships in College," Council on Contemporary Families, February 11, 2016, https://thesocietypages.org/ccf/2016/08/10/; Joseph Padgett and Lisa Wade, "Hookup Culture and Higher Education," in Tasha Orens and Andrea Press, eds., *The Routledge Handbook of Contemporary Feminism* (Routledge, 2019); Lisa Wade, "Doing Casual Sex: A Sexual Fields Approach to the Emotional Force of Hookup Culture," *Social Problems* 68, no. 1 (2021), https://doi.org/10.1093/socpro/spz054; Jennifer Hirsch and Shamus Khan, *Sexual Citizens: A Landmark Study of Sex, Power, and Assault on Campus* (W. W. Norton & Company, 2020); Deborah Rhode, "Sex and Consent on Campus: Definitions, Dilemmas, and New Directions," in "Defining Consent," Stephanie Coontz and Paula England, eds., Council

on Contemporary Families, October 22, 2019, https://thesocietypages.org/ccf/2020/04/21/sex-and-consent-on-campus-definitions-dilemmas-and-new-directions/; and Jessie Ford, "'Consensualish'—What About Sex That Is Unwanted, but Not Physically Coercive?," in Coontz and England, "Defining Consent," https://thesocietypages.org/ccf/2020/11/17/consensualish-lets-talk-about-sex-that-people-dont-want-but-go-along-with-it/.

13. Paula England, "Is a 'Warm Hookup' an Oxymoron?," *Contexts* 15, no. 4 (2016), 58–59, https://doi.org/10.1177/1536504216685114; Elizabeth Armstrong et al., "Orgasm in College Hookups and Relationships," in Virginia Rutter et al., eds., *Families as They Really Are*, 3rd ed. (W. W. Norton & Company, 2024). See also Natalie Kitroeff, "In Hookups, Inequality Still Reigns," *New York Times*, November 11, 2013, https://archive.nytimes.com/well.blogs.nytimes.com/2013/11/11/women-find-orgasms-elusive-in-hookups.
14. Kuperberg and Padgett, "The Date's Not Dead After All."
15. Melissa Hardesty et al., "What Are College Students Talking About When They Say They're 'Just Talking'?," *Emerging Adulthood* 12, no. 3 (2024), https://doi.org/10.1177/21676968241234398.
16. Ray Oldenburg, *The Great Good Place: Cafes, Coffee Shops, Bookstores, Bars, Hair Salons, and Other Hangouts at the Heart of a Community* (Hachette, 1999).
17. Michael Rosenfeld et al., "Disintermediating Your Friends: How Online Dating in the United States Displaces Other Ways of Meeting," *Proceedings of the National Academy of Sciences* 116, no. 36 (2019), https://doi.org/10.1073/pnas.1908630116.
18. Colleen McClain and Risa Gelles-Watnick, "From Looking for Love to Swiping the Field: Online Dating in the U.S.," Pew Research Center, January 25, 2023, https://www.pewresearch.org/internet/2023/02/02/from-looking-for-love-to-swiping-the-field-online-dating-in-the-u-s/. For some more on the pros and cons of dating in the digital age, see Marie Bergstrom, *The New Laws of Love: Online Dating and the Privatization of Intimacy* (Polity, 2022).

    On how individuals' tendency to rely on racial and ethnic stereotypes in their dating choices and how dating app algorithms that sort potential matches on the basis of racial and ethnic similarities constrain people's choices, see Celeste Vaughan et al., *The Dating Divide: Race and Desire in the Era of Online Romance* (University of California Press, 2021). For a fascinating theoretical essay demonstrating that what individuals first find attractive in a potential partner they don't know has very little relationship to their attraction and compatibility once they start getting to know each other, see Paul Eastick et al., "Mate Evaluation Theory," *Psychological Review* 130, no. 1 (2023), https://doi.org/10.1037/rev0000.
19. Eli Tan, "You Don't Need to Swipe Right. A.I. Is Transforming Dating Apps," *New York Times*, November 3, 2025, https://www.nytimes.com/2025/11/03/technology/ai-dating-apps.html.

20. Nicholas Wolfinger and Samuel Perry, "Does a Longer Sexual Resume Affect Marriage Rates?," *Social Science Research* 113 (2023), https://www.sciencedirect.com/science/article/abs/pii/S0049089X22001119.
21. Leslie McCall, "Men Against Women, or the Top 20 Percent Against the Bottom 80?," Council on Contemporary Families, February 18, 2015, https://thesocietypages.org/ccf/2015/02/18/men-against-women/; Christine Schwartz and Hongyun Han, "The Reversal of the Gender Gap in Education and Trends in Marital Dissolution," *American Sociological Review* 79, no. 4 (2014), 605–29, https://doi.org/10.1177/0003122414539682.
22. Michael Noer, "Don't Marry Career Women," *Forbes*, August 22, 2006, https://www.forbes.com/2006/08/21/careers-marriage-dating_cx_mn_0821women.
23. Christine Schwartz and Pilar Gonalons-Pons, "Trends in Relative Earnings and Marital Dissolution: Are Wives Who Outearn Their Husbands Still More Likely to Divorce?," *Russell Sage Foundation Journal of the Social Sciences* 2, no. 4 (2016), 218–36, https://www.rsfjournal.org/content/2/4/218.
24. Killewald Alexandra, "Money, Work, and Marital Stability: Assessing Change in the Gendered Determinants of Divorce," *American Sociological Review* 81, no. 4 (2016).
25. Dan Carlson et al., "Stalled for Whom? Change in the Division of Particular Housework Tasks and Their Consequences for Middle- to Low-Income Couples," *Socius* 4 (2018), https://doi.org/10.1177/2378023118765867. See also Daniel Carlson, "Not All Housework Is Created Equal," Council on Contemporary Families, April 24, 2018, https://thesocietypages.org/ccf/2018/04/24/not-all-housework-is-created-equal-particular-housework-tasks-and-couples-relationship-quality/. For a visual representation of the relationship between dishwashing and marital quality, see the illustration in Stephanie Coontz, "How to Make Your Marriage Gayer," *New York Times*, February 13, 2020, https://www.nytimes.com/2020/02/13/opinion/sunday/marriage-housework-gender-happiness.html. See also Michelle Frisco and Kristi Williams, "Perceived Housework Equity, Marital Happiness, and Divorce in Dual-Earner Households," *Journal of Family Issues* 24, no. 1 (2003), 51–73, https://doi.org/10.1177/0192513X02238520.
26. Lynn Prince Cooke, "'Doing' Gender in Context: Household Bargaining and Risk of Divorce in Germany and the United States," *American Journal of Sociology* 112, no. 2 (2006), https://doi.org/10.1086/506417; Alfred DeMaris, "The Role of Relationship Inequity in Marital Disruption," *Journal of Social and Personal Relationships* 24, no. 2 (2007), https://doi.org/10.1177/0265407507075409; Sarah Schoppe-Sullivan et al., "Associations Between Coparenting and Marital Behavior from Infancy to the Preschool Years, *Journal of Family Psychology* 18, no. 1 (2004): 194–207, https://doi.org/10.1037/0893-3200.18.1.194; Chrustine Stanik et al., "Gender Dynamics Predict Changes in

Marital Love Among African American Couples," *Journal of Marriage and Family* 75, no. 4 (2013), https://doi.org/10.1111/jomf.12037; Yungying Le et al., "Longitudinal Associations Between Relationship Quality and Coparenting Across the Transition to Parenthood: A Dyadic Perspective," *Journal of Family Psychology* 30, no. 8 (2016), https://doi.org/10.1037/fam0000217; Alexandra Chong and Kristin Mickelson, "Perceived Fairness and Relationship Satisfaction During the Transition to Parenthood: The Mediating Role of Spousal Support," *Journal of Family Issues* 37, no. 1 (2013), https://doi.org/10.1177/0192513X13516764; Brian Don et al., "Feeling Like Part of a Team: Perceived Parenting Agreement Among First-Time Parents," *Journal of Social and Personal Relationships* 30, no. 8 (2013), https://doi.org/10.1177/0265407513483105.

27. Daniela Bellina and Gosta Esping-Andersen, "Gendered Time Allocation and Divorce: A Longitudinal Analysis of German and American Couples," *Family Relations* 69, no 1 (2020), https://onlinelibrary.wiley.com/toc/17413729/2020/69/1.
28. Kathleen Gerson, *Why No One Can Have It All: The Collision of Work and Caregiving in an Age of Insecurity*, forthcoming. See also "Why No One Can 'Have It All' and Why That Matters to Everyone," *Sociological Forum* 38 no. 4 (2023), http://doi.org/10.1111/socf.12959.
29. Daniel Carlson, "Reconceptualizing the Gendered Division of Housework: Number of Shared Tasks and Partners' Relationship Quality," *Sex Roles* 86, no. 9–10 (2022), https://doi.org/10.1007/s11199-022-01282-5. See also Carlson, "Mine and Yours, or Ours: Are All Egalitarian Relationships Equal?," Council on Contemporary Families, April 25, 2022, https://thesocietypages.org/ccf/2022/11/08/mine-and-yours-or-ours-are-all-egalitarian-relationships-equal/. My thanks to Dan Carlson for going over his findings with me and sharing charts and graphs that did not appear in the final article.
30. For one example of such findings, see Paul Amato et al., "Continuity and Change in Marital Quality Between 1980 and 2000," *Journal of Marriage and the Family* 65, no. 1 (2003), https://www.jstor.org/stable/3600047.
31. See Carlson, "Reconceptualizing," for a discussion of how inequity in a relationship can create discomfort even for the person who benefits from it. Another example of how taking on more family responsibilities can actually improve men's well-being along with their partner's is found in a 2020 study of how almost two thousand parents divided their "cognitive labor" during the pandemic—who kept track of nonroutine household and family needs, identified options for meeting those needs, and then monitored progress or organized schedules to make sure everything got done. In couples where mothers did the majority of these (often invisible) tasks, they reported higher levels of stress and more depressive symptoms than mothers in couples where the cognitive labor was more evenly distributed. But when couples divided that work more evenly, *both* mothers and fathers reported less

stress and depression. Richard Petts and Daniel Carlson, "Managing a Household During a Pandemic: Cognitive Labor and Parents' Psychological Well-Being," *Society and Mental Health* 13, no. 3 (2023), https://doi.org/10.1177/21568693231169521.

32. Unless otherwise noted, here are the references on the material about same-sex couples in this and the following paragraphs: Kenneth Matos, "Modern Families: Same- and Different-Sex Couples Negotiating at Home," Families and Work Institute, 2015, https://cdn.sanity.io/files/ow8usu72/production/60c48ce374802f4fbfb5ff84b692d244a324d024.pdf; Abbie Goldberg, "'Doing' and 'Undoing' Gender: The Meaning and Division of Housework in Same-Sex Couples," *Journal of Family Theory & Review* 5, no. 2 (2013); Melanie E. Brewster, "Lesbian Women and Household Labor Division: A Systematic Review of Scholarly Research from 2000 to 2015," *Journal of Lesbian Studies* 21, no. 1 (2017): 47–69, https://doi.org/10.1080/10894160.2016.1142350; Samantha Tornello et al., "Division of Labor Among Gay Fathers: Associations with Parent, Couple, and Child Adjustment," *Psychology of Sexual Orientation and Gender Diversity* 2, no. 4 (2015), https://doi.org/10.1037/sgdo000109; Rachel Farr and Charlotte Patterson, "Coparenting Among Lesbian, Gay, and Heterosexual Couples: Associations with Adopted Children's Outcomes," *Child Development* 51, no. 4 (2013), https://doi.org/10.1111/cdev.12046; Charlotte Patterson et al., "Division of Labor Among Lesbian and Heterosexual Parenting Couples: Correlates of Specialized Versus Shared Patterns," *Journal of Adult Development* 11 (2004), https://doi.org/10.1023/B:JADE.0000035626.90331.47.

There is a remarkable difference in the time that men with a same-sex partner and the time that men with a different-sex partner spend with children. Some of this is probably a selection factor, since gay men have to *really* want children in order to make that happen, and the effort it takes probably intensifies the sense of commitment. Still, an analysis of American Time Use Surveys from 2003 to 2013 found that on average, gay fathers spent more time with their children each day than straight or gay mothers or heterosexual fathers! Kate Prickett et al., "A Research Note on Time with Children in Different- and Same-Sex Two-Parent Families," *Demography* 52, no. 3 (2015): 905–18, https://doi.org/10.1007/s13524-015-0385-2. For a visual demonstration of the difference in parental time, see the illustrations Prickett and her colleagues provided for my 2020 op-ed in *The New York Times*: Stephanie Coontz, "How to Make Your Marriage Gayer," *New York Times*, February 13, 2020, https://www.nytimes.com/2020/02/13/opinion/sunday/marriage-housework-gender-happiness.html. For other research on same-sex parenting, see Rachel Farr et al., "How Do LGBTQ+ Parents Raise Well-Adjusted, Resilient, and Thriving Children?," *Current Directions in Psychological Science* 31, no. 6 (2022), 526–35, https://doi.org/10.1177/09637214221121295; Charlotte Patterson et al., "Division of Labor Among Lesbian and Heterosexual Parenting Couples: Correlates of Specialized Versus Shared Patterns," *Journal of Adult Development* 11 (2004): 179–89, https://doi.org/10.1023/B:JADE.0000035626.90331.47.

Despite these advantages, same-sex couples are not immune to the gender socialization that remains pervasive in our society. As I explain in "How to Make Your Marriage Gayer," having a double dose of masculine or feminine socialization in a relationship can pose problems. Women have much more extensive expectations of empathy and emotional support than men, and they monitor relationship quality more closely. This may explain why lesbian marriages, despite their high average quality, are also more likely to break up than gay-male or different-sex marriage. Other studies reveal that although same-sex couples generally use greater positivity than different-sex couples, an exception occurs among male same-sex couples if one partner becomes particularly negative in presenting his side of an argument. On those occasions, his partner often finds it harder to turn down the heat than do lesbian and heterosexual partners, possibly because of the masculine socialization to interpret negative interactions as disrespect. See, for example, John Gottman et al., "Observing Gay, Lesbian and Heterosexual Couples' Relationships: Mathematical Modeling of Conflict Interaction," *Journal of Homosexuality* 45, no. 1 (2003), https://pubmed.ncbi.nlm.nih.gov/14567654/; Giuseppina Holway et al., "Health and Health Behavior Concordance Between Spouses in Same-Sex and Different-Sex Marriages," *Social Currents* 5, no. 4 (2018): 319–27, https://doi.org/10.1177/2329496517734570; Abbie Goldberg and Randi Garcia, "Predictors of Relationship Dissolution in Lesbian, Gay, and Heterosexual Adoptive Parents," *Journal of Family Psychology* 29, no. 3 (2015), https://www.ncbi.nlm.nih.gov/pmc/articles/PMC4460604/. It will be interesting to see what we can learn from the relationship patterns of the growing number of trans, nonbinary, and gender-fluid individuals as they deal with the external challenges facing modern marriages as well as the conflicting demands and habits of conventional gender roles and sexual values.

33. Tom McClelland and Pauline Sliwa, "Gendered Affordance Perception and Unequal Domestic Labour," *Philosophy and Phenomenological Research* 107, no. 2 (2023), https://doi.org/10.1111/phpr.12929.
34. Sarah Thébaud et al., "Good Housekeeping, Great Expectations: Gender and Housework Norms," *Sociological Methods & Research* 50, no. 3 (2021): 1186–1214, https://doi.org/10.1177/0049124119852395. For more on double standards of housework, see Jessica Grose, "Cleaning: The Final Feminist Frontier," *New Republic*, March 19, 2013, https://newrepublic.com/article/112693/112693.
35. Eve Rodsky, *Fair Play: A Game-Changing Solution for When You Have Too Much to Do* (Putnam, 2019).

36. Melissa Milkie et al., "Who's Doing the Housework and Childcare in America Now? Differential Convergence in Twenty-First-Century Gender Gaps in Home Tasks," *Socius* 11 (2025), https://journals.sagepub.com/doi/10.1177/23780231251314667.
37. Researchers have long thought that marriage itself increases gender inequality, possibly because of its long association with rigid gender roles, a view supported by the fact that cohabiting heterosexual couples tend to share housework more equally than married ones. But some new research suggests that nowadays it is childbearing that triggers inequality. Arielle Kuperberg, "First Comes Love, Then Comes . . . Housework?," Council on Contemporary Families, July 16, 2015, https://thesocietypages.org/ccf/2015/07/16/first-comes-love/.

    This process can occur without a couple even noticing it at first. In one study, researchers had 182 different-sex dual-career couples, all committed to gender equity, keep detailed time diaries before the birth of their first child. The diaries confirmed the couples' claims that they shared paid and household work equally. Nine months after the child's birth, both husbands and wives told interviewers they were still sharing the load. But this time their detailed diaries contradicted their verbal reports. "Before the baby was born, a man's average work week (paid and unpaid hours combined) was three hours longer than his partner's. But after the birth of their child, the man's total workload averaged about eight and a half hours *less* per week." Jill Yavorsky et al., "Gender Inequalities in Dual-Earner, College Educated Couples," Council on Contemporary Families, November 23, 2016, https://thesocietypages.org/ccf/2016/11/23/gender-inequalities-in-dual-earner-college-educated-couples-and-the-transition-to-parenthood/. It's easy to understand how the initial illusion of equality could lead a mother first to exhaustion and then to fury when reality sinks in.
38. America is the *only* country among the forty-one nations that make up the Organization for Economic Cooperation and Development and the European Union that doesn't guarantee paid leave for new parents. Fewer than 30 percent of private sector workers in the US have access to paid parental leave, and even unpaid leaves are typically shorter than the minimum of two months of paid leave available to workers in the other forty OECD countries. Kara Dennison, "How U.S. Family Leave Policies Can Catch Up with the Rest of the World," *Forbes*, November 13, 2023, https://www.forbes.com/sites/karadennison/2023/11/13/how-us-family-leave-policies-can-catch-up-with-the-rest-of-the-world; and "Employee Benefits," EBS Latest Numbers, US Bureau of Labor Statistics, https://www.bls.gov/ebs/latest-numbers.htm. See also the 2019 Council on Contemporary Families caregiving symposium, "Parents Can't Go It Alone," https://thesocietypages.org/ccf/2019/12/17/parents-cant-go-it-alone-they-never-have-what-to-do-for

-parents-to-help-our-next-generation-2/. On the expenses connected to raising children in the US, which economists estimate to work out to more than $16,000 a year up to age eighteen, plus requiring very good health insurance, see Nancy Folbre, "The Underestimated 'Price of Parenting,'" *Dollars and Sense,* September 9, 2025, https://www.dollarsandsense.org/the-underestimated-price-of-parenting/.

For more on Americans' work-family dilemmas, the policies needed to address them, and the consequences of not doing so, see Caitlyn Collins, *Making Motherhood Work: How Women Manage Careers and Caregiving* (Princeton University Press, 2019); Anne-Marie Slaughter, *Unfinished Business: Women, Men, Work, Family* (Random House, 2015); Joan Williams, *Reshaping the Work-Family Debate: Why Men and Class Matter* (Harvard University Press, 2010); Stephanie Coontz, "Strengthening the Case for Policies to Support Caregiving," *Signs,* November 30, 2016, https://www.stephaniecoontz.com/node/364. Of forty countries recently surveyed by Market Australia, a company connected to the life-insurance industry, the US came in dead last in policies that promoted work-life balance. Hannah Norton, "The Best Countries for Work-Life Balance in 2024," The Burrow, March 6, 2024, https://www.comparethemarket.com.au/health-insurance/features/best-countries-for-work-life-balance-2024-archive/. See also Marie Holmes, "These Are the Best Countries for Work-Life Balance," *HuffPost,* March 14, 2024, https://www.huffpost.com/entry/best-countries-work-life-balance_l_65f1ba32e4b02ad7de1b36b8.

39. See also Haley Swenson, "Our Best Efforts," *Slate,* March 17, 2024, https://slate.com/human-interest/2024/03/fair-play-household-labor-division-queerness.html.

40. For more on the many reasons that motherhood leads to economic penalties, see Claudia Goldin, *Career & Family: Women's Century-Long Journey Toward Equity* (Princeton University Press, 2021); and Douglas Almond et al., "Large Motherhood Penalties in US Administrative Microdata," *Proceedings of the National Academy of Sciences* 120, no. 29 (2023), https://pubmed.ncbi.nlm.nih.gov/37428937/. Things get even more unequal when parents respond to the growing socioeconomic inequality described in chapters 6 and 7 by having one parent—almost inevitably the woman—devote herself to what sociologists Melissa Milkie and Catharine Warner call "status safeguarding," trying to single-handedly give their child the educational opportunities and mobility-enhancing experiences that a better social safety net would offer to all. International comparisons confirm that rising inequality tends to be associated with increasingly intensive, highly orchestrated parenting practices, recreating gender inequality at home along with psychic costs to both parents and children alike. Melissa Milkie and Catharine Warner, "Status Safeguarding: Mothers' Work to Secure Children's Place in the Status Hierarchy," in

Linda Ennis, ed., *Intensive Mothering: The Cultural Contradictions of Modern Motherhood* (Demeter Press, 2015). On the link between economic inequality and intensive parenting, see Matthias Doepke and Fabrizio Zilibotti, *Love, Money and Parenting: How Economics Explains the Way We Raise Our Kids* (Princeton University Press, 2019), and "The Parent Trap," *Washington Post*, February 22, 2019, https://www.washingtonpost.com/news/posteverything/wp/2019/02/22/feature/how-economic-inequality-gives-rise-to-hyper-parenting/.

41. Quoted in Sarah Blaffer Hrdy's fascinating book *Father Time: A Natural History of Men and Babies* (Princeton University Press, 2024).
42. Sarah Schoppe-Sullivan et al., "Maternal Gatekeeping, Coparenting Quality, and Fathering Behavior in Families with Infants," *Journal of Family Psychology* 22, no. 3 (2008), https://doi.org/10.1037/0893-3200.22.3.389.
43. Sociologist Jaclyn Wong followed the decision-making process and experiences of twenty-one young professional different-sex couples, just starting their work and family life, for six years. She found that it was not enough for a man to pursue his own best career options while being willing to accept whatever his wife decided to do. He had to make decisions about where and what positions to seek for himself on the basis of what locales and working conditions offered good opportunities for her as well, even if these were not the same decisions he might have made on his own. Jaclyn Wong, *Equal Partners? How Dual-Professional Couples Make Career, Relationship, and Family Decisions* (University of California Press, 2023). For an interview with work-family experts on how they organize their own marriages, see Joe Pinsker, "The Gender Researcher's Guide to an Equal Marriage," *Atlantic*, October 6, 2021, https://www.theatlantic.com/family/archive/2021/10/gender-researchers-divide-chores-parenting-at-home/620319/.
44. Sociologists call this "cognitive labor." See Allison Daminger, "The Cognitive Dimension of Household Labor," *American Sociological Review* 84, no. 4 (2019): 609–33, https://www.jstor.org/stable/48595780.
45. Richard Petts, personal communication, May 24, 2024; Richard Petts et al., "Fathers' Time Off Work After the Birth of a Child and Relationship Dissolution Among Socioeconomically Disadvantaged U.S. Families," *Sociological Focus* 54, no. 3 (2021), https://www.ncbi.nlm.nih.gov/pmc/articles/PMC8443147/. See also Ankita Patnaik, "Reserving Time for Daddy: The Consequences of Fathers' Quotas," *Journal of Labor Economics* 37, no. 4 (2019); and other sources in Stephanie Coontz, "Dads Count Too," Council on Contemporary Families, December 3, 2019, https://thesocietypages.org/ccf/2019/12/03/dads-count-too-family-friendly-policies-must-include-fathers.
46. Richard Petts et al., "If I [Take] Leave, Will You Stay? Paternity Leave and Relationship Stability," *Journal of Social Policy* 49, no. 4 (2020), https://

pubmed.ncbi.nlm.nih.gov/33093710/. A separate study of low-income couples found that paternal leave-taking also lowered the divorce risk in this population, despite the powerful external stresses that make such relationships more fragile. Petts et al., "Fathers' Time Off Work."

47. For more on these studies, see Hrdy, *Father Time*; Darby Saxbe and Magdelena Martínez-García, "Cortical Volume Reductions in Men Transitioning to First-Time Fatherhood Reflect Both Parenting Engagement and Mental Health Risk," *Cerebral Cortex* 34, no. 4 (2024), https://pubmed.ncbi.nlm.nih.gov/38615244/; Emily Harris, "Emerging Research Examines How Parenthood Changes the Brain," *MedPage Today*, January 21, 2024, https://www.medpagetoday.com/pediatrics/parenting/108499; Marie Holmes, "The Surprising Way Men's Brains Change After They Become Parents," *HuffPost*, June 13, 2024, https://www.huffpost.com/entry/dads-brain-change-baby_l_6668a095e4b01bc0ceed9231. There is one interesting downside for males that illustrates how malleable our supposedly biologically ingrained responses can be: Men who experience these changes tend to report the same increases in anxiety and problems in sleeping that mothers do. That's not surprising, given that their brains have become so intensely focused on an infant's well-being. Despite this seeming disadvantage, there are indications that the brain changes associated with infant caregiving promote long-term brain health for both men and women as they age. Darby Saxbe, "Dad Brain Is Real, and It's a Good Thing," *New York Times*, June 16, 2024, https://www.nytimes.com/2024/06/16/opinion/dad-brain-fatherhood-parenting.html.
48. Shannon Cavanagh and Asya Saydam, "Maternal Depression Across Early Childhood: Similarities and Differences Across Three Liberal Democracies," *Journal of Health and Social Behavior*, forthcoming.
49. Pepper Schwartz, *Love Between Equals: How Peer Marriage Really Works* (The Free Press, 1995).
50. Lori Gottlieb, https://www.nytimes.com/2014/02/09/magazine/does-a-more-equal-marriage-mean-less-sex.html. This article appeared in print with a less provocative title, "The Egalitarian-Marriage Conundrum," *New York Times Sunday Magazine*, February 9, 2014.
51. Mark Regnerus, "The Death of Eros," *First Things*, October 2017, https://www.firstthings.com/article/2017/10/the-death-of-eros.
52. Sabino Kornrich et al., "Egalitarianism, Housework, and Sexual Frequency in Marriage," *American Sociological Review* 78, no. 1 (2013): 26–50, https://doi.org/10.1177/0003122412472340.
53. Virginia Rutter, "Love and Lust," *Psychology Today*, September 6, 2018, https://www.psychologytoday.com/us/articles/201407/love-lust.
54. Sharon Sassler, "A Reversal in Predictors of Sexual Frequency and Satisfaction in Marriage," Council on Contemporary Families, July 8, 2016, https://

thesocietypages.org/ccf/2016/07/08/a-reversal-in-predictors-of-sexual-frequency-and-satisfaction-in-marriage/; Daniel Carlson et al., "The Gendered Division of Housework and Couples' Sexual Relationships: A Reexamination," *Journal of Marriage and Family* 78 (2016), https://onlinelibrary.wiley.com/doi/abs/10.1111/jomf.12313; Dan Carlson et al., "The Division of Child Care, Sexual Intimacy, and Relationship Quality in Couples," *Gender & Society* 30 (2016). For the findings that women who do disproportionate amounts of household labor report having low sexual desire, see Emily Harris et al., "Gender Inequities in Household Labor Predict Lower Sexual Desire in Women Partnered with Men," *Archives of Sexual Behavior* 51 (2022), https://doi.org/10.1007/s10508-022-02397-2.

In and of itself, sexual frequency is not a good measure of relationship quality. There are two different routes to more frequent sex, write researchers Daniel Carlson and Brian Soller. Male dominance is one. Egalitarian trust is the other. And only the latter predicts high levels of marital intimacy. Daniel Carlson and Brian Soller, "Sharing's More Fun for Everyone? Gender Attitudes, Sexual Self-Efficacy, and Sexual Frequency," *Journal of Marriage and Family* 87 (2019), https://www.onlinelibrary.wiley.com/doi/abs/10.1111/jomf.12524. It's worth noting that having "enough" sex to be happy is not a hard bar to clear. Romantic partners who engage in sex once a week report substantially better well-being than those who have sex less than once a month, but couples who have sex more often than once a week don't seem to get any additional boost in well-being over their once-a-week counterparts. Daniel Carlson et al., "The Division of Child Care, Sexual Intimacy, and Relationship Quality in Couples," *Gender & Society* 30, no. 3 (2016): 442–66, https://doi.org/10.1177/0891243215626709; Amy Muise et al., "Sexual Frequency Predicts Greater Well-Being, but More Is Not Always Better," *Social Psychological and Personality Science* 7, no. 4 (2016), https://doi.org/10.1177/1948550615616462.

55. Virginia Rutter and Pepper Schwartz, eds., *The Gender of Sexuality: Exploring Sexual Possibilities*, 2nd ed. (Rowman & Littlefield, 2011), 33.
56. For this and the next paragraph, see Amy Muise et al., "Broadening Your Horizons: Self-Expanding Activities Promote Desire and Satisfaction in Established Romantic Relationships," *Journal of Personality and Social Psychology* 116, no. 2 (2019): 237–58, https://doi.org/10.1037/pspi0000148; Kimberly Coulter and John Malouff, "Effects of an Intervention Designed to Enhance Romantic Relationship Excitement: A Randomized-Control Trial," *Couple and Family Psychology: Research and Practice* 2, no. 1 (2013): 34–44, https://doi.org/10.1037/a0031719; Arthur Aron et al., "Couples' Shared Participation in Novel and Arousing Activities and Experienced Relationship Quality," *Journal of Personality and Social Psychology* 78, no. 2 (2000), https://doi.org/10.1037/0022-3514.78.2.273; Greg Strong and Arthur Aron, "The Effect of Shared

Participation in Novel and Challenging Activities on Experienced Relationship Quality," in Kathleen Vohs and Eli Finkel, eds., *Self and Relationships: Connecting Intrapersonal and Interpersonal Processes* (Guilford, 2006); Keith Welker et al., "Effects of Self-Disclosure and Responsiveness Between Couples on Passionate Love Within Couples," *Personal Relationships* 21, no. 4 (2014), https://doi.org/10.1111/pere.12058. My thanks to social psychologist Eli Finkel for pointing me to some of this research on marital dynamics. For some suggestions of "love hacks" to revitalize a relationship, see his book *The All-or-Nothing Marriage: How the Best Marriages Work* (Dutton, 2017).

57. Barbara Schneider and Linda J. Waite, "The 500 Family Study [1998–2000: United States]," Inter-university Consortium for Political and Social Research, June 3, 2008, https://doi.org/10.3886/ICPSR04549.v1.

58. For example, psychiatrists discouraged married individuals from maintaining friendships that might "compete" with the marital relationship and encouraged them to put aging parents in nursing homes rather than allowing them to reside with the nuclear family. The popular 1950s play and movie *Marty* was an object lesson on the need for a man to focus on his own marriage rather than any obligations to his mother and aunt or his friendship with old school buddies. See Stephanie Coontz, *The Way We Really Are: Coming to Terms with America's Changing Families* (Basic Books, 1997), 37–38.

59. Natalia Sarkisian and Naomi Gerstel, "Does Singlehood Isolate or Integrate? Examining the Link Between Marital Status and Ties to Kin, Friends, and Neighbors," *Journal of Social and Personal Relationships* 33 (2016), https://doi.org/10.1177/0265407515597564, and "Till Marriage Do Us Part: Adult Children's Relationships with Their Parents," *Journal of Marriage and Family* 70, no. 2 (2008), https://www.jstor.org/stable/40056280; Matthijs Kalmijn, "Shared Friendship Networks and the Life Course: An Analysis of Survey Data on Married and Cohabiting Couples," *Social Networks* 25, no. 3 (2003), https://doi.org/10.1016/S0378-8733(03)00010-8; Michael Johnson and Leigh Leslie, "Couple Involvement and Network Structure: A Test of the Dyadic Withdrawal Hypothesis," *Social Psychology Quarterly* 45, no. 1 (1982), https://doi.org/10.2307/3033672.

60. Sae Hwang Han et al., "Friendship and Depression Among Couples in Later Life: The Moderating Effects of Marital Quality," *Journals of Gerontology: Series B* 74, no. 2 (2019), https://doi.org/10.1093/geronb/gbx046. See also Benjamin Haggerty et al., "The Disconnected Couple: Intimate Relationships in the Context of Social Isolation," *Current Opinion in Psychology* 43 (2022): 24–29, https://doi.org/10.1016/j.copsyc.2021.06.002.

61. Melinda Blau and Karen Fingerman, *Consequential Strangers: The Power of People Who Don't Seem to Matter . . . but Really Do* (W. W. Norton & Company, 2009); Gillian Sandsrom and Elizabeth Dunn, "Social Interactions and Well-Being: The Surprising Power of Weak Ties," *Personality and Social Psy-*

chology Bulletin 40 (2014), https://journals.sagepub.com/doi/10.1177/0146167214529799; Oliver Huxhold et al., "The Strength of Weaker Ties: An Underexplored Resource for Maintaining Emotional Well-Being in Later Life," *Journals of Gerontology, Series B, Psychological Sciences and Social Sciences* 75 (2020), https://pubmed.ncbi.nlm.nih.gov/32055856/; Katherine Fiori, "The Increasing Importance of Friendship in Late Life: Understanding the Role of Sociohistorical Context in Social Development," *Gerontology* 66 (2020), https://karger.com/ger/article-abstract/66/3/286/148324/The-Increasing-Importance-of-Friendship-in-Late. See also Stephanie Coontz, "For a Better Marriage, Act Like a Single Person," *New York Times*, February 10, 2018, https://www.nytimes.com/2018/02/10/opinion/sunday/for-a-better-marriage-act-like-a-single-person.html.

Afterword

1. "Better Life Lab Experiments," New America, February 26, 2021, https://www.newamerica.org/better-life-lab/better-life-lab-collections/better-life-lab-experiments/.
2. Christina Caron, "How Same-Sex Parents Share the Mental Load," *New York Times*, August 25, 2021, https://www.nytimes.com/2021/08/25/parenting/same-sex-relationships.html.
3. Brigid Schulte, *Overwhelmed: Work, Love, and Play When No One Has the Time* (Sarah Crichton Books, 2014).
4. Richard H. Thaler and Cass R. Sunstein, *Nudge: Improving Decisions About Health, Wealth, and Happiness* (Yale University Press, 2008).
5. Thamar J. H. Bovend'Eerdt et al., "Writing SMART Rehabilitation Goals and Achieving Goal Attainment Scaling: A Practical Guide," *Clinical Rehabilitation* 23, no. 4 (2009): 352–61.
6. B. Janet Hibbs and Anthony Rostain, *Try to See It My Way: Being Fair to Your Family When Divorce Seems Imminent* (Avery, 2019).
7. Gottman Institute, gottman.com.
8. Kate Mangino, *Equal Partners: Improving Gender Equality at Home* (St. Martin's Press, 2022).
9. Haley Swenson, "Our Best Efforts: The Debate Over Domestic Labor Is Political. But the Reality, I Found Out, Is Personal," *Slate*, March 17, 2024, https://slate.com/human-interest/2024/03/fair-play-household-labor-division-queerness.html.
10. Katherine Twamley and Charlotte Faircloth, "Understanding 'Gender Equality': First-Time Parent Couples' Practices and Perspectives on Working and Caring Post-Parenthood," *Journal of Family Issues* 44, no. 4 (2023): 1026–48.
11. Eve Rodsky, *Fair Play: A Game-Changing Solution for When You Have Too Much to Do (and More Life to Live)* (G. P. Putnam's Sons, 2019). Rodsky is a

member of the Better Life Lab's Advisory Council. The Fair Play Policy Institute supports the Lab's Care Reporting fellowship.

12. Haley Swenson, "Alexa, How Do I Stop This Meltdown?," *The Persistent*, accessed July 28, 2025, https://www.thepersistent.com/how-to-use-ai-apps-chat-gpt-parenting/.

INDEX